BECOMING QUALITATIVE RESEARCHERS

BECOMING QUALITATIVE RESEARCHERS

An Introduction

Corrine Glesne & Alan Peshkin

University of Vermont

University of Illinois at Urbana-Champaign

Longman

BECOMING QUALITATIVE RESEARCHERS

Longman, 10 Bank Street, White Plains, N.Y. 10606

Associated companies:
Longman Group Ltd., London
Longman Cheshire Pty., Melbourne
Longman Paul Pty., Auckland
Copp Clark Pitman, Toronto

Senior editor: Naomi Silverman
Development editor: Virginia Blanford
Production editor: Linda Moser
Cover design: Joseph DePinho
Production supervisor: Richard Bretan

Library of Congress Cataloging-in-Publication Data

Glesne, Corrine.
    Becoming Qualitative Researchers: An Introduction / Corrine Glesne and Alan
Peshkin.
      p.   cm.
    Includes bibliographical references and index.
    ISBN 0-8013-0295-1
    1. Social sciences—Methodology. I. Peshkin, Alan. II. Title.
H61.G555   1991
300′.1—dc20
                                       91-22604
                                        CIP

3 4 5 6 7 8 9 10-MA-959493

Contents

Tables

Acknowledgments

I would like to acknowledge the American Educational Studies Association for holding its 1986 annual meeting in a hotel with a hot tub. In that hot tub, I met Naomi Silverman, editor at Longman, who gently urged me to consider writing this book. When Alan Peshkin agreed to be a part of the team, the course was set. As editor and, now, as friend, Naomi Silverman receives special acknowledgment. Of utmost importance, however, are the women and men in our qualitative research classes at the University of Vermont and at the University of Illinois. Their questions, thoughts, experiences, and advice have shaped this book the most. In particular, thanks go to Jill Mackler, Gordon Schnare, and Andrea Torello, whose words find their way repeatedly into the text—and to the fall 1990 qualitative seminar class, my writing group, and others who read and commented on a draft. Thanks also go to Golie Jansen of the University of Illinois for her contribution to our writing on theory in this book.

–*C.G.*

Introduction: A Sense of Things to Come

As educators and others who conduct social research have become more familiar with the promise of qualitative inquiry, the demand for acquiring qualitative research skills has grown. In our teaching of yearlong qualitative research courses, we have created and continually modify collections of readings from articles, sections of various textbooks, and our own thoughts and writings. When approached with the suggestion that we write an introductory text that would encompass the process of qualitative inquiry, we agreed. Our guiding principle throughout these pages has been to create a primary text that we would want to use in helping our own students begin to conduct qualitative research. This book focuses on our version of the lore and wit, the basic skills and techniques, requisite to the pursuit of qualitative studies.

In qualitative research, face-to-face interactions are the predominant distinctive feature and also the basis for its most common problems. Through researchers' involvement with the people they study, lives become entwined, with all of the accompanying hazards, challenges, and opportunities that such closeness brings. The prominence of face-to-face interactions necessitates the discussion of rapport, subjectivity, and certain ethical issues. The significance of the relationship between the researcher and the researched even affects how we refer to those whom we want to learn from and about. In quantitative studies, those researched are commonly called subjects. Qualitative researchers, on the other hand, tend to be uncomfortable with the term *subject* because it implies the *acting on* rather than the *interacting with* that at best characterizes qualitative inquiry. Therefore, we prefer the term *others*, as suggested by postmodernists, as well as the commonly used research participants, respondents, and interviewees.

The face-to-face interactions demanded by qualitative research also raise the question of who should do such research. Conventional wisdom has it that the research problem determines the methods chosen. In reality, we see people drawn to qualitative research because they dislike statistics or quantitative techniques or because, as one student stated, "I can do quantitative research, but it isn't *me*."

We suspect that people do have a proclivity for one type of research or another. Qualitative research typically explores what at base is incommensurable. This puts it outside the comfort zone of many researchers. Qualitative researchers must be able to tolerate, and perhaps even to enjoy, ambiguity in their pursuit of complexity. Moreover, they tend to observe what others miss, listen when others talk, and ask questions that others might not think to raise. They also regard themselves as learners who easily become consumed by their wonderment over their world. In the midst of data collection, one student exulted, "I feel like I'm living in the middle of a novel. You never know what will come next."

Finally, qualitative researchers accept the time demands of their consuming interest: the work takes over their lives. In the midst of data collection and analysis, one student reported, "I was driving home, thinking about my research, and missed the exit." Such occurrences are common (although not necessarily limited to qualitative researchers).

Our primary audience is students and other newcomers to qualitative research. Since many students will be working on theses or dissertations, we periodically address some of the particular problems that these students might encounter. Most of the text examples are drawn from educational settings, but we do not limit ourselves to the context of schools or to the needs of scholars of education. The sources of our examples are published works, our own research, and the experiences of our students. In discussing our own research, we use our first names—Corrine and Alan—except when referring to published works. We are most indebted to our students at the University of Vermont and the University of Illinois; they have taught us much about qualitative inquiry. With their permission, we identify their examples by their first names, or, for some, by pseudonyms.

The book guides readers through the research process. Along the way it raises issues, questions, and quandaries with which we and our students have struggled. Readers will therefore learn not only about our own work, but also about the work of the many research novices who have been in our classes and on whose committees we have served. As the students in our classes have noted, and as you will also observe, we find that the most frequent answer to questions raised by qualitative inquiry is, "It depends." In class discussions and in this book, we provide no solutions, find no "truths." Our goal is to raise questions, thereby indicating what is problematic, and suggest guidelines for developing your own judgement in order to learn from and manage the complex issues you may encounter.

From our perspective, acquiring the skill and understanding for conducting qualitative inquiry has three dimensions: reading, reflecting, and doing research. There is no correct order for their performance; ideally, they should be done simultaneously so that the outcomes of each continually interact. Although we can note generally sound points about interviewing and participant observation, for example, data-gathering techniques vary at the hands of different researchers. This variability derives from the researchers' personal characteristics, such as gender, age, personality, temperament, and skill. Thus, to become competent researchers, each of you must acquire the general lore associated with research processes and learn how, in light of your personal qualities, you can best adapt the lore in your own research.

In our own classes, students engage in the adaptation process by keeping a log that describes their practices and, no less important, their critical reflections on these practices, so that they can become increasingly conscious of themselves as they engage in research. The log, in effect, becomes a personal methods book that contains the insights that result from the interaction of reading, reflecting, and doing research. We strongly advocate that you keep a log throughout the whole research process, including the final stages of data analysis and writing. Learning to reflect on your behavior and thoughts, as well as on the phenomenon under study, creates a means for continuously becoming a better researcher. *Becoming* a better reseacher captures the dynamic nature of the process. Conducting research, like teaching and other complex acts, can be improved; it cannot be mastered.

The log is one of several threads to which we refer throughout the text. Another thread is theory, which we discuss within the context of each part of the research undertaking, rather than as a separate chapter. Preexisting theories, for example, may aid in question development—not to shape the study design, but to extend the range of your own thinking. In the early stages of data analysis, you begin developing your own substantive theories about the social phenomenon you are studying. After the data have been collected and analyzed, you may return to the literature to juxtapose your findings and substantive theories with grand theory in order to discuss the contributions that your study provides. Theory, therefore, is a part of various chapters in the book.

Chapters tend to compartmentalize thoughts, giving the impression that data collection, for example, is distinct from data analysis. Although the activities of qualitative inquiry tend to be ongoing and overlapping, we use chapters to focus on one research aspect at a time. We also include chapters on rapport and subjectivity (Chapter 5) and ethics (Chapter 6), matters that must be considered throughout the research process but which are less fully addressed in other introductory texts.

We end this introduction with some notes to instructors of qualitative research courses. We recommend considerable practice of research techniques—on problems of significance to students—in conjunction with reading this book. Ideally, the course is occasion for supervised work on theses and dissertations.

Just as there is no one right way to conduct a study, there is no one right way to learn about qualitative inquiry. A collaborative approach, however, makes sense to us. In keeping with the constructivist nature of qualitative inquiry, knowledge is not acquired didactically; rather, it is developed inductively through dialogue among reading, individual research, and reflection. All participants are both teachers and learners.

Members of our classes come from various disciplines, stages in the educational process, and levels of professional experience. All, however, share the anxiety of being novice researchers. In a collaborative setting, the class becomes a group for criticism and support. In small groups or as a whole, students work on one another's problem statements, interview questions, coding schemes, and writing. They learn to welcome the ideas and suggestions that come through sharing problems, questions, and anxieties. In addition, to our mutual satisfaction, they may conclude as Sally did: "The word *research* used to intimidate me; now it excites me."

On the basis of her experience, Corrine identified five themes characteristic of collaborative, qualitative research courses: Learning collaboratively (1) develops camaraderie; (2) moderates, redirects, and helps make use of the anxiety associated with doing qualitative research; (3) involves humor; (4) is enhanced by diversity; and (5) takes time (Glesne et al., 1989).

CAMARADERIE

Heldke (1988), in her work on co-responsible inquiry, states that participants must be responsive to and respectful of all members in the community of inquiry. In a collaborative class setting, students grow to see one another as active, compassionate knowers who can be trusted with personal insecurities. Joint involvement in a demanding enterprise creates a sense of togetherness. Because a group gets along well, however, does not mean that consensus must prevail. "Points of dissonance" (Miller 1988, 1) raise not only new questions, but also levels of awareness. Students achieve new perspectives, though not necessarily the same perspectives. They learn not only that qualitative research is an interpretive process, but also that interpretation is negotiable. Our model clearly is not that of the solitary searcher who toughs out the problems of scholarship, claiming no allies in the process, accumulating no debts to be announced in the acknowledgments. Obtaining the benefits of indebtedness strikes us as both personally sensible and academically productive.

ANXIETY

Experiencing insecurity throughout all stages of the research process is common to novice and not-so-novice researchers, to whom each aspect of inquiry seems ambiguous and lacking in clear rules or directions. The collaborative environment allows group members to see anxiety as a natural part of the process, not unique to a particular individual. By listening to one another's worries, and by offering reassurances and suggestions for confronting anxiety-producing situations, class participants become more willing to expose and tackle their own insecurities. (See Berg and LeBailly's 1985 paper on ''Anxiety in Research Relationships.'')

HUMOR

Humor facilitates learning, helps to combat anxiety, and encourages participants to be honest with and critical of one another. Through laughter, class members lower their defenses and examine what they might otherwise suppress. We urge you to approach the learning experience as something fully enjoyable. To be sure, that decisions and lives may be affected by research is a serious matter. But learning about the process of research and how to conduct it need not be viewed as a sober undertaking. If, as instructors, we can create a supportive classroom atmosphere that allows students and instructors to explicate insights and laugh at mistakes, then we make it easier to want to learn about and acquire the dispositions, understandings, and skills that qualitative inquiry encompasses.

DIVERSITY

Group diversity contributes to the emergence of new perspectives. Students of different professional disciplines, personal experiences, and research interests contribute to the growth and knowledge of one another. For example, students unfamiliar with the practice of physical therapy will ask questions of the physical therapist's research that insiders might not. Diversity allows each class member to be accepted as a substantive ''expert'' while sharing the role of procedural novice in qualitative research.

TIME

Collaborative inquiry, like qualitative research, is evolutionary. It takes time to discuss individual learnings and thereby arrive at general group learnings. It takes time to develop the camaraderie and the trust needed to expose insecurities. It takes time to meet outside of class on group projects, if that is part of the semester's work. Yet, something about qualitative research and the collaborative process motivates one to find the time necessary to work and rework questions, analytic frameworks, and drafts. If the class can continue over two semesters, so much the better. It takes several semesters to provide an appropriate sense of the nature and practice of qualitative inquiry.

Through collaborative learning, all members of a group learn from the other members' experiences, scholarship, and skills. They may work on a tangible end product, such as a book or a series of articles, but the process produces another important product as well: a community of scholars.

CHAPTER 1

Meeting Qualitative Inquiry

BEGINNINGS

> The people who come to see us bring us their stories. They hope they tell
> them well enough so that we understand the truth of their lives. They hope
> we know how to interpret their stories correctly. We have to remember that
> what we hear is *their story*. (Coles 1989, 7)

A teacher/supervisor so advised Robert Coles as he struggled early on with
becoming a psychiatrist. Although psychiatrists and qualitative researchers
make different uses of the stories they hear, learning to listen well is critical for
both.

Qualitative researchers seek to make sense of personal stories and the
ways in which they intersect. We, the authors of this book, therefore begin
with our personal stories, in hope that once you know something about each of
us, you will more fully understand and interpret our perspectives in the text that
follows.

Corrine's Story

I do not remember "discovering" qualitative inquiry. Where or when I first
heard the term escapes me. The process, however, is one with which I have
been familiar for some time. I grew up in a small, rural, midwestern town and
was always interested in people who were culturally different from me and my
neighbors. I read each month's *National Geographic* and filled my nights with
folk tales from around the world. Books such as *Arctic Wild* (Crisler 1958) and
No Room in the Ark (Moorehead 1959) from my parents' bookshelves supple-
mented library books about travelers, explorers, and adventurers from Charles
Darwin to Genghis Khan.

I gravitated toward anthropology as an undergraduate, which allowed me to continue learning about the many different ways people live. I wrote papers on land tenure in Madagascar and kinship in Sarawak, traced the development of the Chinese novel, and researched the effects of colonialism on the Maori. The more I read, the more I wanted to see for myself. For anthropologists, fieldwork—being present in others' lives—is *the* way to learn about another culture.

Thus began a seven-year, postgraduate trek in which I traveled and worked from Wales to Afghanistan. On a kibbutz in Israel, I pollinated date palms, pruned banana plants, picked grapefruit, and grew increasingly interested in tropical agriculture. Later, I lived in Jerusalem and joined a team of archaeologists for a year. Herodian walls, Roman baths, Byzantine mosaics, and Crusader arches remain vivid images for me because I carefully measured and drew to scale these uncovered structures. I continued with archaeological work in northern Kenya. I camped in dry riverbeds and walked over the tracks of rhinos and lions as I traced the southern migration of people away from the Nile 10,000 years ago. Throughout this period, I kept journals. As I read them now, I am struck by my joy about what I was learning, and my frustration about how to make use of all I experienced. Constantly stimulated by new ways of doing things and different ways of understanding them, I was restless and eager to put it all together in some way. Such desires led me to graduate school with plans to apply anthropology through education.

In graduate school, I took classes in anthropology, international agriculture, and education. I ventured into research courses. *Research*! Research sounded so hard, so formal, so abstract. I have almost lost touch with the Corrine who thought that way. Several courses taught me about experimental and quasi-experimental design and helped me to understand what control groups and dependent and independent variables are. I took statistics and worked with computers on analysis programs. It seemed like a game, which I somewhat enjoyed, but it did not seem real; I could not link this approach to what I had learned about people in my travels. Then I took a course in cognitive anthropology followed by one on in-depth interviewing. The courses focused on question development, interviewing strangers, and keeping field logs. Thus, I returned to my anthropology fieldwork roots. Later, as I prepared to do an ethnographic study in a Caribbean village for my dissertation, I sought out the literature that helped me to make some sense of my own life as well as the lives of others—texts and tales on qualitative inquiry.

Alan's Story

In terms of doing research, I knew that I was not at home in the world of numbers long before I realized that I was at home in the world of words. It was less a case of rejecting numbers than feeling rejected by them. They made me feel like an outsider; they created walls that I could not penetrate. Thus, becoming a qualitative researcher did not begin with a principled, anticipated rejection of one paradigm in knowing acceptance of another. I began by understanding what I could not comfortably do and gradually learned where, in fact, I could be comfortable.

What I needed to do, I understand in retrospect, was to find myself in terms of the conduct of research. Doing research never was in question; how I would do it was.

My dissertation involved questionnaires, observation, and interviewing. I had taken one statistics course as part of my doctoral studies; it was required. I could not see how I could apply anything I had been taught to my investigation of planned change in then East Pakistan, now Bangladesh, where I worked and studied for two years. I concede that the problem was in what I was able to learn about statistics, not in what I was taught. I did not experience a lot of pleasure in the doing; getting there—to the end of a dissertation and a doctoral degree—was not half the fun. As a methodological dud, I floundered, worried a lot, and wanted most to be done.

Within three years of "getting there" I was in Northern Nigeria, a teacher and administrator at the Bornu Teacher Training College in the city of Maiduguri. Halfway through my two-year stint in Nigeria, influenced by Oscar Lewis' (1959) very readable *Five Families* and Barker and Wright's (1951) very unreadable *One Boy's Day*, I began a study of four primary school students, all of the Kanuri tribe, Muslims, and the first members of their family to attend a Western-type school. I trained a separate team of three observers to shadow each of the four children for a full month.

I could not speak the language, which the four children spoke most of the time, and therefore became a vicarious data collector. My observers, who kept complete, running, handwritten notes of everything they saw and heard, were the data collectors. Each day, they would submit their notes, and I would read the notes and prepare questions. The next day's notes included both what the collectors saw and heard, and the answers to my questions. I did not have a name for it then, but I was acquiring "fat data," that heap of words which we so easily collect in the course of qualitative inquiry. I felt good seeing the notes come in daily; in fact, I felt good throughout the research process, which had begun with training my observers, continued with the solving of field problems, and ended with my struggle to arrange four feet of typed notes into a manuscript. I transformed one month of data into one "thick" day in the life of each school child. I had not yet heard about Clifford Geertz (1973) and "thick description," but I had *One Boy's Day* as my guide for using a day to portray a life. The result was my first book, *Kanuri Schoolchildren: Education and Social Mobilization in Bornu* (Peshkin 1972).

This was a nonquantitative book, published in George and Louise Spindler's *Case Studies in Education and Culture* series, but I was no more an anthropologist than I was a qualitative researcher. I had no labels for what I was doing or who I was. Labels would come later. In the meantime, four years after *Kanuri Schoolchildren*, I began the first of my studies of American communities and their schools and came to realize that the best of my research life was built on these facts, the basis of my preferred research procedure: I liked watching, I liked asking questions, and I liked listening. I also enjoyed reading, particularly fiction, which influenced the form of my writing. Eventually, I built a research course around the way I learned and a writing course around the way I wrote. Preparation for each course generated increasing and useful self-consciousness about the research process. Continuing research provided concrete experience to interact with what I was learning through teaching. I learned that I had always been a qualitative researcher.

Now that we have briefly introduced ourselves and our personal journeys into qualitative research, we turn to different research approaches, to different ways of coming to know and understand the world.

WAYS OF KNOWING

Dictionaries define research as a careful and diligent search. We have all been engaged in a variety of careful and diligent searches without necessarily labeling the process research, let alone a particular type of research. For example, Corrine's mother became interested in her family's genealogy. In her search to develop the family tree, she asked questions of great aunts and second cousins; requested that they and other relatives share letters and photo albums; wandered in cemeteries in towns where ancestors had lived; and sent for documents from hospitals, town clerks, and churches. From the formal and informal documents and the words of her relatives, she carefully and diligently traced her family's history, recording both the dates of significant events (births, marriages, deaths) and the stories she heard.

As students some of you may have conducted searches without having been assigned to do so. For example, suppose that as undergraduates living in a residence hall, you and your friends have become increasingly dissatisfied with the selection of food provided by the food service. You complain, but nothing changes. Over a particularly unsatisfactory meal, you and your friends decide to develop a survey for residents. The survey takes shape as a series of statements followed by a five-point scale that ranges from strongly agree to strongly disagree. You type it up, discuss it at a hall meeting, and get the resident hall advisor to make copies, which are distributed via mailboxes. Respondents are asked to deposit the survey in a box outside the dining hall by a certain date. On that date, you and your friends collect the surveys and begin to tally the numbers. By the end of a long evening, you know what proportion of residents responded and how those residents feel about certain aspects of the food service. Armed with your facts in the form of a written report, you distribute a copy to the school newspaper, the university president, and the food service.

As professionals, you may have continued to conduct searches. A middle school English teacher was struck each September by a pattern of frightened, uncertain new students. She had a hunch that teachers, administrators, and older students could do something to ease the transition, but she was not sure what. So she asked her sixth-, seventh-, and eighth-grade classes to write essays about how they felt during their first few days as sixth graders, what made the experience good, what made the experience bad, and what could be changed to make it better. Then, working with the students, the teacher prepared a report for presentation to staff and administration, suggesting steps that the school could take.

In all three of these examples, people are engaged in research. They deliberately set out to collect data for specified purposes. In all three cases better data might have been collected more carefully, but the point is that people do carry out research of sorts in their everyday lives—even though they may not name the approach they use or be aware of how to improve the process so the results are more trustworthy and, thereby, of greater use. In this book, we want to help you improve your approach to qualitative research so that your results are both trustworthy and useful.

Did one of the three examples read more like "real" research than the others? In general, we have been conditioned to think of research as a process that uses an instrument, involves a large number of people, and is analyzed by reducing the data to numbers. This type of inquiry, as demonstrated by the food survey, is termed *quantitative research*. The middle school example and parts of the genealogical search show the researcher gathering words by talking with a small number of people, collecting a variety of documents, and, in the middle school example, observing behavior. Both of these cases use *qualitative* approaches.

Because students and academics are often more familiar with the quantitative approach, the two approaches are frequently compared and contrasted. Quantitative and qualitative researchers do use similar elements in their work, however. They state a purpose, pose a problem or raise a question, define a research population, develop a time frame, collect and analyze data, and present outcomes. They also rely (explicitly or implicitly) on a theoretical framework and are concerned with rigor. Nonetheless, how researchers go about putting these elements together makes for distinctive differences in both the process and the final product.

The research methods we choose say something about our views on what qualifies as valuable knowledge and our perspective on the nature of reality. As will be explained in more detail, quantitative methods are, in general, supported by the positivist or scientific paradigm, which leads us to regard the world as made up of observable, measurable facts. In contrast, qualitative methods are generally supported by the interpretivist paradigm, which portrays a world in which reality is socially constructed, complex, and everchanging.

The different assumptions about the nature of the world affect not only the approach or research methods used, but also the purpose of the research and the roles of the researcher (Firestone 1987). Quantitative researchers seek explanations and predictions that will generalize to other persons and places. Careful sampling strategies and experimental designs are aspects of quantitative methods aimed at producing generalizable results. In quantitative research, the researcher's role is to observe and measure, and care is taken to keep the researcher from "contaminating" the data through personal involvement with the research subjects. Researcher "objectivity" is of utmost concern.

Meanwhile, since qualitative researchers deal with multiple, socially constructed realities or "qualities" that are complex and indivisible into discrete variables, they regard their research task as coming to understand and interpret how the various participants in a social setting construct the world around them. To make their interpretations, the researchers must gain access to the multiple perspectives of the participants. Their study designs, therefore, generally focus on in-depth, long-term interaction with relevant people in one or several sites. The researcher becomes the main research instrument as he or she observes, asks questions, and interacts with research participants. The concern with researcher objectivity is replaced by a focus on the impact of subjectivity on the research process. Table 1.1 compares some of the assumptions, purposes, approaches, and researcher roles inherent in the qualitative and quantitative modes of inquiry. These should not be taken as hard and fast distinctions, but rather as predispositions of the different inquiry modes. (For more discussion on paradigmatic differences, see Eisner 1981; Howe 1988; Lincoln and Guba 1985; Rist 1977; Schwandt 1989.)

Unlike quantitative inquiry, with its prespecified intent, qualitative inquiry is evolutionary, with a problem statement, a design, interview questions, and interpretations developing and changing along the way. The qualitative approach reminds "the scientific sociologist [and the rest of us] that for all his or her neat abstractions, concrete human beings may not neatly bend before them" (Plummer 1983, 7). The open, emergent nature means a lack of standardization; we do not know of and thus do not provide clear criteria packaged into neat research steps. The openness sets the stage for discovery as well as for ambiguity that, particularly for the novice researcher, engenders a sometimes overwhelming sense of anxiety: "Who else should I be seeing?" "What else should I be asking?" "How can I ever assemble all of the pieces into something meaningful?" Hard-to-answer, context-bound questions emerge along with unexpected patterns and new understandings through the evolutionary nature of qualitative inquiry.

TABLE 1.1   Predispositions of Quantitative and Qualitative Modes of Inquiry

Quantitative Mode	Qualitative Mode
Assumptions	
Social facts have an objective reality	Reality is socially constructed
Primacy of method	Primacy of subject matter
Variables can be identified and relationships measured	Variables are complex, interwoven, and difficult to measure
Etic (outsider's point of view)	Emic (insider's point of view)
Purpose	
Generalizability	Contextualization
Prediction	Interpretation
Causal explanations	Understanding actors' perspectives
Approach	
Begins with hypotheses and theories	Ends with hypotheses and grounded theory
Manipulation and control	Emergence and portrayal
Uses formal instruments	Researcher as instrument
Experimentation	Naturalistic
Deductive	Inductive
Component analysis	Searches for patterns
Seeks consensus, the norm	Seeks pluralism, complexity
Reduces data to numerical indices	Makes minor use of numerical indices
Abstract language in write-up	Descriptive write-up
Researcher Role	
Detachment and impartiality	Personal involvement and partiality
Objective portrayal	Empathic understanding

The openness of qualitative inquiry allows the researcher to approach the inherent complexity of social interaction and to do justice to that complexity, to respect it in its own right. Qualitative researchers avoid simplifying social phenomena and instead explore the range of behavior and expand their understanding of the resulting interactions. Throughout the research process, they assume that social interaction is complex and that they will uncover some of that complexity.

To do justice to complexity, qualitative researchers immerse themselves in the setting or lives of others, and they use multiple means to gather data. "They thereby give credence to the contextual nature within which both researchers and their research phenomena abide, and also to the fact that both are . . . shaped by and embody passions and values that are expressed variably in time and place" (Peshkin 1988b, 418). Thereby, they come to understand and are able to show the complexity, the contradictions, and the sensibility of social interactions. "To know a rose by its Latin name and yet to miss its fragrance," stated Eisner, "is to miss much of the rose's meaning" (Eisner

1981, 9). The gift of personal presence is being able to tell the stories of our others.

The quantitative report typically reduces data to numerical relationships and presents findings in a formal, disembodied fashion that follows a standardized form and style. In contrast, qualitative reports are often crafted in ways to "exploit the power of form to inform" (Eisner 1981, 7). Final narratives seek to make the researched phenomena accessible, tangible, and imaginable.

QUALITATIVE/QUANTITATIVE COMPATIBILITY

The positivist paradigm, which dominates natural science investigation in the Western world, has been adapted by social scientists. Until recently, therefore, academic and funding agencies accepted quantitative research methods as *the* way of doing research. Questions about the logic of positivism for social science research, however, are not new. Popkewitz (1984) delineates arguments by John Dewey at the turn of the century, by Karl Popper in the 1940s, and by a number of sociologists (Carl Becker, Alfred Schultz, Max Weber) who argued for field-based studies in the mid-1900s.

For novice anthropologists, fieldwork has been the rite of passage ever since the 1920s, when Bronislaw Malinowski carried out long-term fieldwork among the Trobriand Islanders. Typically, anthropologists sought to study a group of people who lived in a culture that was remote and thus quite different from their own. Although generally within the interpretivist paradigm, many anthropologists aspired to be as "scientific" as possible by incorporating into their studies various quantitative techniques.

In the 1960s, anthropologists increasingly began to study their own home cultures; they also began to reflect seriously on the relationships between inquirer and inquiree as they and others criticized the anthropological discipline for "its historical and ideological role as the hand-maiden of colonialism and neo-colonialism" (Ellen 1984, 3). As both researchers and research participants looked critically at issues of power and control in the research process, they began a shift away from positivism.

Popkewitz places the move from positivism toward interpretive approaches in the larger sociocultural context. Struck by the "contradictions between liberal ideals and institutional processes" in regard to promoting "community" and "personal efficiency," he views changes in the "concepts and methods of study" as "a reaction to the . . . fragmentation in social affairs and the dissolution of moral life" (Popkewitz 1984, 92–93). Our preferred research methods reflect personal choices; they are, however, embedded in our cultural and historical contexts.

Although some social science researchers (Lincoln and Guba 1985; Schwandt 1989) perceive qualitative and quantitative approaches as incompatible, others (Patton 1990; Reichardt and Cook 1979) believe that the skilled researcher can successfully combine approaches. The argument usually becomes muddled because one party argues from the underlying philosophical nature of each paradigm, and the other focuses on the apparent compatibility of the research methods, enjoying the rewards of both numbers and words. Because the positivist and the interpretivist paradigms rest on different assumptions about the nature of the world, they require different instruments and procedures to find the type of data desired. This does not mean, however, that the positivist never uses interviews nor that the interpretivist never uses a survey. They may, but such methods are supplementary, not dominant.

Rather than argue about which paradigm or methods are better, we and others (Eisner 1981; Firestone 1987; Howe 1988) see virtue in a variety of approaches. Different approaches allow us to know and understand different things about the world.

Nonetheless, people tend to adhere to the methodology that is most consonant with their socialized worldview. We are told that the research problem should define whether one chooses a qualitative approach or a quantitative one. This, however, is not how we believe research necessarily is done or even how it should be done. To the contrary, we are attracted to and shape research problems that match our personal view of seeing and understanding the world:

> Our constructions of the world, our values, and our ideas about how to inquire into those constructions, are mutually self-reinforcing. We conduct inquiry via a particular paradigm because it embodies assumptions about the world that we believe and values that we hold, and because we hold those assumptions and values we conduct inquiry according to the precepts of that paradigm. (Schwandt 1989, 399)

As Jill, a student in Vermont, stated, "I felt that I had found a research home when I learned that qualitative research existed." Notwithstanding that you may be taught that there is a preferred way to do research, the particular research mode with which you will find greatest comfort and satisfaction will depend on your personality and background.

THE VARIABILITY OF QUALITATIVE INQUIRY

Varied Modes

Qualitative inquiry is an umbrella term for various philosophical orientations to interpretive research. For example, qualitative researchers might call their work ethnography, case study, phenomenology, educational criticism, or several other terms. As Jacob (1988) elaborates, we can compare the various orientations by addressing their historical roots, assumptions, focuses, and methods. In this manner, Jacob discusses human ethnology, ecological psychology, holistic ethnography, cognitive anthropology, ethnography of communication, and symbolic interactionism. Other orientations include case study, interpretive research, microethnography, and ethnomethodology. Before claiming that your work is phenomonological, for example, we urge you to explore the literature associated with that orientation, and with other orientations, so that you can broaden your knowledge of ways to approach research. This book is oriented to ethnography, which is the anthropological tradition of long-term immersion in the field in which the researcher collects data primarily by participant-observation and interviewing. You should be open to learning about social phenomena from a variety of perspectives and may, therefore, elect to mix techniques associated with different orientations.

In recent years, increased sensitivity to issues of power and control has encouraged a rethinking of research design and implementation. In traditional research, as practiced by both positivists and interpretivists, the authority for research decisions resides with the researcher. Postmodernists and action-oriented modes of research challenge this position, as we will explain. It is an important challenge. Although this text is generally oriented toward more traditional qualitative research, it is influenced by aspects of postmodern ethnography and alternative modes variously referred to as action research, collaborative inquiry, emancipatory research, feminist methodology, and participatory research. Although neither synonymous nor clearly defined individually, these inquiry approaches raise similar questions about how we carry out research. In particular, they cause us to rethink the purpose of research and, thereby, the researcher–researched relationship. Accordingly, we raise some of these challenges to the traditional approach throughout this book in response to our views on what it means to be a responsible qualitative inquirer. To provide some basis for these questions, we will briefly describe the orientation of the postmodern ethnographer and that of one type of action-oriented inquirers, the participatory researcher.

Postmodern Ethnography

Postmodern ethnographers concern themselves with uncovering and ''untangling hidden relations of power and domination with relationship to knowledge'' (Maher and Tetreault 1988, 27). This means looking carefully for ways in which the historical and cultural context shapes the researcher's preconceptions. Postmodernists are also particularly concerned with issues of ''intersubjectivity,'' that is, how researcher and researched affect each other. Continually reflexive, postmodernists look at

> how ethnography is produced, how experiences relate to data, how meanings get imposed on experience, how data are organized and transformed, how texts are written, and how (in the broadest possible sense) the research act is socially constructed. (Ellen 1984, 10)

This perspective calls on researchers not only to describe their interpretations of a social phenomenon, but also to explore their own contextual milieu and consider how the research process is shaping their inner landscape.

In reflecting on the research process, postmodernists consciously choose new metaphors to describe their work. These metaphors have quickly become a part of the general qualitative language:

> It used to be that ethnographic "facts" were "collected," realities were "perceived," and data "presented." The current view is more of one in which field "experiences" are "transformed" into data through encounters between researcher and researched; they are "translated" from one cultural context to another; and they are "constructed" drawing upon the personal and intersubjectivities of those involved. (Ellen 1984, 10)

Rather than write research reports, qualitative researchers translate social experiences and construct narratives.

Participatory Research

Most of the action-oriented alternative modes of research share postmodern ethnography's concern for issues of control and power and its focus on intersubjectivity between researcher and researched. The postmodern ethnographer does not, however, necessarily seek to change some aspect of society through the actual research process the way that the action-oriented researcher does. The researcher's role often becomes that of a facilitator who works collaboratively with research participants, although the forms and extent of that collaboration vary. In some cases, participants are involved in every aspect, including establishing research priorities, collecting data, interpreting data, and taking actions toward solving an identified problem. (See Dubell 1981; DuBois 1983; Gitlin, Siegel, and Boru 1989; Lather 1986; Maguire 1987; Mies 1983; Reason 1988; Reinharz 1983; Roman and Apple 1990; Whyte 1991.)

In participatory research, for example, ideally all research participants are co-researchers who combine investigation, education, and action (Maguire 1987). Together a group of people investigate social problems of mutual concern, as Maguire (1987) did with battered women in the Southwest, or as Belenky, Bond, and Weinstock (1991) did with young rural mothers in the Northeast. The investigation becomes an educational endeavor through analysis of the problems' structural causes. It then becomes a process of collective action aimed at social change. Ideally, the researcher–researched relationship is marked by negotiation, reciprocity, and willingness on the part of all participants to change and be changed.

Drawing heavily on the work of Paulo Freire ([1970] 1988), participatory researchers regard research as "praxis," or reflection plus action. "Social value'' becomes the criterion for determining whether or not a research question should be pursued. Three goals shape their work: (1) to develop critical consciousness, (2) to improve the lives of those involved, and (3) to transform societal structures and relationships (Maguire 1987, 29). Often these ambitious goals are not met, but they remain a guiding set of standards for participatory research work.

Although the alternative modes of inquiry promise to contribute much to the researched community as well as to the larger society, the approaches are not problem free. Particularly when the primary researcher is an outsider, there are difficulties associated with defining the research focus, creating collaborative groups where no formal organization exists, and knowing when and how to leave or end the research project. The identified problems and strengths of these alternative modes suggest that much potential lies in the concept of practitioners (e.g., teachers, nurses, social workers) as researchers who investigate, with others, their own ''backyard'' (Bissex and Bullock 1987; Ebbutt 1985; Goswami and Stillman 1987; Griffiths 1985; Hustler, Cassidy, and Cuff 1986; Miller 1990; Mohr and MacLean 1987). Practitioners who couple basic research theories and techniques with an action-oriented alternative mode can develop collaborative, reflective data collecting and analysis teams for their own practices and thereby better the socio-political-economic context in which they dwell.

WHAT IS TO COME

Qualitative inquiry is everchanging. ''It reminds me of a dot-to-dot exercise that I use with my first graders,'' said Mary. ''One dot of information leads me to another dot, and, in the end, some sort of pattern becomes evident.'' There are many ways to connect the dots, however. Susan, another student, had a difficult time dealing with the ambiguity that new ''dots'' presented. After collecting data for a semester, she stated, ''I'm ready to throw the whole project out because I've come up with so many new questions. This process has blown me away. I feel like I need to go back and begin all over again.'' Susan is right. You know best what you should look for, what questions you should ask, and what methods you should use at the end of your study. The process of getting to that end, however, takes you through a terrain that eventually becomes clearer overall, while growing more complex in detail. We hope that the combination of your own inquiry, field log, and reading of this text will help you to grasp the phenomenon of your research with the clearer understanding and sense of complexity that are the gifts of qualitative inquiry.

CHAPTER **2**

Prestudy Tasks: Doing What Is Good for You

Researchers make many decisions before they begin collecting data through fieldwork. These decisions generally are embodied in a research proposal prepared for possible funding agencies or for a dissertation committee. The sections of this chapter raise issues for discussion in the research proposal (see also Marshall and Rossman 1989). Although we do not advocate a particular format for proposal writing, we do urge careful attention to these prestudy decisions. In their proposals, researchers present the possibilities of their study, deliberate on each aspect of the research, anticipate the requirements of their fieldwork, and create guidelines by which to work.

Cobb and Hagemaster (1987) succinctly discuss nine criteria that a student and committee should consider in developing and evaluating a qualitative research proposal:

1. the students' expertise in doing what they propose,
2. the research problem and/or research questions,
3. the purpose and significance of the proposed research,
4. a review of the relevant literature,
5. the context,
6. the sampling design,
7. the data collection methods,
8. the data processing and analysis methods, and
9. the provision for the use of human subjects.

Surely, you should address these categories comprehensively, but with the understanding that the resulting proposal is somewhat tentative—a forecast of things to come but not in contractual terms. Your plans will probably change as your fieldwork progresses and the opportunities of the field emerge. If you are inflexible, resolutely tied to your prestudy plan, then you may forego the serendipity that the process offers. Yet without a plan, your studies may flounder, suffer many false starts, and needlessly extend the inquiry. The tentativeness of a proposal may be greatly reduced, however, if written after preliminary pilot fieldwork has been completed that sufficiently informs the researcher about the promise of the field situation. If the opportunity exists, this is the preferred procedure.

THE RESEARCH TOPIC

The first research decision is to determine what you want to study. Unless you are working on a project conceptualized by someone else, you must figure out which issues, uncertainties, dilemmas, or paradoxes intrigue you. It is your passion for your chosen topic that will be a motivating factor throughout the various research aspects, some of which are more intrinsically interesting than others. You tap into your subjectivity, of which passion is a part, to find topics appropriate to your interests. The topic, however, should not be so personal that it is of little interest to anyone else; nor, as Douglas (1976) warns, should it be in an area where you have major emotional problems. You must be able to distinguish the line between your passion to understand some phenomenon and your overinvolvement in very personal issues that need resolution.

Distinguishing the difference between a topic for research and one for psychoanalysis is not always easy. For example, one student, who was also an instructor in a small community college, was about to begin a research class when he received word that his teaching contract was not renewed. Understandably, he was angry and disturbed. Consumed with thoughts on this matter, he decided that for his research project he would interview people at his institution to develop a better understanding of why he was dismissed. The class convinced him not only that such an investigation would be limited in scope, but also that he was unlikely to get honest and complete answers from interviewees. In the end, he explored another interest: attitudes of prison guards toward the private tutoring of inmates, a topic that, as he gathered and analyzed his data, brimmed with fascinating possibilities for continued study.

Asking yourself how your proposed research arises out of your life history and whether you are setting out to prove something that you already believe to be true helps to test your emotional attachment to a topic. Ken, an elementary school principal who had held several different principalships, wanted to investigate the relationship of job stress to administrative turnover. Reflecting on the role of subjectivity in his research, Ken wrote:

My topic is perfect, I thought. The turnover rate for school administrators is incredible, I know the subject firsthand, I have dozens of contacts in the field, and stress is on everybody's agenda, both public and private sector. This is definitely a topic for the 1990s.

So what's the problem? I care too passionately about the results. I devoutly want the study to prove that school boards and superintendents should show some compassion for building administrators. I want taxpayers to recognize the limitations of personnel, resources, and supplies, which make the job of principal so frustrating. I want parents to see that a partnership between school and home is in the best interests of the children. I want to prove that the narrow-minded bigots who persecuted, criticized, harassed, and hounded me were wrong. This is clearly no way to begin an unbiased study.

Interestingly, however, I did not realize the full extent of my personal prejudices until I presented my initial ideas to the qualitative methods class. I was angered and shocked to be accused of having an ax to grind—of having reached my conclusions before I began my research. I was particularly angry because I recognized that they were right.

Ken wanted to justify his own experience. Although he needed to be interested in his research topic, his emotional attachment precluded the open, exploratory learner's attitude that is necessary for good data collection and analysis.

Emotional attachment may manifest itself in other ways. If the very thought of approaching your research participants causes severe anxiety attacks, then you should ask yourself why. Debbie, a special education teacher new to her school and district, was experiencing resistance to designing a project that involved interviewing her administrators and supervisors. Finally, she realized that she was threatened by the thought of exposing herself to her professional superiors in her novice researcher role. She considered alternatives, shifted her focus, and set up a study that required obtaining data from teachers rather than from administrators.

Not everyone works effectively under the same conditions. If you are overly intimidated by the thought of going into the field, then consider reshaping your study in a more inviting way. For example, you may feel unprepared to conduct a study involving persons who differ considerably from you in age, social class, or ethnicity. Or your problem may be too large, your field site too complicated. Some of your intimidation may be the result of feelings or problems that you need to overcome; others may represent feelings and problems beyond your capacity to remedy. The qualitative inquiry process, by nature, is replete with anxiety-producing occasions without the researcher unwittingly setting up more.

Practical issues such as time, place, and money must also be considered. The conceived study may be appropriate in academic terms but impossible to conduct given practical limitations. Do not begin with a topic so vast in scope that you could never reasonably afford the time or money to complete it.

Although the planned scope for a research topic should be realistic, neither too broad nor too narrow, the researcher cannot always know the ideal scope until data collection is underway. For example, Purvis (1985) originally planned to look at all forms of adult education provisions for working-class women in nineteenth-century England. As she collected and examined documents, however, she realized she had to narrow her study, but how she should focus her research was unclear. Should she investigate forms of adult education provided by the middle class, or types of adult education organized by working-class women themselves? Should she look at all forms of adult education, or concentrate on a few specific areas? Should she limit her inquiry to education in rural areas or in urban areas, or should she address regional differences? Purvis' range of choices suggests the alternatives available as you consider a research focus; you will find good arguments for supporting many different focuses within the same general area of study.

THE PROBLEM STATEMENT

Once you have selected your research area, clarify it further by writing a problem statement. The problem statement presents the overall intent of the study and indicates how open or closed the study will be. In general, quantitative studies identify sets of variables and seek to determine their relationship. Qualitative inquiry, on the other hand, generally searches for "understanding" of some phenomenon. Depending on what your literature review reveals, however, your problem—otherwise thought of as a statement of the intended contribution of your research—can relate to description, verification (of existing theories, hypotheses, generalizations, or practices), evaluation, or prescription, as well as understanding.

A research project is an effort to remedy the ignorance that exists about something. Thinking about what you do not know, as well as what kind of light you hope to shed, is useful for giving direction to your research adventure. In working out the problem statement, it helps to begin by jotting down all of your questions about your topic. When categories for inquiry are exhausted, look at the questions as a whole and figure out the central or overarching question. Then look at all of the other questions and consider how they can be categorized into subquestions that will assist in investigating the central question (see Bissex 1987).

You will write and rewrite your problem statement, seeing it, at best, as tentative: expect it to change. Give it to friends and advisers for their reactions. Sharpen the specific questions you anticipate asking in interview sessions and look for the interaction between your topic and the questions, so that both topic and questions grow clearer in the exchange.

In the early stages of data collection (ideally, in a pilot study), you may gain understandings of your topic that cause you to change your problem statement. A student interested in interaction among children from different cultures began a participant-observation study in a university child-care center. After observation and reflection on her notes, she realized that gender, not ethnicity, was the important issue at the center. Such changes in research focus may indicate poor planning, but they are also likely to indicate new learning. It is important to be open to such learning, so that the best possible marriage between researcher and topic will result. That the research problem may change is no reason to avoid carefully thinking through your interests and hunches from the beginning. Reading available literature facilitates this process. It, too, is part of getting started.

REVIEW OF THE LITERATURE

Knowledge of the literature will help you to judge whether your research plans go beyond existing findings and may thereby contribute to your field of study. Some qualitative researchers argue against reviewing the literature until after data collection has begun, for fear that the researcher will be unduly influenced by the conceptual frameworks, research designs, techniques, and theories of others. Although we acknowledge this possibility, we think that the benefits of reviewing literature before data collection outweigh the possible harmful effects.

Reading about the studies of others in a way that is useful to your own work requires a particular frame of mind. First, collect, scan, and read the literature to verify that you have chosen a justifiable topic. For example, the many dissertation studies that have investigated why parents send their children to fundamentalist Christian schools have identified and discussed a range of explanations. Another study on this topic, even in a state where no such studies have taken place, could contribute little more of interest. Try to warrant your own project on the basis of what has been done and what has not been done.

Second, use the literature to help find focus for your topic. Existing studies show what is known about a general area of inquiry and what is missing. A review of the Christian school literature suggests that very little is known about the lives of adults who as children attended a fundamentalist Christian school (Glesne and Peshkin, forthcoming). To what extent do they live within the boundaries of the doctrine espoused by their schools? Someone interested in Christian schooling could make a significant contribution by studying this population.

Third, the literature can help to inform your research design and interview questions. Learn from the successes and failures of other researchers investigating similar phenomena. For example, what questions were raised, but poorly worded? What questions were not asked at all? Were the questions asked of a usefully varied group of people? Did the researcher spend enough time to establish rapport and to probe for more than surface responses? What questions worked and thus merit reusing?

Fourth, remember that in qualitative inquiry reviewing the literature is an ongoing process that cannot be completed before data collection and analysis. The data often suggest the need to review previously unexamined literature of both substantive and theoretical nature. For example, before Corrine began fieldwork in the Caribbean (Glesne 1985), she reviewed rural development literature in addition to agricultural and educational studies and documents pertaining to the eastern Caribbean. During her time in the field, but particularly after focused time on data analysis, she began to read extensively about dependency theory, which explained economic and power relationships between nation states. Dependency theory became central to her literature review section, and the rural development literature receded in importance. Indeed, it seems most productive to regard a review of the literature in interactive terms. You can learn different things from the work of others depending on what you already have learned and on what you need to know. You may find yourself both dismayed and pleased to benefit later from material read earlier but overlooked because you lacked the experience to recognize it as beneficial.

In conducting your literature search, cast a wide net. Do not confine yourself to your topic, nor to your discipline. If, for instance, your topic involves the use of French in schools by Franco-Americans, then you will want to collect literature on schooling and bilingualism in general. Anthropologists, sociologists, psychologists, and educators often write on the same topics, but from different perspectives. Try to seek sources from all possible disciplines.

You should not, however, let the widening circles of possibly applicable literature preclude your entry into the field. Remember that the data collected and the data analysis will also inform your literature search. Ernie was preparing to collect data on professionalization in the field of physical therapy. He reflected on his dance with the literature:

> First of all, I needed to define what professionalization was. Then I felt the need to read enough sociology to understand how people achieved it, which got me into the field of professional socialization. Then if you do achieve it and act it out, you are into the area of professional power and influence. After reading literature about that, I thought I needed to understand professional ethics and how that linked with the idea of the development of community. Finally, I realized that if I didn't go out to the field, I'd spend the rest of my life saying, "Next month, I'll be ready."

Remember that being ready to go to the field is often a state of mind, affected by, but not necessarily related to, having completed the preliminaries.

USE OF THEORY

Social scientists define theory in different ways. Some of their positions are attributable to their alignment with either the positivist paradigm or the interpretivist paradigm. Positivists assume that phenomena are best understood by objective observations or measurements that produce empirically verifiable results; they view theory as a set of propositions that explain and predict the relationships among phenomena. The most prevalent positivist definition of theory comes from Homans (1964), paraphrased by Denzin (1988, 49): "Theory refers to a set of propositions that are interrelated in an ordered fashion such that some may be deducible from others, thus permitting an explanation to be developed for the phenomenon under consideration." The ultimate goal of this form of theorizing is to develop universal laws of human behavior and societal functioning.

Glaser and Strauss (1967) criticize the positivist's conventional deductive approach to research, opposing the focus on verification for theory development and the a priori definition of concepts and hypotheses. In *The Discovery of Grounded Theory*, they propose an inductive strategy whereby the researcher discovers concepts and hypotheses through constant comparative analysis. They advocate theory generation through discovery, and call the results "grounded theory." However, they also accept the positivist's position that the ultimate function of theory is explanation and prediction.

Interpretivists such as Geertz (1973) and Denzin (1988) offer yet a different understanding of theory, which is neither explanation nor prediction. It is interpretation, or the act of making sense out of a social interaction. Theory building proceeds by "thick description" (Geertz 1973), defined as "description that goes beyond the mere or bare reporting of an act (thin description), but describes and probes the intentions, motives, meanings, contexts, situations and circumstances of action" (Denzin 1988, 39).

Interpretivists see the goal of theorizing as providing understanding of direct "lived experience" instead of abstract generalizations. Originating in phenomenology, "lived experience" emphasizes that experience is not just cognitive, but also includes emotions. Interpretive scholars consider that every human situation is novel, emergent, and filled with multiple, often conflicting meanings and interpretations. The interpretivist attempts to capture the core of these meanings and contradictions (Denzin 1988, 18). Interpretivists would agree with Coles' understanding that "What ought to be interesting . . . is the unfolding of a lived life rather than the confirmation such a chronicle provides for some theory'' (Coles 1989, 22).

This discussion of theory hints at the difficulty that a researcher may experience in deciding the role of theory in a study. Theory is formulated at different levels of abstraction: One researcher may refer to sets of propositions as theory, while another regards theory as a conceptual framework for reaching understanding. Moreover, some authors tack on theory at the beginning or end of a study, while others make it an integral part of the entire process.

In addition to Glaser and Strauss' (1967) grounded theory, which the researcher discovers, we identify four types of theory that the researcher uses. These vary according to levels of abstraction and scope of applicability. The first three types are from Turner's (1985) classification scheme, and the fourth follows Denzin's (1988) definition of a conceptual framework. The four types of theory are empirical generalizations, causal or theoretical models, middle-range propositions, and conceptual frameworks.

Empirical Generalizations

Empirical generalizations are found in both quantitative and qualitative studies. This type of theory is at a low level of abstraction; it consists of outcomes (empirical generalizations) from related studies and mainly functions to raise questions or provide rationale for new studies, and to compare and contrast with study findings. A review of literature related to the study's main concepts provides the base for working with empirical generalizations.

Causal or Theoretical Models

Studies framed in terms of models go by many names: path, input–output, causal, block-recursive. Causal or theoretical models are more complex than empirical generalizations in that more variables are involved to explain variance, so that the scope of empirical generalizations is expanded. Primarily quantitative studies make use of this form of theory, although qualitative studies may seek to investigate or expand some aspect of a theoretical model.

Middle-range Propositions

What sets middle-range theory apart from empirical generalizations and causal or theoretical models is that it ''pertains to variables that exist for more than one empirical case'' (Turner 1985, 26). ''Middle range theories try to explain a whole class of phenomena—say, for example, delinquency, revolutions, ethnic antagonism. . . . They are therefore broader in scope than empirical generalizations and causal models'' (Turner 1985, 27). Qualitative researchers often make use of middle-range theories as a framework for both asking questions of their study and discussing aspects of their findings. For example, Alan made use of Goffman's (1961) total institution concept while planning, analyzing, and writing up his study of a fundamentalist Christian school (Peshkin 1986).

Conceptual Frameworks

In a conceptual framework, "descriptive categories are placed within a broad structure of both explicit and assumed propositions" (Denzin 1988, 49). These frameworks inform both the methodological and the substantive aspects of many qualitative studies. In such studies, the entire process, with all of its elements, is a reflection of the conceptual framework. The theory of symbolic interactionism and phenomenology are examples of such conceptual frameworks.

In summary, theory, sometimes referred to as the latest version of what we call truth, is used in a variety of ways in qualitative research. Typically, qualitative research is neither invariably nor explicitly driven by theory, but researchers often use empirical generalizations or middle-range propositions to help form initial questions and working hypotheses during the beginning stages of data collection. As they begin to focus on data analysis, they may seek out yet other theories to help them examine their data from different perspectives. Qualitative research may or may not eventuate in statements of theory that are grounded in the data. Finally, some consider the entire research process as theoretical.

SITE SELECTION

With your topic selected and the process of reviewing relevant literature and theories begun, you must decide where to conduct the study, who the study's participants should be, what techniques to use to gather data, and how long to spend in the field. Each decision needs careful prestudy thought, but, as with the problem statement, each is subject to change as data collection proceeds and informs you. No guiding list of rules exists for these decisions, yet that does not mean that anything goes. Literature, documents, discussions with potential research participants, guidance of experienced researchers, and your own good judgment all contribute to sound decisions.

When making site and participant selection decisions, some conventional wisdom is applicable. Unless you are conducting a form of action research, it is not advisable to conduct your study in your own backyard—within your own institution or agency, or among friends or colleagues. Such studies are attractive, however, for a number of presumed reasons: You would have relatively easy access; the groundwork for rapport would already be established; the research would be useful for your professional or personal life; and the amount of time needed for various research steps would be reduced.

Novice researchers are understandably tempted to undertake backyard studies, but they soon become fully aware of the problems generated by their involvement in and commitment to their familiar territory. Previous experiences with settings or peoples can set up expectations for certain types of interactions that will constrain effective data collection. Remember that you already have a role in your personal or professional nonresearch capacity—whether as colleague, supervisor, or friend. In your research role, you will relate to known persons as your research "others." This switch may prove confusing to both parties.

Carolyn, for example, was interested in handicapped children and interviewed special education supervisors about their work. She herself was a mother of a handicapped child. She said of her interviewees, "They couldn't disassociate my research role from my role as a parent of a handicapped child." Instead of giving careful answers to her questions, they tended to say, "Well, you know what it's like," or "We've talked about this before."

Gordon is a school principal whose project involved interviewing students in his school:

> Ah! the innocence of the novice researcher! Feeling smug with my own cleverness for choosing a subject both near and dear, I set out to do my research. What could be easier? I was a well-established, well-regarded principal in a small community. Principals are supposed to study student achievement. Thus I had not only the right, but the professional imperative to visit classrooms and interview students if these activities would bring about improvement in the educational program. I knew each subject individually, my teachers respected me (I had hired most of them), and I had control of scheduling. Best of all, I was the main gatekeeper for the school. Thus, through my role as principal, I had the opportunity, the right, and the resources to make short work of interviews and observations. What could go wrong?
>
> Well, several things. First of all, as principal I was on duty anytime I was in the building and crises didn't go away just because I was doing qualitative research. Thus my good intentions to make observations and do interviews were regularly shattered by irate parents, students with personal problems, broken boilers, and wayward buses. Second, as a principal it was my responsibility to protect the education of children wherever possible. How, then, could I justify taking children out of class to interview them about achievement when half of them were reputed to be underachievers? Third, as the primary disciplinarian in the school, I became involved in a long-term disciplinary process with two of my subjects, and I lost valuable data because I was unable to interview them. Finally, as principal, I felt

pressure not to upset rapport with teachers, so I found that I tried not to rock the boat any more than I had to. I think I lost valuable data by not interviewing them about their views on the underachievement of students.

What did I learn from all this? First of all, I've found that it's a good idea to go away from home to do your research. Research should be undertaken at least far enough away so that your job role does not interfere with your activities. Second, conduct your research where you are not so emotionally close to your subjects that it distorts your design, preferably someplace where you have not worked and lived for many years.

Backyard research can also create ethical and political dilemmas. As an established insider, succumbing to the temptation to be a covert observer may lead to guilt or anxiety over that role. Also, interviews frequently uncover what can be termed "dangerous knowledge"—information that is politically risky to hold, particularly for an insider. Such problems are not limited to backyard research, but they do seem to proliferate there.

If you do not research your own backyard, then how do you go about selecting a site? Often, the selection of research place or places is built into the problem. A colleague, for example, is studying what happens when a Japanese firm moves into a predominantly white, small American city. His interest grew out of year-long negotiations that took place in several small midwestern cities before a Japanese car industry selected one as its base. He then knew where his site would be.

Some research problems do not call for a specific research site; they simply require a setting within some specified geographical boundaries. For example, a study of working single mothers who had been on welfare within the past year does not necessarily involve selecting a single study site, but convenience suggests limiting the selection of study participants to nearby locations.

Commonly, however, researchers have to develop a rationale for selecting one or more sites for data collection. Perhaps the phenomenon you wish to investigate exists to some extent everywhere. Do you choose an exemplary site or an average site? What criteria determine exemplary, average, or other classifiers? If you select an "effective" school, must you also look at an "ineffective" school? How many sites should you select? To make such decisions, you must look again at your research interests and carefully reflect on what you want to study. You may need to try out, or pilot, tentative site selections.

For example, Alan wanted to continue his series of school and community studies by looking at an ethnically diverse school and community. He set two criteria for site selection: (1) a community with only one high school and (2) a community that contained high percentages of African-Americans, whites, Hispanics, and Asian-Americans. The research problem led him to California, a state with considerable ethnic diversity. From state publications, Alan obtained a list of all school systems in California, which included ethnic stratification and the number of high schools in each district. He then visited each of the possible sites and selected one on the basis of two important criteria: (1) would the school and community accept him, and (2) would he feel comfortable working there?

SELECTION OF RESEARCH TECHNIQUES

Qualitative researchers depend on a variety of methods for gathering data. The use of multiple-data-collection methods contributes to the trustworthiness of the data. This practice is commonly called "triangulation" and may also involve the incorporation of multiple data sources, investigators, and theoretical perspectives in order to increase confidence in research findings (see Denzin 1988).

Three data gathering techniques dominate in qualitative inquiry: participant observation, interviewing, and document collection. Within each technique, a wide variety of practices can be carried out, some more common than others. For example, in participant observation, some researchers use videotaping as a means to replay, slow down, and freeze observed interactions. Many, however, rely on their senses, the results of which are relayed through their pens and stored in their field logs. Some researchers use props such as card sorts or pictures as stimuli for specific information in interviews. Most only ask questions.

These data gathering techniques are discussed in later chapters; the point here is that, ideally, the qualitative researcher draws on some combination of techniques to collect research data, rather than a single technique. This is not to negate the utility of, say, a study based solely on interviews, but rather to indicate that the more sources tapped for understanding, the more believable the findings.

To figure out what techniques to use, again consider carefully what you want to learn. Different questions have different implications for data collection. In considering options, choose techniques that are likely to (1) elicit data needed to gain understanding of the phenomenon in question, (2) contribute different perspectives on the issue, and (3) make effective use of the time available for data collection.

SELECTION OF STUDY PARTICIPANTS

Since most research situations are too vast to interview everyone or to observe everything, you will need to devise a selection strategy by which to choose events, times, and people. Committee members and funding agencies often expect the research proposal to delineate clearly how many and which persons will be interviewed, as well as how many and which situations will be observed. The researcher is therefore tempted to develop complex selection matrices. A study of university students might combine criteria such as gender, age, years in program, and major, but should not invest too heavily in such a process. Stratification means thinking in terms of important variables related to the problem; thinking of important stratification criteria is a good place to begin. The open nature of qualitative inquiry, however, precludes the ability to know either all of the important selection criteria or the number of observation or interview sessions necessary to gather adequate data. The selection strategy evolves as the researcher collects data.

For example, as Carol begins her study of the leisure styles of later-life widows, she assumes that leisure is affected by social class, years of education, employment status, and leisure options locally available. Varying her selection of study participants by these attributes helps her to learn more about her topic. Nonetheless, as Carol begins collecting data, she learns of other criteria that appear to affect leisure styles—such as how recently the women were widowed—and must include these in her selection strategy.

As she spends time in the field, Carol may decide that there is too much variation for her to understand the leisure styles of all later-life widows. She would therefore narrow her focus to one group, such as high school educated, working, recently widowed, urban women. Doing so would simplify her selection of participants and allow her to go deeply into the leisure behavior of a reasonably homogeneous group. What struck Carol as ideal at the planning stage of her project would then be replaced by something both useful and feasible.

To exemplify further the various paths that selection of study participants and research techniques might take, we present two cases drawn from the beginning stages of dissertation studies. In any one area of inquiry, you can learn different sorts of things, all of which may be worth knowing. Ask yourself, "What is it that I'm personally disposed to do? What is it that I want most to learn?" The direction finally settled on will depend on the focus selected as worthwhile and feasible. As with site selection, such decisions can sometimes be made only after preliminary work in the field.

Consider the case of Sue, who is interested in the teaching of ethics in nursing programs. She must decide if she wants to focus on ways in which ethical issues are taught in different nursing programs, or if she would rather investigate nurses' perceptions of their own education in ethics.

If Sue were to focus on ways in which ethical issues are taught, she would do participant observation, interviewing, and document collection. Her need would be to get as many perspectives as possible on the pedagogical process. To select her sites, she might lay out all of the nursing programs within the most contiguous geographic area because of the practical limitations of time, transportation, and money. Of the programs available, she would then find out which ones have instructors who either offer courses in ethics or integrate ethical training into other courses. With the number of programs further narrowed, she might decide that, based on her own experience, there could be a difference in how two-year and four-year programs handle the teaching of ethics. Next she would divide her list into four possible groups: two-year programs with ethics integrated into the curriculum, and two-year programs with ethics courses, four-year programs with ethics integrated, and four-year programs with ethics courses.

As Sue collects and reflects on data from one or more sites, new selection criteria may emerge. She may perceive differences in ethics courses that include practical work and those that do not. She may decide to stratify her selection on the basis of who teaches the courses: non-nurses, nurses with two-year degrees, and nurses with advanced degrees. Selection criteria for research sites and respondents would develop from the literature, and from Sue's experience, data collection, and reflection.

Returning to the second option, Sue might decide to focus on nurses' perceptions of their ethical education, rather than on ways ethics is taught. This focus would likely involve much interviewing and little, if any, participant observation. Sue might select one community as her site, acquire a list of all registered nurses, and then begin to select some criteria for initial grouping. If she decides to group by nursing specialty, she might then work on gaining access to pediatric nurses, emergency ward nurses, and nurses in general practice clinics. After interviews with a nurse in each group, she might use her data to consider other criteria for stratifying and selection. She might also decide to shadow several nurses. The research goal is not to describe the norm but to learn about the range of behavior related to the research focus, in order to gain understanding of the complex phenomenon in question.

Consider now the case of Tom, who is interested in sexual harassment policies in institutions of higher education. If he were to study formal policy formation in order to understand sexual harassment codes, then he would collect data primarily through content analysis of documents and through interviews with administrators and, perhaps, university lawyers. He might decide to limit his study to developing a national portrait of sexual harassment policy in state universities. By limiting his investigation to state universities, however, Tom would miss how other higher education institutions deal with sexual harassment. Or, Tom might stratify higher education institutions within his region by type—such as state, private, religious, two-year, and four-year—and then gather data through document collection and interviews with people from different types of institutions.

Instead of focusing on sexual harassment policy development within different types of institutions, Tom might decide that his real interest centers on the perceptions, attitudes, and concerns of different groups within an institution. He would then collect data primarily through interviews and documents from one or two institutions. To select interview participants, he might stratify the university population by position—that is, by student, faculty, staff, and administration—and further stratify by gender. As he interviews, he must attend to the suggestions of other groups and other kinds of people that he might include in his population. The focus of his attention would be the impact of sexual harassment policy on the lives of people in the institution. Each of Tom's several possibilities is a viable choice; at some point, he must narrow his research focus.

In order to begin selecting participants from various stratified groups, qualitative researchers often use "snowball" or "network" techniques. They make one contact and use recommendations to work out from there. For instance, Annette wanted to learn about welfare-to-work transitions of poor African-American women in a midwestern town. She made her first contacts through the minister of a church and the professionals in a local social welfare agency. Her first interviewees gave her the names of others to interview. Although not systematic in the beginning, Annette was able to develop criteria for further stratification from these early interviews; she made enough contacts to help her find potential participants.

Several questions remain. How many persons must you interview? How much must you observe? How do you know when to stop? There are no magic answers. In the numbers game, depth is traded for breadth. For in-depth understanding, you should repeatedly spend extended periods with a few respondents and observation sites. For greater breadth, but a more superficial understanding, carry out one-time interviews with more people and one-time observations in more situations.

Finally, participant selection, for all of its resemblance to subject sampling, is dissimilar because the intentions are different. The sampling of quantitative research is conducted with numbers and variety that support the use of statistical techniques and the prospect of making generalizations. Although qualitative researchers make generalizations (see Wehlage 1981; Stake and Trumbull 1982), they do not depend on a particular numerical basis for their generation. Moreover, the strategy of participant selection in qualitative research rests on the multiple purposes of illuminating, interpreting, and understanding—and on the researcher's own imagination and judgment. (For more discussion on sampling and selection, see Goetz and LeCompte 1984.)

THE TIME FRAME

You cannot know with certainty how long your research will take. Invariably, you will underestimate the amount of time needed. For example, gaining access to a school may drag on because the school board did not address the researcher's plans on the evening scheduled. Introduction to the school's teachers is delayed because the teacher's meeting was canceled. People re-schedule interviews at the last moment, or they don't show up. Unexpected assemblies or field trips change observation schedules.

Despite the delays, do not become discouraged. Rather, remember that unless researching your own backyard, you are external if not alien to the lives of the researched. You are not necessarily unwanted, but, because you are not integral to the lives of your others, you are dispensable. You will complete your research tasks, but normally later than you expect.

Returning to the previously discussed student projects allows examination of how time might work in different research situations. If Tom were to collect and examine sexual harassment policies from a number of universities, he would count on others to send him the documents. If they did not comply, he would then follow up with written or telephoned reminders. Some researchers resist seeking out or following up delinquent respondents; others approach the search process in detective fashion, as a game to ferret out the reluctant in order to achieve the highest possible response rate.

For example, a colleague and friend, Bob Porter (1984), attempted to resurvey 200 participants in a college survey conducted ten years earlier. His search for the original participants familiarized him with high school alumni associations and churches throughout the nation. He learned that 2 participants had died, but of the remaining 198, he eventually traced 196.

The story of Bob's search for one of the women he never found demon-strates the extent of his tracking. Through old college records, Bob traced the woman's family to a small town in Colorado. Her high school had no knowl-edge of her current whereabouts. From an answer on the earlier survey, Bob knew that the woman was raised in the Catholic Church, and so he called the small town priest. The priest remembered where the family had lived and gave Bob the name of a family who lived across the street from their old home. Bob called the neighbors, who remembered the family and described them as reclusive. In probing for clues, Bob learned that the family had always raised Afghan hounds. He tried one more call—to the Afghan hound society. When it was unable to help him, he decided he could let that one go. But through phone calls and follow-up letters, Bob eventually received back 182 of the 196 questionnaires he sent out.

Tom has an easier job because he already knows the whereabouts of the institutions he wants to include in his study. Most likely, however, he will have to be persistent in order to obtain the response rates he desires.

If Sue decides to look at the teaching of ethics in schools of nursing, then she will have to consider time in a number of ways. If she plans to visit schools within driving distance, then she will need to allow time for poor weather. Snow, ice, and fog could lengthen or postpone her trips and cancel the classes she meant to observe. Sue must also consider the semester schedules of the various schools and juggle her visits with official school breaks and teacher-planned activities.

Even with both school and teacher schedules in hand, unforeseen events change the nature of planned visits. For example, another student made arrangements well in advance to interview a principal. She arrived, however, just after the principal discovered that someone had stolen all of the keys to the school. The principal was far from ready to discuss team teaching, the researcher's topic; he postponed the interview. One always needs to allow extra time for data collection. If Sue, for instance, attempts to collect all of her data in two months through tightly scheduled, two-day visits to ten nursing programs, then she will be setting herself up for high stress and mental anguish. Furthermore, she probably will not collect all of the data that she desires and her project deserves.

Institutional structures affect schedule planning. For example, the elementary and high school setting is more structured than the university setting. The scheduling of bells to demarcate set periods assists researchers in planning whom they can interview or when they can observe and for how long. Alan usually interviews high school students during their study hall periods. In a recent study, he was at a school that had abolished all study halls. Finding time for student interviews during the school day meant making arrangements with teachers, arrangements that were subject to all of the vagaries of the typically overscheduled American high school.

The control respondents have over their time within an institutional framework varies. In general, it appears that individuals who hold higher places on the institutional hierarchy have greater autonomy to declare when they are free. Yet they often are busy individuals who reschedule appointments as a matter of course. Those in lower places on the hierarchy often have little autonomy to set a time to talk. When Lynne interviewed the custodial staff of a university, she had to work through the physical plant manager. He helped develop a schedule, communicate the research intent to the staff, and release individuals for interviews. As a result, Lynne felt caught between management and the workers, grateful to the manager for access and to the workers for their stories, but unsure of how to report the data she received. A way around this situation would be to interview people when they are not at work, although that can create other problems.

In thinking about the time needed for participant observation, find out whether the institution has cycles or seasons of activity, and if it has episodic occasions that affect what goes on. If so, your observations should take account of the different phases of the cycle, as well as of the different occasions. This does not mean that observations need to occur every day, but it does mean that time, as well as places and people, must be sampled. Findings from classroom observations made during the first quarter of a school year are likely to differ from those made in the fourth quarter. Classroom observations made only on Mondays may present a very different picture from observations made on other days of the week. Teachers and their students may interact quite differently in September than they do in December, as they may before football games, proms, and all the other big events that temporarily stand a school on end.

Despite the problems that individual researchers face in estimating the time they need to carry out their research, we recommend developing a timetable. Doing so helps to assess the needs of the possible research aspects and to anticipate the requirements of each: arrangements to be made, letters to be written, people to be phoned, and places to be visited. Although somewhat integrated with data collection, analysis and writing should receive at least as much scheduled time as data collection; it is relatively easier to collect data than it is to shape them satisfactorily as words on a page. Finally, the timetable serves as a reality check on the feasibility—given the inevitable constraints of time and finances—of your choice of research methods, sites, and participants.

The timetable is a useful tool, but, like all qualitative research tools, it must remain flexible. In face-to-face interactions, unforeseen circumstances occur that can considerably delay your plans. On one hand, this can be perceived as a source of frustration and anxiety. On the other, the unforeseen is part of the world of exploration, and researchers, if open to what one can learn from occurrences that deviate from their plans, may use it to acquire better data and a better understanding of the people and setting under study.

THE PILOT STUDY

A pilot study can test many aspects of your proposed research. It does so under circumstances that don't count, so that when they do count, you can put your best foot forward. Pilot your observations and interviews in situations and with people as close to the realities of your actual study as possible. Ideally, pilot study participants should be drawn from your target population.

Researchers enter the pilot study with a different frame of mind than they do when going into the real study. The idea is not to get data per se, but to learn about your research process, interview schedule, observation techniques, and yourself. Clarify your piloting intentions for the respondents. For example, ''I would like to interview you with these questions and then talk to you afterward about the questions themselves: How clear are they? Are they appropriate? What else should I be asking?'' The pilot participants need to know that they are part of a pilot and not an actual study. Of course, their role is to answer the questions you ask, but with the intent to improve them. This is one of many times when you must teach your others how to perform as participants in your research.

Less obvious than learning about your research questions and getting a general sense of the nature of your research setting is the need to learn how to be present in that setting. What roles can and should you play in addition to that of researcher? Does the researcher role itself have ramifications that are peculiar to a particular place, ranging from the serious matter of needing clearance from the institution's head for all changes in research routine, to the less serious but still important matter of how to dress. In the course of three studies, each of them in settings with different standards, Alan had no beard and wore no suit and tie, had no beard and wore suit and tie, and had a beard and wore no suit or tie. Learning an institution's rules and expectations, its major actors, and its taboos can direct you to personal behavior that will help you to gain access, and keep it.

How many people need to be in the pilot? Again, there is no specific answer. The number and variability should be sufficient to allow you to explore likely problems, as well as to give you clues on stratification criteria. That is, if level of education is important to your topic, then do your questions work differently with people with a college degree than with those who never graduated from high school? Use the pilot study to test the language and substance of your questions, and the overall length of your interview. Use it to determine how your introduction to the study works: Is it too long or not detailed enough? What else do people want to know? Does it inform as broadly as necessary to reassure your others about your proposed project?

Use the pilot study to test your observation techniques: How do those who are observed respond? What would make them feel more comfortable? Can you take field notes as you observe or should you write them up after observation periods? Use the pilot study to test yourself: How do you present yourself? How do you relate to others? How do you establish rapport? Finally, use it as a chance to inform yourself about the topic itself. What other criteria might be important for selecting research participants? What kind of political or ethical problems might arise against which precautions are needed?

Through pilot studies, Alan looked at a variety of denominational schools in order to begin understanding the differences among them. He narrowed his focus to fundamentalist Christian schools. Then, through pilot studies in several fundamentalist Christian schools, he learned that they are guarded places, sensitive to the presence of non-Christians. The pilot studies were significant in preparing Alan to anticipate the possible uneasiness of the educators in the Christian school he studied.

The pilot study readies you for gathering data. With the results of the pilot, you may revise your research plans, your interview questions, and even your way of presenting yourself.

THE COVER STORY

Pre-data-collection tasks are not complete without a developed cover story. Cover stories are written or verbal presentations of yourself. Different interactions with your others require different introductions of varying levels of detail. You tell the same basic points to everyone, but what else you tell certain individuals depends on the circumstances. The school superintendent needs to know more, and will most likely want to know more, about your study than the teachers and students. Your cover story expands and contracts as fits the case, so that the teacher being observed from the back of the room may receive different reassurances than the teacher being interviewed.

Observing puts the researcher in a passive role, but the teacher needs to feel reassured about what the researcher is doing "back there," what is being scribbled, and what will happen to the scribblings. Interviewing puts the researcher in the active role of asking questions, which makes confidentiality and anonymity more palpable issues. Also, with its format of questions and answers, interviewing resembles a test and can cause interviewee anxiety about "right answers." Reassuring participants that they cannot fail, that they cannot be wrong, is necessary. They need to be told that to "do right" they must simply remember and disclose what they can; verbalize their opinions and feelings; and remain comfortable when they do not remember something or have nothing to say to a question. Reassure them that it is your question that is unclear, not their thinking. The cover story does more than tell what your study is about; it prepares your others to take part most effectively for data collection.

All cover stories address the following twelve points:

1. who you are,
2. what you are doing,
3. why you are doing it,
4. what you will do with the results,
5. how the study site and participants were selected,
6. any possible benefits as well as risks to the participant,
7. the promise of confidentiality and anonymity to participants and site,
8. how often you would like to observe or hope to meet for interviews,
9. how long you expect that day's session to last,
10. requests to record observations and words (by notes, tape recording, or videotaping),
11. clarification that you are present not to judge or evaluate, but to understand, and
12. clarification that there are no right or wrong answers to your questions, and that they are the experts and teachers.

The extent to which you elaborate on each point depends on what you are doing with whom. In addition to covering these points, you should be prepared for other questions that your others might have, such as, "Can I see the data?" or, "Will I get a copy of the final report?" Anticipate such questions and be able to give reasonable answers and explanations without promising more than you can deliver.

An ethical dilemma often occurs with presentation of the cover story. Do you disclose the full research intent if doing so might alter the behavior and answers of respondents? Alan, interested in respondents' perceptions of and attitudes toward ethnicity in a multiethnic school, did not in the beginning disclose this specific research purpose, believing that he would get less natural behavior if he did so. He did not focus directly on ethnicity until he had observed for a semester and had had several interview sessions with his respondents to gather other types of data. Given the obvious thrust of his questions at that time, his strategy involved nondisclosure of interest in ethnicity for a while, followed by quiet, understated disclosure. Although we do not subscribe to a single presentation-of-self standard that fits all circumstances, we emphasize that honesty is the best policy and that it is paramount to disclose research plans from the start. This may be done in a general manner that becomes more specific as the study unfolds. (For more discussion of this issue, see Chapter 6.)

GAINING ACCESS

With all of these preliminary tasks taken care of, you are almost ready to begin your research. But first, you must gain access, which sometimes is a simple matter, sometimes not (Peshkin 1984). This section discusses the process of gaining access in general. As with the other aspects of qualitative research, what you do in practice will depend on the context and the researcher–participant relationship.

Access is a process. It refers to your acquisition of consent to go where you want, observe what you want, talk to whomever you want, obtain and read whatever documents you require, and do all of this for whatever period of time you need to satisfy your research purposes. If you receive full and unqualified consent, then you have obtained total access. If your access is qualified somehow, then you must explore the meaning of the qualifications for meeting research expectations: Should you redefine your research? Should you select another site?

If the study involves some sort of organization or agency, then you must first make contact with its "gatekeepers," the person or persons who must give their consent before you may enter a research setting, and with whom you must negotiate the conditions of access. Since there may be several different gatekeepers, making contact can be complicated, involving different persons at different times. If, for example, you want to study a particular elementary school, do you go first to the principal, the superintendent, or the school board? It is risky to start anywhere but at the top of the hierarchy because acceptance by those in the lower ranks may be negated by those higher up. Yet it is also risky to gain acceptance at the top because others may feel ordered to cooperate or may think that you are somehow politically aligned with one of several factions.

It helps to have an ''informant,'' an insider who knows the individuals and the politics involved, to advise you in making access decisions. Successfully traversing the often sensitive territory of your research field may require not only your own good sense, but also that of an experienced insider who, you happily discover, likes assisting you in the many ways that good informants do. (For more on informants, see Chapter 3.)

If you are concerned with individuals unrelated to any organizational structure, then you must make direct contact with these potential participants. Whether approaching gatekeepers or a series of individuals, you want them to say, ''Yes, your study sounds interesting. You are welcome.'' Such a response is more likely if you are introduced by an intermediary whom the gatekeepers or potential participants know and respect. The others then have a way to check you out—to find out informally who you are, what you are like, and whether they would mind having you around. When there is no intermediary, and even sometimes when there is, gaining access to people within a site is best achieved by first ''logging time.'' Just being around, participating in activities, and talking informally with people gives them time to get used to you and learn that you are ok. This approach leads to better data than one in which a superior requests a subordinate to cooperate with you. For example, asking the principal to arrange a schedule for interviewing the school's teachers can be an efficient way to obtain teacher cooperation, but not necessarily an effective one.

When meeting the gatekeeper, be prepared to negotiate your access. This involves presenting your cover story, listening and responding to concerns and demands, and clarifying overarching issues. First, make clear that your data—field notes and interview transcripts—belong to you, the researcher (or, in some cases, to the researcher and the respondent); claim this ownership in the interest of preserving the anonymity and confidentiality that you promise. Second, make clear what you will deliver. This relates to your responsibility to meet respondents' expectations for things such as receiving drafts that they may review and critique, final reports, or consultation about their problems. Third, make clear the emergent possibilities of qualitative research. In other words, make sure the gatekeeper understands that, although you enter his or her domain with a problem statement, the problem may shift during the course of research and other issues may surface which could require more discussion and renegotiation of access. The necessity of renegotiating all or some part of your relationship to your research site is not farfetched. Gaining access is an initial undertaking, but maintaining access is another matter; it may be occasioned by changes that occur in the expectations and needs of both researcher and researched at any time in the course of the research process.

Just as problem statements and interview questions evolve over the course of fieldwork, so too does trust. Trust needs to be developed before people can be willing to release certain kinds of information. For instance, if you are interested in college students on academic probation, then you should probably wait until after several interviews before requesting access to their academic files. Saying no often conjures feelings of defensiveness and discomfort. You do not want to put your others in this position; nor do you want to be told no.

Despite utmost care, rejections do occur. It is easy to overreact and become paranoid when faced with negative responses to requests to interview, sit in class, or attend a meeting. Although the negative response may be real, resist concluding from it that you will not be allowed to do the other things you have requested. The rejection may be unrelated to anything you have done or could have done, but it is, nonetheless, a signal to reflect on what you are doing and perhaps experiment with other approaches. For example, the same person who is intimidated by the primary researcher may be perfectly willing to have research assistants observe and interview. While Alan was working on the ethnicity study, one teacher told him that she was glad that his co-worker Jim (younger and just out of graduate school) was in her class because he was not threatening and she was accustomed to his presence in her room. She did not want Alan to observe because he was the "big man" and she would be too nervous.

RESEARCHER ROLES

As a researcher, you need to define clearly your research roles. This definition is situationally determined, depending on the context, the identities of your others, and your own personality and values. There are, however, predispositions that all qualitative researchers should carry with them into research situations. First is the researcher's role as researcher. You are a researcher when you are sitting in the back of a classroom taking notes or in the midst of a lengthy interview; you are also a researcher when you talk informally in the grocery store with someone in your study. All of the places in which you present yourself communicate to your others how a researcher acts. As a researcher, ever conscious of your verbal and nonverbal behavior, you are more than usually attuned to your behavior and its impact. This degree of awareness may be uncomfortable to manage, particularly in the early days of your field contacts. Awareness to the degree of great nervousness or paralysis, doing nothing from fearing to do wrong, is of course extreme. What we urge is a useful level of self-consciousness that has you habitually attend to your behavior and its consequences. With such feedback, you have the basis to modify less-than-productive behavior. We also recommend that you seek feedback from persons in the research setting, particularly from your informants, who can see you as you cannot see yourself.

Although often anxiety-producing, the researcher's role can also be ego-gratifying. Students in our research classes discuss how they deal with their new credentials as researchers. After being in the field for a while, they find themselves saying to colleagues, "Well, my research shows that. . . ." They are asked to give presentations; they begin receiving clips of relevant articles and notices from colleagues and friends; and they begin to gain pleasure from their research role.

The second research role is the researcher as a learner. It is important to have this sense of self from the beginning. The learner's perspective will lead you to reflect on all aspects of research procedures and findings. It also will set you up for a particular type of interaction with your others. As a researcher, you are a curious student who comes to learn from and with research participants. You do not come as an expert or authority. If you are so perceived, then your respondents will not feel encouraged to be as forthcoming as they can be. As a learner, you are expected to listen; as an expert or authority, you are expected to talk. The differences between these two roles are enormous.

Whether or not researchers should be advocates is a debated topic. Traditionally, if researchers had a stake in their topic, or took a position on it, then the trustworthiness of their data was suspect. In contrast, the ideal of participatory research is for researcher and researched to be engaged in an interactive, action-oriented process. We support action-oriented and advocacy research but urge novice researchers to begin with a nonadvocacy, nonprescriptive role. The relationship you and your others develop should be marked by reciprocity, trust, mutual respect, and learning, but, at this point, not by advocacy and action. If so moved by problems that action must be taken, then complete the research, redefine your relationship with your others, and get involved.

During data collection, expect to feel—all at the same time or in close sequence—that you are not learning enough, that you are learning more than you can ever deal with, that you are not learning the right stuff, and that you are learning great stuff but do not know where it will lead or how it will all fit together. Anxieties about data collection will change as you engage in each aspect of the research process. Anxieties about how everything will fit together signals that you have begun seriously to consider the meaning of the data. As coding and data analysis proceed, you will invariably become anxious about how to organize everything into written form.

Accompanying all of the various forms of anxiety is the feeling that your research is running your life. In this research-heightened condition, you will see nonresearch settings as potential research sites. Informal events will trigger thoughts about your research, and those near to you may come to know another person. "I learned about creative chaos," said Andrea, in the midst of her research; "I was organized in my research, but my house was a total mess. One day I took my son to school without his shoes. My mind was simply on other things.''

Neither this nor any other specification of prestudy tasks can exhaust the possibilities of what you personally might anticipate and do before you begin to collect data. You may engage in exhaustive, detailed planning; or you may be comfortable with preparations well short of exhaustiveness. In this, as in so much of research, you need to find yourself, your style, so that you will learn what works for you. Getting ready to conduct your study is not an end in itself. It is a means to the end of data collection. The next two chapters address such activity: participant observation and interviewing.

CHAPTER 3

Being There: Developing Understanding Through Participant Observation

After a hot, still day, the evening was delightfully cool. Ina, Elija, and Marcus, Corrine's young, Rasta-aspiring friends, had just entered her house in the Caribbean valley. They had been to a "sing" up on Mango Ridge. A Methodist missionary group from the United States was in the valley for the evening to preach and spread the Word. It was an occasion for a gathering—something out of the ordinary—and many attended. Ina told how a young woman asked him if he had accepted the Lord as his personal savior. Ina had said yes and produced a detailed conversion story when she asked for the particulars. All three friends laughed at this and the other invented tales they had told of evil deeds and repentance.

Corrine laughed with them, but she felt uneasy. After several months in the Caribbean valley, she suddenly wondered what was real and what was made up in the stories she had been told. Ina, Elija, and Marcus assured her that, although they made up names and made up jobs in their earliest conversations, they no longer did this. After all, she was living in the valley with them; she was "practically Vincentian."

Participant observation provides the opportunity for acquiring the status of "trusted person." Through participant observation—through being a part of a social setting—you will learn firsthand how the actions of your others correspond to their words; see patterns of behavior; experience the unexpected, as well as the expected; and develop a quality of trust with your others that motivates them to tell you what otherwise they might not. Interview questions that develop through participant observation are connected to known behavior, and their answers can therefore be better interpreted. Although participant observation ideally continues throughout the period of data collection, it is particularly important in the beginning stages because of its role in informing us about appropriate areas of investigation and in developing a sound researcher–other relationship. Our discussion on participant observation focuses first on the process and then on the researcher. (See also Bogdan 1972; Burgess 1984; Fetterman 1989; Jorgensen 1989; and McCall and Simmons 1969.)

THE PARTICIPANT-OBSERVATION CONTINUUM

Participant observation ranges across a continuum from mostly observation to mostly participation. It can be the sole means of data collection or one of several. Although your actual participant-observer role may fall at any point along this continuum, you will most likely find yourself at different points at different times in the data collection process.

Psychologists typically carry out research entirely at the observer end of the continuum. This role is more in keeping with the traditional scientific paradigm, wherein the researcher has little to no interaction with those being studied. For example, the researcher may observe children in a university day-care program through a one-way glass. Similarly, the observer may sit on a city park bench, notebook in hand, observing town square activities. At the complete observer end of the continuum, your others often do not know that they are being observed.

"Observer as participant" is the next point on the continuum. The researcher remains primarily an observer but has some interaction with study participants. When we studied the fundamentalist Christian school (Peshkin 1986), we interacted with students and teachers, but for a semester we were primarily observers, taking notes from the back of a classroom. We did not teach; give advice; or assist teachers, students, or administrators.

In contrast, Corrine was more of a "participant as observer" during her work in St. Vincent (Glesne 1985). She was interested in nonformal education and interacted extensively with her others throughout her year's residency in their village. She assisted in agricultural work, socialized, and became an intermediary, if not an advocate, in interactions with agricultural agencies. A paradox develops as you become more of a participant and less of an observer. The more you function as a member of the everyday world of the researched, the more you risk losing the eye of the uninvolved outsider; yet, the more you participate, the greater your opportunity to learn.

The "full participant" is simultaneously a functioning member of the community undergoing investigation and an investigator. In order to learn about the politics and workings of a social welfare agency, for example, a researcher may seek employment with such an agency. Doing so is not as easy as first perceived because the researcher must manage two, sometimes conflicting, roles. Jan Yoors, in his book *The Gypsies*, describes the dilemma of becoming a full participant: "I was torn between two worlds and unable to choose between them despite the Romany saying that *Yekka buliasa nashti beshes pe done grastende* (with one behind you cannot sit on two horses)" (Yoors 1967, 47).

Where on this continuum *should* you place yourself? Your answer depends on the question you are investigating, the context of your study, and your theoretical perspective—to restate some of the contingencies underlying our much-used response. What applies to so much of the conduct of qualitative inquiry applies here: What is best done is less a case of what is established as right than of what your judgment tells you is fitting. If you are interested, as Woolfson (1988) is, in the nonverbal interaction between medical doctors and their patients during the initial, symptom-description phase, then you need to observe as unobtrusively as possible. Woolfson operated a video camera from outside the room where doctor and patient sat.

The context of the study can also affect your position on the participant-observer continuum. Because neither of us is a fundamentalist Christian, we could never, without more deception than we could justify, be full participants in our study of the Christian day school. In his study of ethnicity in a California high school (Peshkin 1991), Alan found himself moving from his usual "observer as participant" role to more of a "participant as observer" because he was easily and readily incorporated into the lives of the people there. Your place on the continuum also depends on your theoretical perspective. Many who reject the conventional scientific paradigm as inappropriate for the study of social phenomena also reject research techniques that are noninteractive in nature.

PARTICIPANT-OBSERVATION GOALS

Some people and some places are much studied. People can become jaundiced by the presence of outsiders who stay too short a time to get the picture that local folks have of themselves. Robert Caro, author of a book on Lyndon Johnson, describes his entry into the thinly populated county where Johnson grew up. At first the local people did not trust him. Too many reporters and journalists had already come for a day or a month and had invariably misrepresented the place and its people. Caro says,

> The people felt—and they were right—that they were being used, and that the things that were being written didn't accurately reflect and convey the country they loved. When I moved there, as soon as I said "I love it here and I'm going to live here and I'm going to stay here as long as it takes to truly understand it," their attitude really changed. (Caro 1988, 227)

In contrast to the general journalistic tendency to swoop in and swoop out, the ethnographic researcher means to stay long enough to get the native's point of view.

The main outcome of participant observation is to understand the research setting, its participants, and their behavior. Achieving this outcome requires time and a learner's stance. Hymes states:

> Much of what we seek to find out in ethnography is knowledge that others already have. Our ability to learn ethnographically is an extension of what every human being must do, that is, learn the meanings, norms, patterns of a way of life. (Hymes 1982, 29)

"Rather than studying people," agrees Spradley, "ethnography means learning from people" (Spradley 1979, 3).

As a learner, you are not in the research setting to preach or evaluate, nor to compete for prestige or status. Your focus is on your others, and you work to stay out of the limelight. To maintain this stance, be flexible and open to changing your point of view. Bateson describes the importance of this attitude in the lives of her parents (Gregory Bateson and Margaret Mead) and in anthropological fieldwork in general:

> In anthropological fieldwork, even when you take with you certain questions you want answered or certain expectations about how a society functions, you must be willing to turn your attention from one focus to another, depending on what you are offered by events, looking for clues to patterns and not knowing what will prove to be important or how your own attention and responsiveness have been shaped. (Bateson 1984, 164)

Through participant observation, you also seek to make the strange familiar and the familiar strange (Erickson 1973). The strange becomes familiar in the process of understanding it. To make the familiar strange is often more difficult because you must continually question your own assumptions and perceptions, asking yourself: Why is it this way and not different? Overcome your disposition to settle into a way of seeing and understanding that gives you the comfort of closure at the price of shutting down thought.

In the end, your new understandings—achieved through your learner's stance, your flexibility, and your emphasis on making the strange familiar and the familiar strange—provide new vantage points, new ways of thinking about some aspect of social interaction.

THE PARTICIPANT-OBSERVATION PROCESS

In everyday life you observe people, interactions, and events. Participant observation in a research setting, however, differs in that the researcher carefully, systematically experiences and consciously records in detail the many aspects of a situation. Moreover, a participant observer must constantly analyze his or her observations for meaning (What is going on here?), and for evidence of personal bias (Am I seeing what I hoped to see and nothing else? Am I being judgmental and evaluative?). Finally, a participant observer does all of this because it is instrumental to the research goals, which is to say that the observer is present somewhere for particular reasons. In your ordinary, everyday life, you may be a good observer of the interactions around you, but you do not consciously record and analyze what you hear and see in the context of particular goals that direct your behavior.

Early Days of Fieldwork

The first days in the field are the most anxiety-producing, as you question whether people will accept you and whether what you are doing is "right." The early days are also exciting and full of new learnings, but the many unknowns can create stressful situations.

Do not feel the need to "get in" with everyone, everywhere. Look for easy openings, that is, with friendly, welcoming people. Spend time with them, but never to the neglect of others at the site. Spend enough time with them, however, for them to get to know what you are doing, how you will be present, and what it is like to have you present—so that they can reassure others about you.

Figure out where the safe places are in the setting—safe because they are not controlled by any one person. In a school, this might be the cafeteria, the teachers' lounge, hallways, and the grounds outside the school. Spend time in these places, getting to know people and letting them get to know you, so that they will feel comfortable with you and will be more apt to respond positively when you ask to observe in "their" space.

Look for entry into closed places that in some ways are controlled by a person or group, possibly by arranging for introductions through mutual friends. Do not seek administrative-ordered permission to enter closed places in institutions, such as schools; if formal permission is given, do not take it as a proper invitation. Instead, arrange for the administration to announce your presence; then, address all of the teachers with your cover story, clarifying that you want to come to their classes but that you will not do so unless they agree. Before school in-service sessions are a fine time to introduce yourself and your project.

If the teachers do not routinely introduce you to the students during your classroom visits, ask if you can do so the first time you come to a class. This allows you to reassure the teacher and the students that you are there to observe, not to judge or evaluate. You can also more easily interact with students because they know who you are and why you are there.

When visiting classrooms, arrive at the beginning of a period and leave when the period is over. Be unobtrusive; do not call attention to yourself. Take notes only when doing so is understood and accepted by the teacher. Do not leave without a word of thanks to the teacher. If you are lucky, you will be invited back "anytime."

Finally, guard against bringing preconceived opinions to your participant observation. This is particularly easy to do if you are or have been a teacher, nurse, or social worker yourself and then become a participant observer in a similar site. Even though you were once "there," you cannot safely assume that you know what the people are like in your research site. All schools, hospitals, and social work agencies are not the same. For example, Sandy taught in a school where teachers were very critical of professors from a nearby university. Therefore, when she began participant observation in a school in another university town as part of her dissertation research, she was hesitant to identify herself with the university—when in fact the school chosen for her study had a good working relationship with the university. Do not assume that you know nothing about schools, hospitals, or village life, but do assume that you have to learn about the particular site and its people.

Observations

When you begin your role as a participant observer, try to observe everything that is happening: make notes and jot down thoughts without narrow, specific regard for your research problem. Study the *setting* and describe it in words and in sketches, using all your senses. How does the setting sound and smell? In what ways does a setting change from place to place throughout your research site? For instance, if you are doing research in a K–12 school, then in what ways is the first grade setting similar to and different from a twelfth grade classroom? Work on making the familiar strange. For example, if you notice that classroom doors tend to be left open (or closed), then ask yourself what this signifies.

Take note of the *participants* in the setting. Who are they in terms of age, gender, social class, ethnicity? How are they dressed? What do they do and say? Who interacts with whom? Make note of the conversations you hear.

Take note of *events*, differentiating between special events and daily events; then look for *acts* within those events. In the fundamentalist Christian school, for example, the first event of every day was a teachers' meeting. What kind of greetings do teachers offer during teachers' meetings, and to whom do they offer them? What do they informally talk about with one another? What kinds of questions do they ask of the principal? In other words, what "acts" make up the "event" of a teachers' meeting?

Another category for observation is people's *gestures*. How do students show enthusiasm and boredom? How does the teacher? What gestures help the principal to deliver his or her points? Observe which gestures jump out at you, which you take for granted, and which you might be misinterpreting. If a child lies with her head on the desk while the teacher is talking, is she sleepy, bored, or concentrating?

Cross-cultural research brings with it the recognition of either new gestures or new meanings to familiar gestures. A whispered "pssst" in the Caribbean can be a friendly "hello." Sucking air in through one's teeth with an upward motion of the head, however, is not the desired reaction to one of your serious comments—it signifies disregard, disagreement, or disdain. But you need not go to another country to find differences in how gestures are used. Native American children may opt for collaborative work assignments and avoid ones that draw attention to individual success (Sindell 1987). African-American children may seek eye contact with the teacher but at a different rate than white children do (McDermott 1987). Just as teachers, to be effective, need to be aware of cultural differences in gestures, so too do researchers.

As a participant observer, then, consciously observe the research setting; its participants; and the events, acts, and gestures that occur within them. In the process, note what you see, hear, feel, and think. Unless you are doing a case study that concentrates on a few people, focus your attention on behavior rather than on individuals (Glaser and Strauss 1967); this will assist you in abstracting to similarities and differences across individuals and events. For example, Ginny chose to practice her observation skills in the lounge of a squash facility during a men's round-robin tournament. After a period of jotting notes, she began to see a pattern:

> The winners of matches seem to stand or walk around after the match is complete. The losers always sit immediately. Blue headband wins. Red sits. Blue goes off to find a towel and water. Blondy, who had mentioned a head problem earlier, wins a match with Glasses. Glasses sits down. Blondy walks around and asks the director who is winning.

Ginny continued with more examples and concluded with questions about the behavior of male winners and losers during sports competition. She was able to move from the individuals in her observation, to their behavior, to thoughts about the more general behavior of men in sports events. (See also Bogdan and Biklen 1982 for an excellent discussion of field observations.)

Field Notes

Notebook Form.   The field notebook or field log is the primary recording tool of the qualitative researcher. It becomes filled with descriptions of people, places, events, activities, and conversations; and it becomes a place for ideas, reflections, hunches, and notes about patterns that seem to be emerging. It also becomes a place for exploring the researcher's own biases.

The actual form of the field notebook varies with the preferences of the individual researcher. Some arrange everything chronologically in spiral-bound notebooks; others keep loose-leaf notebooks so that different kinds of notes can be easily separated; yet others take notes on pads of paper, later transferring them to computer files. Alan used to complete data gathering with a large box full of spiral-bound notebooks, until his research in Riverview, California, when he replaced his notebooks with 5 × 8 cards. He limited one point to a card and gave each card a date and a topic label, such as "Filipino," or a general label for later categorizing. Since during data analysis Alan always organized his field notes onto 5 × 8 cards, he reasoned that he might as well start out with them that way. Not only does this save the laborious process of cutting up photocopied field logs and attaching them to cards, but it also motivates him to develop preliminary categories or codes early on.

Writing directly on cards may be a good method for those who can work from their handwritten notes. Those who prefer to transcribe everything into their computer are increasingly served by computer programs that assist in the coding and sorting of data (more on this later).

What form you choose for keeping notes is not important. That you keep a field notebook, however, is vital. (See Sanjek's [1990] edited volume *Field-notes*.)

Making Notes.   Lofland (1971) distinguishes among mental, jotted, and full field notes. Mental notes are made of discussions or observations when pulling out one's notebook would not be prudent. In the fundamentalist Christian school, since we did not take notes during chapel, we made mental notes and wrote them up later. Jotted notes may be done in private or in public. They are the few words jotted down to help remember a thought or a description that will be completed later on. The full field notes are the running notes written preferably throughout the day, but sometimes, depending on the circumstances, after the observational period.

If possible, carry a notebook with you at all times and make it known that, as a researcher, you will write in your notebook. Your role will become that of inscriber, and soon it will be expected that if anything at all is going on, you will write it down. Of course, not all situations lend themselves to full note-taking. Agar (1973) could not take his notebook with him when doing research on drug addiction in New York City. Even in safe places, some researchers suggest that you should ease into writing. While doing research in a school, you may say that you plan to take notes, but this does not necessarily mean that you should or will do so at the outset of your fieldwork. You may want to spend from a few days to a few weeks just hanging out, getting to know the people and the place before you judge that it is acceptable to begin note-taking and determine just when and where it is acceptable to do so.

All notes should be expanded later, preferably the same evening. Some studies indicate that you can sleep on a day's events and retain your recall abilities, so that you could write up field notes the morning after participant observation. Ability to remember the details needed for field notes declines rapidly after that period of time, however.

Allot ample time for working on field notes. If you are making only mental or jotted notes, some researchers suggest that you give as much time to writing up your notes as you did to being in the field. If you are taking full field notes, then allow several hours to read through your notes to clarify and expand on them and to add your reflective thoughts and ideas. If this all seems rather much, we reassure you that your ability to write quickly and to observe and remember what you saw and heard does improve with practice. We further reassure you that you will be pleased with the trouble you take to prepare clear, ample notes when later you sit down to analyze and write. One caveat: Your comfort zone may be breached by the demands of notekeeping. Find a balance between preparing notes that support your research needs and preparing them to an extent that makes research a seriously aversive act.

Descriptive Notes. Your field notes should be both descriptive and analytic. In recording details, strive for accuracy, but avoid being judgmental. Make sure that your notes will enable you, a year later, to visualize the moment, the person, the setting, the day. Summarizing observations into succinct abstract statements will not do the job. For example, after observing a class, you might be tempted to write, ''The class was disorderly and noisy.'' This statement does not present a clear picture of the classroom, and it is judgmental because it relies on the researcher's conceptions of ''disorder'' and ''noise.'' The following statements are more concrete in their descriptiveness:

> The fifth grade class contained fifteen girls and twelve boys. When I entered, they were clustered loosely into six groups. One group of four girls was trying to see who could blow the biggest bubble with their gum. A group of five boys was imitating a Kung Fu movie they had seen on tv the evening before. . . .

When you observe and describe the interactions taking place, you invariably look for patterns in what at first you might perceive as chaos and disorder. Check your field notes for vague adjectives such as *many* or *some* and replace them with more descriptive words. Look for and replace with descriptions words that convey an evaluative impression, that obscure rather than clarify, such as *wonderful, mundane, interesting, doing nothing, nice,* or *good*.

Make note of the dialogue that occurs. In particular, focus on words frequently used in or unique to the setting. Such terms help in wording interview questions and often become ''native'' or participant-generated analytic categories in the final write-up. Be alert for familiar words that assume very different meanings from your usual understanding. Corrine spent a month in St. Vincent before she understood that Vincentians did not use the word *country* to describe any nonurban area. Instead, they used "up country" to refer to the windward or eastern side of the island. A young man who lived in the capital city, Kingstown, but went "down leeward" (to the western side of the island) every weekend to help his grandmother on her land could honestly answer that he could not remember when he was last "in the country."

Drawing sketches also helps you to visualize a setting. Focus on where people and inanimate objects are located in space. Are there patterns? Do they change over time?

Your eyes, ears, and hands join forces to capture the details of a setting in your field notes, particularly early on in your fieldwork, when you are trying to capture an overall picture of the setting and its people. Through note-taking, you reflect on the appropriateness of your problem statement and become increasingly focused. Then, what you record and what you omit will begin to depend on your ever-refined, ever-clarified purpose. If you decide to emphasize, for instance, the interactions of international children in a university day-care center, then you do not need to describe in detail the teacher's curriculum. If, however, you are looking at the role religion plays in Christian schools, then you do note where in the curriculum religion does and does not play a part.

The following is an example of descriptive notes from Corrine's field log of the St. Vincent setting in which she lived:

The valley stretches from the sea four-and-a-half miles inland until lost in the interior's 3,000-foot peaks. At 6:00 A.M. on a November Sunday morning, the bay is already a scene of relaxed activity. As a light rain develops, old men move into the fishermen's bamboo shelter. One curses another about his chickens. At the mouth of the river, men, women, and children gather to catch tree-tree (fish no longer than one's fingernail) by weighting burlap sacks on the river bottom with stone and then covering the sacks with "bush" (branches of trees and shrubs). The small fish seek the shelter of the leaves but are caught when the fabric is suddenly lifted from the water. On down the black sand beach, young women and children sit where the water meets the shore. Young men swim to a fishing boat anchored farther out, climb aboard, and talk as the boat gently rocks with the rising and falling sea. A rainbow stretches from beyond a "board house" (house made of wood) on a point of land bathed in yellow light to the middle of the sea. In the other direction lies the valley, green and pastoral, with rugged hills covered in clouds.

A lane lined by sprouting fence posts leads into the valley. Cattle, horses, and sheep intermingle on the lush, river-mouth land. Thorny, palmlike trees stand out on the nearby cliffs. They soon give way to coconut palm, mangoes, breadfruit, and citrus trees. A mile into the valley, where most of the villages are, one forgets the immensity and varied moods of the nearby sea and is only aware of the enfolding mountains, often misty with rain.

Villages sprinkle the two miles of arterial road which, after the last village, winds on up into the mountains a short distance before becoming a track for walking and climbing to land terraced and planted primarily in eddoes or bananas. The fields continue as the land slopes steeply, but then give way to natural vegetation.

These descriptive notes were intended to portray the context in which more focused observations and conversations took place. They set the scene for discussion of the life of young people within that valley. They do not analyze or try to explain what was going on; they only describe.

Analytic Notes.   Analytic notes are sometimes called ''observer comments,'' but they should be more than comments. After each day of participant observation, the qualitative researcher takes time for reflective and analytic noting. This is the time to write down feelings, work out problems, jot down ideas and impressions, clarify earlier interpretations, speculate about what is going on, and make flexible short- and long-term plans for the days to come. Of course, reflective and analytic thoughts may come to you during participant observation and at other times as well. It is important to make note of these thoughts— to write ''memos'' to yourself (Glaser and Strauss 1967). Otherwise, the thoughts are apt to slip away. Mark these memos in some way to identify them easily as your own thoughts and wonderings. Analytic noting is a type of data analysis conducted throughout the research process; its contribution ranges from problem identification, to question development, to understanding the patterns and themes in your work. Bateson says of her mother, Margaret Mead,

Margaret always emphasized the importance of recording first impressions and saving those first few pages of notes instead of discarding them in the scorn of later sophistication, for the informed eye has its own blindness as it begins to take for granted things that were initially bizarre. When something occurs to you, *write it down*, she said. (Bateson 1984, 165)

This is good advice to follow.

The following six guidelines are, in a sense, tricks of the participant-observer's trade gained through experience. They are lore about the process of ''noting'' as a participant observer, some of it inapplicable if you use a word processor.

1. When taking notes by hand in a notebook, write only on one side of the paper. This reduces confusion if notes are later photocopied and cut into chunks for data analysis.
2. Leave ample margins on either side of your notes for coding and for afterthoughts.

3. Create your own form of shorthand to assist you in note-taking. For instance, in our field notes *Christian* soon became Xn, *student* S, *knowledge* K, *teacher* T, and *school* sch. We also used the same shortened forms for similar prepositions and other commonly used words, relying on the context to differentiate them. Thus, *became* and *because* were both noted as b/c, *with* as w/, and *without* as w/o. If you know shorthand, then you may see this made-up shorthand as inefficient; if not, then our advice is to develop your own system.

4. When taking jotted notes, do not discuss your observations with someone else before writing up full field notes. Such talk not only dissipates the need to get your observations and thoughts down on paper, but also can modify your original perceptions. This does not mean that you should not compare your interpretations with others, but first record your own observations and reflections.

5. Even if you have been taking full, running notes throughout the day, your work is not done when the school bell rings or the sun sets. Read through the day's notes. Fill in remembered descriptions, clarify and expand briefly noted events or actions, and then reflect on the day and write your thoughts.

6. Invariably, unplanned occasions provide data relevant to your research question. Include these casual encounters in your field notes. Qualitative research is not delimited by time or space, even though when focusing on an institution such as a school, data collection generally occurs within set hours in a set location. This does not preclude collecting data in other places at other times.

Finally, let us reassure you that variety in observations does not mean that someone got it wrong. Journalist Joan Didion (1988) describes how both she and her husband wrote very different books about El Salvador despite being together all of the time that they were there. Differentiating between "institutional" and "cultural" studies of pupils, Ball states, "The landscape looks different depending on the particular hill you happen to choose to stand on" (Ball 1985, 28). Our subjective dispositions may direct us to a variety of different things. This variety reveals the multiple realities of any social phenomenon, which together provide a fuller picture of the people, the times, and the place. Mary Catherine Bateson observes,

> You record carefully what your attention has allowed you to see, knowing that you will not see everything and that others will see differently, but recording whatever you can so it will be part of the cumulative picture. (Bateson 1984, 164)

Other Fieldwork Allies: Informants, Photographs, and Documents

Informants.   Anthropological and sociological ethnographers often develop a close working relationship with a member of the researched group. This person is, in ethnographic terms, an "informant." The informant plays a variety of roles, limited only by researcher imagination and informant willingness and capability, such as making introductions, alerting the researcher to unexplored data sources, and helping to develop theories grounded in the data. Although it has not traditionally been the case, the informant role today is sometimes carried out by a "native" collaborator who plays the role of partner in all aspects of the research process.

In Alan's study in Mansfield, Illinois (Peshkin 1978), a teacher volunteered himself as informant, asking, "Do you want to know what really is going on here?" And in the Christian school study (Peshkin 1986), one student slowly emerged to play this role over the course of many interview sessions. By all indicators, the student was a faithful Christian, but he had reserved some type of autonomy that was expressed in his particularly forthcoming conduct. In his own way, he too was peripheral to his institution, although, unlike Alan, he was an insider as well.

Informants are indispensable partners in the conduct of qualitative inquiry. There will be much that you could not know without the interpretive knowledge, sensitivity, and insights of insiders, from the development and wording of interview questions to understanding hierarchies of power and authority.

In fact, you may need more than one informant, and you may have recourse to different informants at different times in your research process. Informants, unlike members of a rogue's gallery, do not line up for selection. Knowing that you need informants, be on the lookout for them; be ready to nurture the relationship with those willing and able to serve in the role; and be ready to receive and appreciate them for the treasures they are. In this, as in your other research relationships, you must be attuned to the responsibilities of reciprocity with your informants, and to the need not to offend or abuse as you develop what ideally is a mutually rewarding association. (For extended accounts of informants in the lives of famous anthropologists, see Casagrande 1960.)

Photographs.   Photography and videotaping techniques can enhance observation, and they can be employed in a variety of ways. For microanalysis, or focusing on one aspect of everyday interaction, videotaping is invaluable. For example, Pat wanted to understand how low-income mothers help their children to learn. She had access to videotapes of such mothers and their children in laboratory-play situations, and she observed the tapes over and over. Then she interviewed the mothers, using her observations as a guide for question development. Through her observations and interviews, Pat developed a detailed coding manual that incorporated both behavioral and cognitive information for analyzing the videotapes.

The qualitative researcher remains open to creative ways to enhance data collection. Special educator Bruce was interested in familial perceptions of their children with handicaps. He gave a roll of film to each family and asked them to take pictures of the child and family members in everyday activities. A member of his research support group suggested that he give the families another roll of film and ask each member to take five pictures that for him or her symbolize the child but without the child in the picture. He could then interview each family member about his or her pictures and perhaps uncover items that he would not see or otherwise ask about.

Photographs also provide useful data for the historical background of your study. Alan asked residents of his rural school-community study (Peshkin 1978) to show him their family albums, which contained pictures dating back as far as seventy years. Such pictures not only captured the past in a special way, but they also served, as in Bruce's research, as the basis for interviewing. The utility of photographs, like the utility of informants, is limited only by your imagination (see Becker 1986a; Bogdan and Biklen 1982; Fetterman 1989).

Documents.   Archaeologists reconstruct life in past times by examining the documents left behind. These documents, usually called artifacts, provide archaeologists with the basis for hypotheses about how people fed, clothed, and housed themselves; with whom they communicated; and how they thought about gods and an afterlife. Archaeologists cannot observe and participate in the everyday life of their others; they cannot interview men and women and children. Yet, from the records people leave behind, archaeologists can re-create their probable lives.

You have it easier than the archaeologist because you can both observe people in their normal interactions and ask them about the meanings of their actions. This is not to suggest, however, that you should ignore documents as a source of data. Documents corroborate your observations and interviews and thus make your findings more trustworthy. Beyond corroboration, they may raise questions about your hunches and thereby shape new directions for observations and interviews. They also provide you with historical, demographic, and sometimes personal information that is unavailable from other sources.

As a society that venerates the written word, we have many types of written documents. Diaries, letters, memoranda, graffiti, notes, memorials on tombstones, scrapbooks, membership lists, newsletters, and newspapers are all potentially useful documents. A comparison of graffiti on the bathroom doors in the fundamentalist Christian school (only two statements observed all year, both witty but tame) with that found in the community's public school (many and of various natures) reinforced the image of the Christian school students that our observations and interviews had provided us.

Students in the Christian school, as with students everywhere, passed notes to one another during classes, then crumpled them and left them behind. These notes became artifacts in our research—consistent with our other findings. Compare, for example, the substance of the message from a Christian school student (in the first letter below) with that from a public high school student (in the second letter below):

Joe,

I'm not the kind of girl who lets a guy boss me around. I don't like any guy doing that to any girl. . . .

If you save me a seat at lunch, I'll sit with you. . . .

I'm not going to meet you anywhere on my bike 'cause Mom will somehow find out and I'd be in big trouble.

Plus, I'd feel very bad 'cause I'd have to lie about where I was going and what I was doing . . . . Talk to you later.

Rachel
(Peshkin 1986, 155)

Fran,

I'm gonna kick this girl Nicky's ass in 3rd period. She has a smart ass mouth! I'm 'bout to hit her in it.

Are you going to the class meeting today? I might. I'm going to the junior prom, my mom's going to get a dress for pregs but in style.

Bell just rang finish later.

Lisa
(Peshkin, unpublished letter 1986 fieldwork)

To understand a phenomenon, you need to know its history. Reviewing a town's newspapers and institutional newsletters are one way to get started. A town's library archives are a good place to begin, but you will most likely get access to even more useful historical documents by letting it be known that you are interested in old letters, scrapbooks, and minutes of meetings. Such matters often work in a network fashion; once you find someone delighted by your historical interests, that source will usually lead you to someone else.

You can ask research participants to produce documents for you: to keep diaries, journals, or other kinds of records. If working in a school, you may be able to collaborate with teachers so that assignments simultaneously meet the needs of students, teachers, and researcher. For instance, if you are interested in children's self-concepts, then you may be able to persuade English teachers to ask their students to write self-portraits and then let you read them.

Notwithstanding your comfort with the written word, do not forget other forms of potentially useful documents, such as films, drawings, paintings, and music. While in St. Vincent, Corrine asked the children who found her home an entertaining hangout to draw themselves as they imagined they would be when grown. From these drawings she pulled out themes for comparison with the themes that emerged from interviewing young adults. She also analyzed the reggae and calypso music played in St. Vincent (particularly that composed by Vincentians for Carnival) for its agricultural and educational messages; her findings were consistent with hunches gleaned from participant observation and interviews.

Documents provide both historical and contextual dimensions to your observations and interviews. They enrich what you see and hear by supporting, expanding, and challenging your portrayals and perceptions. Your understanding of the phenomenon in question grows as you make use of the documents and artifacts that are a part of people's lives.

THE PARTICIPANT OBSERVER

The participant observer's role entails a way of being present in everyday settings that enhances your awareness and curiosity about the interactions taking place around you. You become immersed in the setting, its people, and the research questions. One way to test if you are being there appropriately is whether or not you are seeing things you have never noticed before. After Andrea began her study of a community, she wrote the following in her field log:

> I went to a local restaurant for breakfast, caught myself watching the gathering of men at the breakfast bar, and found myself wondering for the first time: Who are those men? Why do they come here? How come I never noticed them before? Should I find out who they are—perhaps they represent some potential research rock yet unturned? I enjoy this newly honed sense of seeing.

After a period of time in the field, another test is whether you find within yourself a growing determination to understand the issues at hand from the participant's perspective. This indicates that you have been able to suspend your personal judgment and concerns. In the words of Sigmund Freud: ''I [Freud] learnt to restrain speculative tendencies and to follow the unforgettable advice of my master Charcot: to look at the same things again and again until they themselves begin to speak'' (Malcolm 1987, 95).

Another gift of immersion is that everything you read and hear can be connected, or at least considered for connection, to your phenomenon. (For more on connectedness, see Gould 1990, 3–6.) Ideas are generated and notes pile up. It is a time of transformation, when a research persona emerges with a life of its own. This persona is the one that fits your research field. It is not that you become some unrecognizable other person, but that, as you respond to the needs of being present somewhere in the role of researcher, you learn that you cannot just be the person you are in other settings playing more familiar roles. You are more and less yourself, moved to unexpected behavior in order to capitalize on research opportunities and constrained from ordinary behavior that would interfere with your progress.

Anxiety: A Research Companion

Immersion in and connectedness with someone else's life do not occur without tensions and problems. After finding a place to live in the Vincentian village, Corrine wrote the following in her field log:

> I am moved into the house—complete with bats that fly out of the sink drain, a cockroach apartment complex in the kitchen cabinets, a strange smell of something dead under the kitchen floor, bat races in the ceiling every morning at four A.M., no refrigeration so that even bread does not last the night without molding, and a toilet which leaks.
>
> Moving in is easy, though, compared with moving out into the community to begin observation and informal interviews. I finally forced myself outside around nine A.M., although I was ready to go at 7:30— I just couldn't make my feet walk out the door. I felt out of place, näive, unsure. . . .

Although Corrine's work took place in another culture with its attendant novelty and strangeness, immersion into an unfamiliar setting within your own country can be as anxiety-producing. Expect to feel like a somewhat awkward newcomer, as people rightfully wonder who you are, why you have come, what you will do, and what sort of nuisance you might prove to be.

New participant observers often feel timid, sensing that as invaders of someone else's territory, they are unwanted and unnecessary. It is true that, unless engaged in collaborative research, you are neither invited nor necessary. If, however, you retain that timidity, then you will limit your success because you will be too restrained about where you go, who you see, what you ask, or how much time you take. With a little effort and time, plus some skill, this awkwardness passes, your presence becomes ''natural,'' and you begin to feel at ease. You need not become an essential presence to feel at ease and be welcomed; you just have to behave well, fit in with the local behavioral norms, and be agreeable, interested, polite, and respectful. In fact, you may find yourself behaving "better," that is, more properly than you otherwise do in your nonresearch life.

Feeling at ease does not, however, happen all at once with all participants in all sites, and it may never happen with some people in some places. Occasionally, overcoming timidity and fitting in may mean finding a role in the setting where you contribute in some way, although such roles are not always necessary, not always possible, and not always useful. What you do and how it is received depends on your skills, research needs, research participants, and setting.

Once accepted into the research setting, your companion anxiety latches onto new worries: Are you talking to the right people, observing the right events, and asking the right research questions? Soon after beginning his study in Riverview, California, Alan noted the following in his field log:

> Titles keep popping into mind. This process begins earlier in each study. It is more than just a game. I really don't know what I can, should, or want to do. What stories does the place support? Today I got the first of my sinking feelings that I'm lost. The place is too big for me, and I won't be able to handle it.

Alan was able to "handle" it, and he did learn at least some of Riverview's stories. Anxiety of varying degrees is our constant companion: we need to acknowledge its presence, take account of its messages, and then continue our work.

In addition to courting anxiety, researchers face mental and physical fatigue from overdoing, especially from "overbeing," which is a sense of always being on stage and therefore on best behavior. Fatigue generally finds researchers after they have been in the field for an extended time; burnout becomes a possibility. When feeling overwhelmed with fatigue, it is clearly time to consider interspersing work with breaks of various sorts taken both inside and outside the field.

Participating

As discussed earlier, how much of a participant you can or should be in a study varies. Horowitz takes issue with the implication that the researcher is essentially free to choose the degree and form of participation:

> I will argue that fieldwork roles are not matters dictated solely, or even largely, by the stance of the fieldworker, but are instead better viewed as interactional matters based on processes of continuing negotiation between

the researcher and the researched. Together, the qualities and attributes of the fieldworker interact with those of the setting and its members to shape, if not create, an emergent role for the researcher. (Horowitz 1986, 410)

Research others often assign the researcher a role in keeping with their own conceptual frameworks. Horowitz was identified as a "lady" (which meant she was sexually unavailable) and as a "reporter" by the young male gang members she studied. The roles allowed her access to considerable information, but kept her from some areas of discussion and participant observation. In St. Vincent, Corrine became the "agriculture lady" who relayed messages to both governmental and nongovernmental agricultural organizations with which she had contact. Alan found himself functioning in a "teacher" role several times. The following is an example from his field log:

> The class was devoted to students writing paragraphs to go with their thesis paragraph, already submitted. The thesis paragraph contained a quote from Huck Finn, a statement given to them about Twain, and their opening statements. The students worked on their own or came to Jane [their teacher] for a reaction to their paragraphs. Then they started coming to me and kept coming for about half the period. They seemed to have decided that I was functioning as if I were a teacher.

Alan worried about this role:

> I've never been co-opted to a teacher's role before. I like doing it, but I do have misgivings. Kids may forget that I'm the book-writing guy to whom they can say anything with impunity, if what they think of when they see me is that I'm some sort of teacher, not quite like their regular one, but a teacherlike person, nonetheless.

Balance the costs and benefits of your participation. What you do in an effort to reciprocate may conflict with your role as researcher. If, for example, a teacher asks you what you see from the back of her classroom, and you respond with advice or reinforcement, then you assume a judgmental expert role and risk losing your credibility as a nonjudgmental researcher. If you are enlisted as a free substitute teacher and do well with a class, then you make teachers aware of your teaching assets and, possibly, their teaching liabilities. If a class needs a driver for a field trip and you volunteer, then you may be overdoing the good-person role because of the resultant time drain on your work. Being the field trip driver, however, may provide an opportunity to observe students and teachers in a different context than the usual one. Do participate, but in a way that does not get you inextricably incorporated in a setting's ongoing affairs. If you become incorporated, then you might have to take a position that alienates you, that makes you reactive, that makes you take sides.

Remaining Marginal

Ethnographic researchers are sometimes called "marginal natives" (Freilich 1977) because, although they grow close to their others, they generally remain sojourners who are physically and psychologically at the margin of life in the research setting. In physical terms, the researcher attends events but stays on the fringes, at the back of classrooms and meetings.

Although researchers and participants interact freely, the interaction usually is within a frame of guarded intimacy. The researcher does not take charge or play the role of change agent or judge, but stays at the psychological margins of interactions. Remaining marginal "allows one to continue to spend time with groups when they are no longer friendly" (Horowitz 1986, 426) with each other. The point of the margin is that it offers the vantage of seeing without being the focus of attention, of being present without being fully participant, so that you are free to be fully attuned to what occurs before you, which, after all, is the point of being there.

As participation increases, marginality decreases, and you begin to experience what your others see, think, and feel. This can be absolutely worthwhile; no amount of advantageous marginality can replace the sense of things that participation offers. The best strategy is a judicious combination of participation and observation, as dictated by what you hope to understand.

Gaining and Losing Self

"In short, she could not unself herself and become other people" (Pritchett 1987, 134). This criticism was said of writer Rebecca West and her failure to become an actress when she was young. In a sense, qualitative researchers are like actors; they must be able to "unself" themselves as they enter the lives of other people. They do not "become" other people, but they do manage the impressions that they give.

Participant observation places researchers in the lives of others in a self-consciously instrumental way. Participant observers are not merely visiting with the hope to see the sights, have a good time, and, in passing, learn a little about how the natives live. Researchers have ends-in-view, purposes—however incipient—that underlie their presence in particular settings and direct their behavior while there. The inescapable truth is that researchers are not merely present as they would be in other ordinary circumstances of their lives. Given purposes to pursue, they shape their behavior to be efficacious in light of these purposes, managing selves that are instrumental to gaining access and maintaining access throughout the period of study in a way that optimizes data collection.

Participant observers are selectively present in that they hold back their words and watch carefully what they say when they do talk. They strive to attain an optimally nonreactive presence in order to minimize the shaping of research participants' self-presentation in clear reaction to the researchers as stimulus.

You have control over your words and actions, but less control over other aspects of yourself—sex, age, religion, and ethnicity. But even with seemingly unchangeable characteristics such as gender or ethnicity, you do have some choice in how you present yourself. For example, Daniels elaborates on her "learned responses" to behave "appropriately" when working as a woman sociologist among Army officers:

> Certain behavior was considered inappropriate or even insulting from women: a firm handclasp, a direct eye-to-eye confrontation, a brisk, businesslike air, an assured manner of joking or kidding with equals were all antagonizing. Most galling of all was my naïve assumption that, of *course*, I was equal. It was important to wait until equality was *given* me. When I learned to smile sweetly, keep my eyes cast down, ask helplessly for favors, and exhibit explicitly feminine mannerisms, my ability to work harmoniously and efficiently increased. (Daniels 1967, 275)

Most research situations do not call for such extreme impression management. In St. Vincent, Corrine always wore a skirt because shorts and slacks were not considered appropriate dress. In the Christian school, Alan shaved his beard, and we both carefully removed any minced oaths from our speech, such as "gosh," "darn," or "gee." Researchers often have to work for their acceptance, and this frequently entails a nonaggressive style or, as Lofland puts it, becoming "a socially acceptable incompetent" (Lofland 1971, 101). The extent to which you should modify behavior for research purposes is difficult to define: Where are the boundaries of integrity? When does adaptation go too far? In everyday life, you present yourself differently in different situations. Research is one more occasion for fashioning a presence, albeit more self-consciously than is ordinarily the case. At some point does this impression management become a lie and transgress the boundaries of ethical warrant?

A number of people have collected research data through covert participant observation and, in so doing, monitored carefully their presented self. Dalton (1959) worked covertly as a firm manager to investigate management; Homan (Homan and Bulmer 1982) studied a Pentecostal sect as if he were a novitiate; Sullivan (Sullivan, Queen, and Patrick 1958) lost weight, altered age, and adopted a "new personality" in order to study Air Force recruits; and Humphreys (1970) studied homosexuals by taking on the role of "watch queen" in public restrooms. Researchers who study the powerful, the illegal, and the marginal often have used covert means of gathering data.

Although some (Douglas 1976) would argue that ordinary social life is characterized by deceit and impression management, others say that no research act should consciously deceive. Covert research is fraught with questions and problems, discussed to some extent in the ethics chapter (Chapter 6). On one hand, some argue that the rights of subjects override the rights of science, and that covert observation is harmful to subjects, researcher, and the discipline. On the other hand, some believe that a measure of deception is acceptable in some areas when the benefits of knowledge outweigh the harm, and when the harm has been minimized by following conventions of confidentiality and anonymity.

Being Effective

Learning to be an effective participant observer takes some doing. We suggest that you begin by asking what there is about your identity or persona—such as gender, age, ethnicity, or country of origin—that might affect your access and data collection. Are there ways in which you can monitor yourself to gain more information? Second, before entering a setting as a participant observer, investigate the scene or use informants to discover normal attire and acceptable behaviors. You will make mistakes in your research interactions, but being prepared lessens the probability of major mistakes. Third, as you begin your role as a participant observer, be on the lookout for ways to adjust or accommodate yourself so that you "fit in" in a manner instrumental to gathering data. For example, this may mean brushing up on the latest music when working with teens, or keeping up with football scores when working in a male-dominated education department in the Midwest. Fourth, as participant observation continues, be aware of the different groups in the setting and carefully consider whether or not to become aligned with any one group. Unless your focus narrows so that you are concerned with only one group, such as the athlete student group, then it is probably best to remain unaligned. Finally, a natural disposition is to share what you learn with others whom you know would be interested. Don't. Learning to be judiciously silent is critical, so that everyone who talks to you knows that he or she can safely tell you anything.

Bittersweet Times: Disengaging

Leaving the field may be a bittersweet time. You are glad to be done and have your life return to normal; you can finally get to the neglected tasks in other aspects of your life; and you can once again spend time with family and friends. Still, you are sad because something you have invested highly in is over. You may be leaving good relationships and good times. Even if you never personally accepted your others' ideology, most likely you came to empathize and enjoy interacting with them. It may be that you will never return to the setting under the same circumstances.

You may feel dislocated when you return full time to pre-fieldwork life. After all, you have adjusted to living properly in someone else's life. You may also feel different about yourself; long-time immersion in someone else's life enhances your general self-awareness and tells you about yourself as a field-worker. You feel relief at not always having to be watchful, yet you find yourself reevaluating your "normal" life through comparisons with the life-style of your research participants. You miss people, places, and ways of doing things. Of course, leaving an African village is different from leaving a secondary school in the city in which you normally live, but departure from both places tends to be bittersweet.

CHAPTER **4**

Making Words Fly: Developing Understanding from Interviewing

We conceptualize interviewing as the process of getting words to fly. To be sure, they do not fly with the regularity and predictability of balls emerging from batting-practice machines that baseball teams use. Interviewing is a human interaction with all of its attendant uncertainties. As an interviewer, you are not a research machine, but you do "pitch" questions at your respondents with the intent of making words fly. Unlike a human baseball pitcher whose joy derives from throwing balls that batters never touch, you toss questions which you want your respondents to "hit" and hit well in every corner of your data park, if not clear out of it—a swatted home run of words. As a researcher, you want your "pitches"—your questions—to stimulate verbal flights from the important others who know what you do not. From these flights come the information that you transmute into data—the stuff of dissertations, articles, and books.

Getting words to fly is the subject of this chapter. It is a simple matter to express: Develop a clearly defined topic; design questions that fit the topic; ask the questions with consummate skill; and have ample time to "pitch" the questions to forthcoming, available, and knowledgeable respondents. We offer our own experience and that of others (see, for example, Bernard 1988; Brady 1976; Burgess 1984; Enright and Tammivaara 1984; Fetterman 1989; Gorden [1969] 1975; Hyman 1975; Patton 1990; Spradley 1979; Wildavsky 1989) that speaks to this matter of getting words to fly.

What type of interaction is the interview? An interview is between at least two persons, but other useful possibilities include one or more interviewers and one or more interviewees. Interviewing more than one person at a time sometimes proves very useful: Some young people need company to be emboldened to talk; and some topics are better discussed by a small group of people who know one another (see McMillan 1989 and Van Galen, Noblit, and Hare 1988–1989).

Researchers ask questions in the context of purposes known fully only to themselves. The respondents, the presumed possessors of information, answer questions in the context of dispositions (motives, values, concerns, needs), which the researchers need to unravel in order to make sense out of the words that their questions generate. The questions, typically created by the researchers, may be fully established before interviewing begins and remain unchanged throughout the interview. Questions may emerge in the course of interviewing and may be added to or replace the preestablished ones; this process of question formation is the more likely and the more ideal one in qualitative inquiry.

The questions you bring to your interview are not set within a binding contract; they are your best effort before you have had the chance to use them with a number of respondents. However much you have done to validate the utility of your questions, you should think of them tentatively, so that you are disposed to modify or abandon them, replace them with others, or add new ones to your schedule. The more fundamentally you change your interview schedule, however, the more frequently you may have to return to people whom you thought you had finished interviewing in order to ask them questions that emerged in interviews with others. In general, it is not advisable to say final good-byes to respondents; leave the door open to return.

Interviews can figure in a research project in different ways. In the positivist tradition, they can be the basis for later data collection, as in the form of a questionnaire. Not knowing enough about the phenomenon of interest, researchers interview a sample of respondents in the hope of transforming what they have learned into the necessary items and scales. Schuman (1970), also in a positivist vein, advocates the interview as a validity check of the responses given to questionnaire items. For example, what do respondents mean when they select ''strongly agree'' or ''strongly disagree'' as their response to some item? Probing in depth with a small sample of respondents who account for what they meant when they disagreed or agreed can indicate whether different respondents perceived the question in reasonably similar terms, as well as what underpins their reactions to it. In the interpretive tradition, the interview can be the sole basis of a study, or it can be used in conjunction with data from participant observation and documents.

Given the contact opportunities of ethnographic research, you may ask questions on the many occasions when something is happening that you wonder about. You inquire right then and there without formally arranging a time to ask your questions. Interviewing, in contrast, is a more formal, orderly process that you direct to a range of intentions: you ask about that which you cannot see or can no longer see. For example, you are interviewing when you seek facts about something that already has happened, using the reporter's who, what, where, and when questions. Jan Myrdal (1965), in *Report from a Chinese Village*, reconstructs—through interviews with many people—the transition in rural China between the passing of Chiang Kai-Shek's regime and the ascendancy of Mao Zedong. Mary F. Smith (1954), in *Baba of Karo*, re-creates—through interviews with one person—the life of a Nigerian woman of the Hausa tribe.

You might also interview in search of an explanation for why something happened. Interviewing puts you on the trail of understandings that you may infer from what you observe, but not as the actors themselves construe their actions. You cannot, that is, except through interviewing, get the actor's explanations. Nor, moreover, without interviews, can you learn about their probable future behavior—what they will do, or their probable conjectural behavior—what, if such and such were the case, they might do. You might also interview in search of opinions, perceptions, and attitudes, for example, asking teachers their opinion about the substance of the state-mandated changes in the middle school science curriculum. How do they perceive the impact of the changes on their work as teachers? What is their attitude about this impact? Concerned about the utility of the state's curricular mandate, you might conduct interviews to obtain data that will be instrumental for under-standing teacher conceptions of science and the obstacles to implementing proposals for reform.

The opportunity to learn about what you cannot see and to explore alternative explanations of what you do see is the special strength of inter-viewing in qualitative inquiry. To the above sets of circumstances add the serendipitous learnings that emerge from the unexpected turns in discourse that your questions evoke.

DEVELOPING QUESTIONS

What is the origin of the interview question? In our own work, the experience of learning as participant observer precedes recourse to interviewing and is the basis for forming questions. The things we have seen and heard about the people and circumstances of interest to us therefore become the "irritants" around which we construct our questions. Of course, participant observation does not and cannot always precede question making. What then? We turn to our topic and ask, in effect: If this is what we intend to understand, what questions must we direct to which respondents?

Among the more important sources of questions is the theory, implicit or explicit, underlying some behavior. Daren, for example, planned to investigate what he called "the returning dropout," young people who dropped out of high school but later returned to study in an adult education program. Daren's questions originated from his knowledge of the literature and from his reasoning. Over time, they were modified by pilot testing and through consultation with other researchers and informants. They reflected theoretical considerations. He asked, for example:

1. why returnees left school in the first place (suggests a connection between leaving and returning to school),
2. how parents reacted to their decision to drop out (suggests the likelihood of a parental role in leaving and returning),
3. whether they have friends who also dropped out (suggests that peer influence could motivate leaving and returning),
4. how they learned about the adult education program (suggests the possible influence of the source of knowledge about the program), and
5. whether treatment of students and contents of instruction were different in the adult program than in their high school program (suggests the appeal of some particular features of the adult program compared with the high school program).

These discrete questions do not amount to a theory; they do, however, point toward an understanding of the complex phenomenon of returning to school, which is a precursor to theory. In short, with the answers Daren received from each of his returning dropouts, he advanced his ability to explain why dropouts return to school.

By whatever means obtained, the questions you ask must fit your topic: the answers they elicit must illuminate the phenomenon of inquiry. And the questions you ask must be anchored in the cultural reality of your respondents: the questions must be drawn from the respondents' lives. Thus, when Sarah interviewed student teachers about their classroom practices, she knew what to ask because she had both sat in their prepractice teaching methods class and later watched them perform in their own classrooms. But she also could have known what to ask by having taught a teaching methods class and supervised student teachers. In both cases, she could enhance the experiential foundation from which she generated questions by use of knowledgeable informants, such as former student teachers and supervisors of student teachers, as well as by reading the relevant literature.

View the preinterview process of question construction as a continuing interaction between your topic and questions and the informant that you enlist to play several facilitative roles in this process. Do not treat question development and use as a simple, straightforward process of topic, to questions, to pilot testing, to revision, to interview, although this linear representation contains most of its primary elements. What this representation ignores is the repeating feedback loops and the contribution of your facilitative others—those friends, informants, and advisers who give you the benefits of their insights and critiques. Such facilitators are the *sine qua non* of sensible question development, if not of all research from inception to completion.

Think of the prepilot testing period first as a three-way interaction between the researcher and the tentatively formulated topic and questions. Tentative because in so thinking the researcher is optimally open to what is known to be most realistic: that both topic and questions will change. Second, think of prepilot testing as a four-way interaction when the facilitators enter the picture. Before this happens, however, write questions, check them against your topic, possibly revise your topic, and reconsider the questions.

The accumulating impact of this seemingly interminable effort is your growing investment in the products of your effort and, therefore, your increasing incapacity to assess the worth of what you have accomplished. This incapacity characterizes all researchers, however experienced. Enter those called the "facilitators," the researcher's agreeable peers, who will read drafts of your questions in light of what you communicate as the point of your study. They bring their logic, uncontaminated by your investment of self, to the assessment of your questions, and give you the basis for returning to your work table to create still one more draft. Such facilitators tell you about grammar, clarity, and question–topic fit. In addition, some informant-facilitators may be informed by experience with the people and phenomena of your research topic and thus can ascertain if your questions are anchored in the respondents' cultural reality. No doubt, the most effective facilitators are the persons for whom your questions are meant. Your greatest challenge is to create useful questions, ones whose answers provide you with pictures of the unseen, expand your understanding, offer insight, and upset any well-entrenched ignorance.

Simultaneous with the challenge of creating substantively appropriate questions is the more mundane issue of mechanics, which, if left unaddressed, can minimize or defeat your purpose. Your questions must be free of words, idioms, or syntax that will interfere with your questions and the respondents' understanding of them. Your questions must be relieved of the leading and the loading that inadvertently, perhaps because of their ubiquity in your nonresearch question life, can creep into your research language forms.

Some years ago, television evangelist and presidential aspirant Pat Robertson mailed out as a "questionnaire" a thinly disguised solicitation for funds. Robertson's question, "Are you shocked by rape, murder, and other brutal acts of violence on TV?" is a loaded one because it assumes that television shows do in fact present such events. We do not contest the presence of such events, but we contend that it is poor form to ask research questions in this way because they ignore the fundamental point of whether the presumed facts contained in the question are indeed perceived as facts by the respondent.

Questions with assumptions have other problems. "Don't you suspect," Robertson continues, that "the writers and producers of today's programs have conspired to undermine the values of America?'' This is a leading (and loaded) question. Its "Don't you suspect" come-on is designed to press the unsuspecting down the righteous path of agreement. Foundation and government coffers aside, researchers may not be charged with trying to get their hands on anyone's pocketbook, but they may be accused of leading come-ons with "don't you think" and "isn't it the case that" constructions.

Creating questions without recourse either to the advice of facilitators or to the testing of a pilot study is a mistake. The properly organized pilot, with respondents drawn from the actual group that you mean to study, is a crucial prelude to the successful conduct of interviews. Urge your pilot respondents to be in a critical frame of mind so that they do not just answer your questions (the intent is not to collect data) but, more important, that they reflect critically on the usability of your questions.

During a pilot study, you test your questions, your ways of relating to your respondents in general, and your ways of interviewing them in particular. Do not confine this testing process to a formally designed pilot study period, because your "real" interviews will also provide continuing opportunities for learning and revising. Since formal pilot studies are not always feasible, you might design a period of piloting that encompasses the early days of interviews with your actual respondents, rather than a set-aside period with specially designated pilot respondents. Such a period, if conducted in the right frame of mind—the deep commitment to revise—should suffice for pilot-testing purposes.

The questions below are drawn from the study that Alan conducted in the pseudonymous Riverview High School (Peshkin 1991). He planned to explore how, if at all, ethnicity figured in the life of a high school. They are not intended as model questions, but as types of questions that can be raised for qualitative inquiry.

Some questions were addressed to each group interviewed—counselors, teachers, students, and parents—others were designed for a particular group only. One set of questions for counselors was planned to encompass three or more interview sessions. The introductory interview covered background data and explored the process of becoming a counselor; it was intended as a time to become acquainted, build rapport, and ease the counselor into the role of interviewee. In the next session, planned as an after-school meeting, the counselors were told, "I'd like to get a general picture of what you do in the course of a day, not necessarily the very special things, just the routine type of things. Take today, for instance. What did you do?" (Included with this introduction were these notes to the interviewer: "Make a list of these things. Get elaboration of anything not perfectly clear. Categorize discrete activities.") Spradley (1979) refers to this type of question as a "grand tour" question.

The idea was to complete this picture as a setup for the third session, which opened with a review of the types of activities the counselor reported and a request to the counselor to add anything that the list omitted. Then, the counselor was told, "Ok, now I'd like to take these activities one at a time and learn something about their operation. Were the student a Filipino girl [the type of student was, alternately, a Filipino, Hispanic, African-American, or Italian boy or girl], what would your thinking be about how the matter is best handled?" The payoff was to learn if and how counselors differentiated their professional behavior on the basis of a student's ethnicity. Alan assumed that it would take at least two sessions to establish rapport and set up the necessary structure of concrete objects (the list of a counselor's ordinary activities) in order to elicit effectively a report of behavioral distinctions on the basis of ethnicity. A common mistake in interviewing is to ask questions about a hot topic before promoting a level of rapport that allows respondents to be open and expansive.

Another mistake is to ask questions about something that is too vague to elicit the most comprehensive response. The record of the counselor's day is the concrete object toward which further questions were directed. Other such objects can be obtained by asking the respondent to recapture something by imagining it. The interviewer's task is to create circumstances for the most fruitful imagining.

For example, if you want to understand how nurses with varying years of experience construe the initial entry period into their profession, you could say, much as might a hypnotist: "I'd like to have you go back to a time in your professional life that you've probably not thought about for years. Remember when you finished your schooling? You found a position and were ready to begin your first day on the job," and so on. The idea is to provide mood and props for interviewees to recall something likely to be long unthought about. For your purposes, you want them to recapture time, place, feeling, and meaning of a past event. The straightforward "Let's talk about the early days of your work as a nurse" just might fail to get the words to fly.

Another type of concrete object would be a quotation that you select from another source that contains ideas on which you wish your respondents to comment. The value of the quotation is that it allows you to attribute to someone else ideas that are usefully provocative but that you would prefer not be put in your own voice. Alan did this in his study of a Christian school. He used a quotation from Jerome Bruner's (1960) *Process of Education* that contrasted education which inculcated in students a way of viewing the world with education that helped students to find their own way of viewing the world.

A procedure similar to that used with counselors was followed with the high school teachers. Alan began a line of inquiry with a general, exploratory, multipart question: "I'd like you to put yourself in the position of my adviser.

I'm a brand-new teacher, never taught here before, and I want to start the school year with the best start possible. What would you advise me about the students: What are they like? What do I need to do to get along with them?" Using the same format, the student lead was followed by soliciting advice about parents, teachers, and community. This question elicited virtually no reference to ethnicity. Some questions and at least one interview session later, Alan asked, "Is the ethnic identity or culture of students ever a factor in your work as a teacher?" Once answered, this global question was followed by specific ones that asked if the students' ethnicity influenced what teachers taught; how they taught, disciplined, and counseled students; and what textbooks they chose. This line of inquiry was somewhat more productive of comments on ethnicity than the first, but not nearly as productive as the third, which, again some questions and one session later, took the following form: "I'd like to return to being a new teacher and ask your advice again. I need some general information about the different groups of students who attend school here. Let's take one group at a time. You're making generalizations. Filipinos [then Hispanics, African-Americans, and Italians]—in general, what are they like?" This was followed by, "Any advice for teaching them?"

Was it the question format that made the difference in productivity? Was it the respondents' enhanced awareness of Alan's research purposes, or the greater rapport established by the time he asked the third set of questions? Whatever the explanation, though each line of inquiry produced useful results, it took a third try—which was not part of the original interview schedule—for teachers to learn from their own comments that not only did they think that they were color blind, and that "kids are just kids," but they also made distinctions based on student ethnicity.

In the several examples of questions above, note the difference in the voice or subject of the questions. The two advice examples have teachers speaking to a hypothetical newcomer, an indirect form compared with asking the same teacher, "What do you do in the case of . . . ?" The advice-question format elicits possibly more idealized responses. In contrast, the question that asked teachers if ethnicity was a factor in their own behavior with students was more direct. The point is that you have a choice of voices, and thus of degrees of directness and generality. You can ask "do you," "do teachers like you," "do teachers in your school," or "do teachers in general." The scope of the voice increases with each example as, accordingly, the degree of personal disclosure decreases. Whenever you judge your question to be too personal to be asked directly, you can use another voice, and assume that the longer the respondent talks, the more likely he or she is speaking in a personal voice.

Framing questions in terms that your respondents understand is essential. When Joyce conducted her study of perceptions of counseling services by a group of African-American residents, she learned that they did not talk about counseling but about "needing to talk" or "needing help." In the ethnicity study, Alan learned what terms the students used to refer to ethnicity. In one of the early interview sessions, students were told the following: "From the looks of the kids here I see that there are lots of different races and nationalities and ethnic groups. Before we go on to some other questions, I'd like to be sure what word or words you use to describe the different groups of kids. Is it races? Or nationalities? Or ethnic groups? Or what?" Then, in order to be able to make accurate reference to each student during later questions, Alan followed the above with, "Do you consider yourself to be part of one or more of these groups?"

Interviewing that is preceded by or accompanied with participant observation creates chances to derive some questions from sheer fortuity. One day in class Alan heard a student tell a story to other students that ended with, "It's stupid to trip off of people's color." This statement became the first line in a question that began with, "I heard a student say . . ." and continued with: "What do you think this means? Could it mean anything else? Do people trip off of color in Riverview? In Riverview High School?" If students answered yes, they were asked: "How common is it? Why do they do it? Do some do it more than others?"

That some questions are designated as warm-up questions suggests that others are best asked at the end. When you are reasonably comfortable with the form and substance of your questions, begin to give attention to their order. Which belong at the beginning because they are easy to answer and answering them will reassure respondents that your questions are manageable? Which belong at the beginning because they are foundational to what you will ask later, or because they will give you the time needed to promote rapport? Which questions should be asked in special sequence? Which should be kept as far apart as possible because you want to minimize an interactive effect? Which should be asked at the end because they are of a summary or culminating nature? Of course, we all know what happens to the best-laid plans of researchers. Having made a case for ordering your questions, we hasten to add that your logical order may be sundered by the psychological order that emerges from your respondents' answers. Not needing to keep things straight, as you see it, they may talk in streams of language that connect to various of your questions, but in no way resemble your planned order. So be it: Make a virtue out of unavoidable necessity.

Conceiving the entire first meeting with students as a warm-up session, Alan used the following question toward the end of his meeting: "Let's say that you wanted someone to become friends with you. Which of your personal characteristics would be important for this person to learn about if you wanted him or her to get to know you really well?" To assist their responses, students then received a card containing a list of personal characteristics, including one reference to their ethnicity: "that you are Filipino [or Hispanic, African-American, or Italian]." Including this characteristic on the list was the earliest stab at learning about the place of ethnicity in the identity of the students. It was tucked away in a context that did not call attention to it, with the idea that, by placing it in a context of relevant personal attributes, students would more accurately indicate its place in their identity.

In time, questions with ethnicity as the central focus were increasingly introduced. One very large question set easily occupied one complete interview session, which typically in a school study lasts the length of one school period. The lead-in for the set required placing the interviewee in the role of adviser to a new student who is preparing to join Riverview High School for the fall semester, and who is of the same age, sex, and ethnicity as the interviewee. Prospective students (the helping prop for the question) would want to know what to expect at Riverview High School and would ask, "As a Filipino guy [girl] at Riverview High School, is it likely that I will: (1) be friends at school with [Hispanics, African-Americans, whites]; (2) be friends away from school with . . . ; (3) be very close friends with . . . ; (4) be called names by other students; (5) find each ethnic group equally willing to accept me?" The list was long, and it grew longer in the course of interviewing and continuing participant observation. The question set compelled students to think about their ethnicity more fully and systematically than they ever had before and, possibly, than they ever will again.

Interviewing will be that type of experience for many of your respondents; it is unavoidable. Take all the care at your disposal to insure that the experience will be risk-free. Note one more aspect of this question set: It did not invite respondents to speak about themselves. Rather, the subject was a hypothetical person like themselves. Again, questions may be given different voices: what something is like for you, for your friends, for Filipino males [females] at Riverview High School, for Filipino males [females].

In the ethnicity study, all interviews with students and others ended with several global questions. One type, the "magic wand" question, was a fishnet: "If you could change Riverview High School (its students, teachers, or curriculum) in any way you wanted, what, if anything, would you change?" After weeks of interviewing, typically with one session a week for four or more weeks, and with ethnicity gradually becoming more prominent in the questions, Alan wondered what references to ethnicity would turn up through this question. He also wanted to see what could be learned by asking about change. Another equally general question set to teachers was, "You know that we're trying to develop a complete and realistic portrait of your school, a portrait that does full justice to it. (1) What else should we know that we haven't asked? (2) What have we overlooked? (3) Have we underemphasized important things? (4) Have we overemphasized unimportant things?"

SETTING UP TO INTERVIEW

Several matters must be settled before your interviews can proceed. Where will you conduct your interviews? Convenient, available, if not appropriate locations need to be found. Retreat from selecting quiet, physically comfortable, and private locations only when you must; they are generally most appropriate. When respondent convenience is the overriding consideration, agree, knowing that their willingness to cooperate with you may be contingent on how unbothersome it is to see you. Defer to your respondents' needs because their willingness is primary, limited only by your capacity to conduct an interview in the place that they suggest. If, for example, a location's lack of privacy dampens or defeats open discussion, or if its noise level precludes hearing, then the available site is not workable. If meeting where radios or televisions blare—the normal background sound in many homes—your gentle request will generally suffice to get the sets turned off. An office set aside for the researcher on a regular basis is ideal for interviews with students conducted at school. Otherwise, you may have to use your creativity and move around, depending on the time of day—the lunchroom, auditorium, backstage, campus picnic table, and weight-lifting room are possible places. Teachers, counselors, and administrators are easier to meet because they have classrooms and offices.

When will you meet? Convenient, available, and appropriate apply also to the time of the interview. By appropriate, we mean a time when both researcher and respondent feel like talking. Again, however, you take what you can get and defer to the preferences of the respondent. School-based interviews usually follow a teacher's free period schedule and a student's study hall period. Barring these class-time opportunities, before and after school and lunchtimes are other possibilities. Consider evening meetings if they are a teacher's preference. To meet counselors and administrators requires fitting into their schedules when free of appointments.

How long will your interview last? An hour of steady talk is a useful rule of thumb to guide appropriate length before diminishing returns may set in for both parties. There are exceptions, for example, when less time is available to the respondent. Take what you can get, while trying to promote regularity—of location, time, and length of interview—so that you can say to your respondent at the interview's end, "Same time and place next week?"

How often will you meet? This is variable, although most studies require multisession interviews to obtain trustworthy results. Just how many will depend on the length of the interview schedule, the interest and verbal fluency of the respondent, and the probing skills of the researcher. Respondents understandably want to have some idea of how often they will meet with you. We suggest that you say, "At least two times, and maybe more, certainly no more than is comfortable for you. And you may—without providing any explanation—stop any particular session or all further sessions.'' Then, it is your challenge to make the interview experience so rewarding that having more than two sessions, if needed, is unproblematic to the respondents. We discuss how to do this later on in this chapter.

How will you note your studies? Whether by hand, audiotape, or video-tape is a matter of your needs and the respondents' consent. Most will agree to the use of a tape recorder, and for most research purposes an audio record is fully sufficient. Depending on the sensitivity of your topic and the unease of your respondents, you may want to wait until the end of the first session—by which time you have proved to be innocuous, if not enjoyable to be with—before you ask for permission to tape-record.

Tape-recording requires an electrical outlet or a rechargeable battery pack; using batteries is acceptable but somewhat risky. Give due attention to the quality of your cassettes, tape recorder, and microphone. Tape recorders that permit a hand-held on–off switch to be attached allow you to turn off the tape recorder unobtrusively when the talk turns to medical insurance and you are interested in teacher effectiveness. Tape recorders that make a sound when the end of the tape has been reached save you from continuous peeking at the tape to check its proximity to the end, and from calling attention to your taping. Most recorders have built-in microphones, which are less effective than an external microphone; best of all are lapel microphones that can be attached to both researcher and respondent, particularly if there is sound around your interview site or you are interviewing persons who are soft-voiced or who make fidgety noises that will be amplified on your tape.

Also on the subject of equipment, we greatly recommend a transcribing machine with headphones and a foot pedal for reversing and advancing the tape, so that your hands are free to transcribe (see Fetterman 1989). Whatever means can be afforded to minimize the agony of transcribing tapes—estimate five-plus hours per ninety-minute tape done by an experienced transcriber—should be seized. The good times of data collection can quickly pall if the transcribing doldrums set in. To avoid them, don't assume that you must have a verbatim transcript. Reflect carefully on your needs. Replay your tapes on the way home from interviews. Browse through tapes and reserve judgment about how much you need transcribed. In these ways, you also gain some idea of how you are doing as an interviewer, what you need to improve, what you have learned, and what points you need to explore further. If you wait until you have completed all of your interviews before hearing your tapes (or reviewing your notes), then you have waited too long to learn what they can teach you.

It is not quite a tossup as to whether you note by hand or tape recorder. With handwritten notes, you are closer to being done writing when your interview is done; this is their distinct advantage. Also, noting by hand is less obtrusive and less intimidating to some persons. But be aware of the message your respondent may deduce whenever you stop taking notes: the risky, ''I no

longer am noteworthy.'' You will also feel less in control of the interview
when, as you handwrite notes, your attention is focused on the struggle to keep
up with the respondent's talk (even knowing that this generally cannot be
done), and you can only intermittently maintain eye contact and attend to all of
the verbal and nonverbal cues that have bearing on your procedure. Interviewees may generally be patient and slow down, even wait for you to catch up
if you explain your desire to capture their words as fully as possible. The tape
recorder, however, provides a nearly complete record of what has been said
and permits easy attention to the course of the interview. For this ease, you
may pay a price in the transcribing process, unless you can hire someone to do
it (an unlikely possibility) or your research purposes allow you to make a
selective record rather than a verbatim one, much as you do when you take
notes at a lecture or from a book.

Regardless of the means you select to record your interview, keep an
account of every interview that includes the following: old questions requiring
elaboration; questions already covered; where to begin next time; special
circumstances that you feel affected the quality of the interview; reminders
about anything that might prepare you for subsequent interviews; and identification data that at a glance give characteristics (such as age, gender, ethnicity, socioeconomic status, experience, or occupation) that have bearing on
your respondent selection. This identification data allow you to monitor the
respondents you have seen, so you can be mindful of whom else to see.

THE NATURE OF INTERVIEWING

Conducting interviews is well within the capacity of most researchers, although it is clearly true that some people take to it naturally, and readily get
better and more proficient. Others, less naturally inclined, take longer to
become adequate interviewers; and still others begin inept and remain inept,
despite concern and practice—this form of verbal interaction at odds with their
souls.

Interviewing, as well as other modes of data collection, is not for everyone. Moreover, it is not quite the same process for all practitioners, any more
than teaching, nursing, counseling, or drawing a picture is. Its variability
derives from who is conducting the interview with whom, on what topic, and at
what time and place. Interviewing, in short, brings together different persons
and personalities. As you move from respondent to respondent, the nature of
the interaction will change, as will, depending on the topic discussed, the
location of the interview and the temper of the times. If you are an Anglo
American researcher interviewing a Mexican official of the Mexican-American
Political League on the subject of farm workers, in the league's business office
during the heated times of a strike, you will conduct an interview that is

imaginably different than if you are a Mexican researcher, interviewing the same officer, on the same subject, in your office, at a time when labor peace prevails.

But even if all variables were the same and just the researcher changed, the interview process could be expected to be observably different—albeit possibly equally good, for there is no one person who is exactly the right interviewer, any more than there is in the case of teachers, nurses, or social workers. We each have personal strengths and weaknesses that form the basis of our interview style. It makes no more sense to take on the style of someone else than it does to try to become like someone else. Just as in nonresearch life, some persons engender nearly instant trust; they can safely ask direct, probing questions on hot topics early in an interview relationship. Some can make blunders and get excused over and over because they are eminently forgivable. Some create such an atmosphere of good cheer and nurturance that respondents line up to be interviewed by them.

Do not mourn who you are not; learn who you are and how you operate, and make the best of it. Do not expect the same reception from all respondents. They will take to you as variably as people do in general. This means that some will always give you better results, and others may not be helpful at all. Of course, your unsuccessful interview encounters should not occur always with the same type of person. It would never do to have your unsuccessful respondent group be confined, for example, to middle-aged males who always vote Republican.

Interviewing is a complex act. We say this to produce not faint hearts but, rather, realistic users who will be fair to themselves, especially in the nervous early days of interviewing when it might be easier to conclude, "This is not for me" than to exult, "What a wonder I am." Interviewing is complex because of the number of things that are happening simultaneously. Because there are so many acts to orchestrate, effective interviewing should be viewed the way that good teaching is: you should look for improvement over time, for continuing growth, rather than for mastery or perfection.

Several acts occur simultaneously. Of course, first and foremost is your listening. Interviewers are listeners incarnate; your machines can record, but only you can listen. At no time do you stop listening, because without the data your listening furnishes, you cannot make any of the decisions inherent in interviewing: Are you listening with your research purposes and eventual write-up fully in mind, so that you are attuned to whether your questions are delivering on your intentions for them? If they are not, is the problem in the question, in the respondent, or in the way you are listening? Has your question been answered, and is it time to move on? If so, move on to what question? Should you probe now or later? What form should your probe take? Do you need to probe further the results produced by your probe? Have your questions been eliciting shorter and shorter if not monosyllabic returns, possibly suggesting irritation with the topic or tiredness? The spontaneity and unpredictability of the interview exchange precludes planning your probes ahead of time; you must, accordingly, think and talk on your feet, one of those many interview-related skills that practice improves.

You listen and you look, aware that feedback can be both nonverbal and verbal. You observe the respondent's body language to determine what effects your questions, probes, and comments are having, in order to decide whether you will adjust your conduct accordingly. Do you see indicators of discomfort, and is the source of that discomfort the physical conditions of your interview site or the topic to which you are stimulating a response? Do you see signs of boredom, annoyance, bewilderment? What might be their source and their remedy, and is it within your means to find a remedy?

If you see an uncomfortable respondent, is the cause within your means to control? Dick wrote in his log about causes that were beyond his control:

> I arrive at school on a day when classes have been called off because of a power outage at 7:30 A.M. on a cold winter day. The principal is afraid because it came back on some time afterward, but not before she had made the decision to call off school. Parents will be angry because they had to make alternative arrangements for child care when the child could have been in school.

Dick needed to decide whether to proceed as planned with his interview.

Although listening and looking are critical, you forego their gains unless you remember. You want to remember your questions to avoid constantly looking down at your list, and so you won't be taken off guard when your questions are being taken out of order. You want to remember what has been said—by you and your respondent—in this session and in previous ones. You want to recall what you have heard, so that you can pick up on past points in order to make connections, see gaps and inconsistencies, avoid asking some questions, or rephrase other questions when you know that your first stab at questioning fell short of your expectations and needs. You must of course remember to bear in mind your expectations and needs—your yardstick of worth—so that what you are listening to is being assessed in respect to your research purposes. Flying words and worthy words are necessary conditions for judging your interviews to be successful. We suggest visualizing in text the words you are hearing so that you are alert to the payoff of your respondent's words.

You must remember not only your yardstick of textual worthiness, but also your role as controller of the quality of the respondent's experience. Are you attending to aspects of the interview that make it not just agreeable but pleasurable for the respondent? Just as your pleasure may be confined to the verbal goods you receive, your respondents' pleasure derives from the satisfaction of talking to you. How satisfied respondents are can affect their willingness to continue to talk to you, the effort they put into their talk, and, significantly, what they may tell other interview candidates about being your interviewees.

Related to controlling the quality of the respondent's experience is remembering to control your negative emotions. Although expressing such emotions may be permissible in ordinary conversations, the interview is not an ordinary conversation; hence, you do not have the license to manifest your anger and irritation at the ''disagreeable'' views you are hearing. When Bonnie learned from interviewing nurses that they often are seriously uninformed about the care and treatment of older, confused patients, she could not vent her feelings to the nurses and maintain her role as a researcher. The venting may be acceptable and consistent with her role as a caring nurse, but not with her role as a researcher. Keeping roles separate is hard but essential if you mean to collect any data, let alone usable data. Moreover, you may be disappointed with the quality of your respondent's answer; nonetheless, mask any feelings that express this disappointment and look for positive means to improve the quality of your respondent's answer.

Finally, remember to keep track of time, so that time remains for you to make some usefully culminating statements, such as, ''Here is the ground we covered today. I was pleased to learn about such and such. Would it be ok for next time if we went back to this and that point before we turn to the subject of the declining market for fresh ostrich eggs?'' In this way, you review and pave the way for your next interview session. You keep track of time so that you can keep your promise to talk only for an hour and avoid overstaying your welcome. Be a person of your word. Take the time to negotiate and verify the details of your next meeting, and be punctual for each appointment.

To listen, look, and remember in the comprehensive terms suggested here require developing your concentration. This means shutting off the myriad other aspects of your life so that you can fully attend to the needs of your interview. Achieving the appropriate level of concentration can be physically and emotionally draining, particularly in your early days as an interviewer. Accordingly, a depletion of your personal resources is yet one more of those things that occur simultaneously while interviewing. It is not excessively farfetched to say that if you are not tired at the end of an interview session, then you might wonder about the quality of the session.

INTERVIEWER ATTRIBUTES THAT MAY CONTRIBUTE TO SUCCESSFUL INTERVIEWS

We at once disclaim any suggestion, even the merest hint, that the many attributes we describe below collectively ensure high-quality interviews. We simply find them useful in our own work. Some stand to reason. For example, *anticipatory* means being prepared: How can being prepared not be desirable? Others, such as *rapport*, are embraced by conventional wisdom: How can one interview without rapport? Finally, others are inherent in our sense of the interview process. *Paradoxically bilateral* comes to mind, which is to say that we think there is a decidedly one-sided character to the bilateralism of a good interview.

We urge you to acquire all of these attributes, although to what extent you must master them, which ones have primacy, or which others may be substituted we do not know. For us, these attributes have stood the tests of use, reason, conventional wisdom, and congruency with our conception of the effective interview. Each completes the sentence "The good interviewer is. . . ."

Anticipatory

As a good interviewer, you look ahead and ask, "What does the situation call for?" Some of the specifics about what to anticipate already have been mentioned. Your cover story is an example, in which you consider both what true things you must say in order to present yourself and your project cogently, and how what you say may vary from situation (the superintendent of schools) to situation (the parents of students). What materials and equipment do you need to assemble for your interview session? Who should you see next, in light of what you have been learning and not learning, and what arrangements need to be made to set up an interview relationship? Anticipation feeds off the results of taking stock, an activity that might well be included at the end of the day in the daily task of log writing. Reflecting on each day is preparatory to anticipating what is next, both broadly in terms of your inquiry, and narrowly in terms of your next day's activities.

Alert to Establish Rapport

Is it conceivable that you can learn anything of consequence from anyone, save the uncontrollably loquacious, without rapport? We think not. Since rapport will be discussed in Chapter 5, we will only say here that rapport is tantamount to trust, and trust is the foundation for acquiring the fullest, most accurate disclosure a respondent is able to make. Indeed, many of the attributes below contribute to rapport, though they may be intended to accomplish something else, as well.

You promote rapport by the interest you show in what your respondents say. Showing interest is an easy way to reward; by your verbal and nonverbal behavior you demonstrate that you are enjoying what you are hearing. The simple fact is that almost everyone gets satisfaction from being able to evoke interest in their listeners. Furthermore, although your expression of interest promotes rapport, its pointed carefulness also communicates just what it is that interests you. Your interest shapes the respondent's behavior by selectively reinforcing the respondent's discussion of some topics and by setting the procedure for discussion (e.g., careful, elaborate, replete with explanations). Such researcher shaping of the others' behavior is an ongoing part of the research process. It is the researcher's obligation to assist the researched to play a role—one that ordinarily we can assume he or she has never played before. Clearly, you will shape behavior, even when not intending to, by the form and content of your questions, and by the nature of your reactions to the answers you get.

Naïve

Naïve is the term that characterizes the researcher's special learner role. It entails a frame of mind by which you set aside your assumptions (pretensions, in some cases) that you know what your respondents mean when they tell you something, rather than seek explanations about what they mean. Often, the hazard is that your research is on a topic about which you may know a great deal through study and personal experience. What you know is the basis for assumptions that preclude you from seeking explanations and that shut down your depth-probe inclinations (which derive from the conviction that you cannot really know what is in the mind of others). If you second-guess your respondents, then you forego the chance to say, "Tell me more." The difficulty in being naïve is that assumptions generally are useful for simplifying our relations with others. How boorish and painful it would be to keep asking, "What do you mean?" In your research capacity, you need not be relentless in asking this question in the many guises that you can give it, but you must be alert to the value of being naïve.

Claudia faces the hazard of not being usefully naïve in her study of families at risk of losing their children. She is an "expert" on the subject; she trains people to work with such families. Her expertise may obviate her asking some questions, and, as well, her respondents from discussing matters that they assume she already knows. Claudia must convince her respondents by all she says and does, both before and during her interviews, that she is a learner, not an expert. Not being naïve interfered with Ned asking his extension agent respondents to explain what they meant when they spoke of "small landholders." He failed to ask because he had once been an extension agent, used the term himself, and thereby assumed he knew to what amount of land the term applied. But because the meaning of what respondents said would change depending on the amount of land involved, the referent of the expression had important consequences.

Pat reflected on her role as interviewer and learner:

> I found that I enjoyed the interviewing process, but I had to be careful not to make it into a performance where I was the "star interviewer." Instead, I

had to be aware that I was just the "seeker of knowledge." This became an important distinction for me when I first started because I had been concerned with how I would do as the interviewer—I had to shift my attention from me to the topic at hand, and when I did this successfully, I found the interview to be enjoyable and meaningful.

Casting yourself as a learner correspondingly casts the respondent as a teacher. For many, this is a flattering role that enhances the respondent's satisfaction with being interviewed, and satisfaction begets rapport. More than just developing rapport, when you are a learner, you get taught.

Analytic

Analysis, we cannot emphasize too much, does not refer to a stage in the research process. To the contrary, it is a continuing process that should begin just as soon as your research begins. It follows, then, that interviewing is not simply devoted to data acquisition. It is also a time to consider relationships, salience, meanings, and explanations—four analytic acts that not only lead to new questions, but also prepare you for the more concentrated period of analysis that follows the completion of your data collection.

Gloria interviewed women who had left and then returned to the university. All had children. One woman told her that being away from home so much required that her husband change his participation in family life. Hearing this should have set bells ringing in Gloria's mind, but the bells did not ring. She was not listening analytically. The respondent's husband had to redefine his role as father. Gloria needed to focus on the husband's behavior: include questions about it, probe it, and consider its need and meaning for other family members. By not listening analytically, she could not capitalize on what she was hearing.

As much as you might try to give your interviews the character of a good conversation, you must not forget that research talk differs from other talk because it is driven by research purposes. The distinguishing mark of a good interview is not good conversation but good data. When your data collection is complete and you enter a period of extended data analysis, you will find the analysis easier if all along you have been listening analytically and converting the results of ongoing analysis into further questions and notes that capture thoughts and ideas.

Paradoxically Bilateral: Dominant but Also Submissive

The traditional imbalance of the researcher–researched relationship is much contested, notably by postmodernists and action-research scholars. Oakley, a feminist methodologist, says that

> in most cases, the goal of finding out about people through interviewing is best achieved when the relationship of interviewer and interviewee is

> nonhierarchical and when the interviewer is prepared to invest his or her
> own personal identity in the relationship. (Oakley 1981, 41)

Nonhierarchical relationships may be possible in participatory research where researcher and researched define the research problem. In most instances, however, the researcher maintains a dominant role that reflects his or her definition of the inquiry purposes. As long as the purposes are his or her own, the researcher sustains a power imbalance that may or may not get redressed, depending on the researcher's opportunity for and commitment to reciprocity. The researcher's awareness of the respondents' needs figures into the relationship between them, which causes the researcher to be duly and unpatronizingly understanding, empathetic, supportive, and, if possible, contributory in terms that reflect the respondent's conception of personal needs. Hierarchical relations are not inevitably devoid of mutual warmth and caring.

The researcher's terms of dominance emerge in the intent to control the direction, shape, and flow of the interview. By skillful assertiveness, try to keep your respondents on your track, bringing them back to it when, by your standards, they stray. Your dominance, however, will be distinctively countered by the demands of optimizing the respondents' positive reactions to the interview: that is, are they physically, mentally, and emotionally comfortable with, if not pleased and rewarded by, the interview? Good listening, which is at the heart of effective interviewing, is an act of submission. That is, listening in an interview situation requires literally giving oneself over to what the respondent is saying and feeling and wondering about. Good-listening interviewers are tuned in to their respondents, fixed and fully attentive to what they are saying.

Some degree of this quality of listening is generally desirable in ordinary life circumstances. We expect more of it from close friends than from acquaintances. It comes naturally to some people. For others, it must be developed— and it can be.

Sociologist Jack Douglas (1985) speaks of the need for researchers to be subordinate to their interviewees because interviewees hold the knowledge and the power. Indeed, your respondents have the power to reject your request for an interview, to terminate interviews once begun, to refuse to answer some questions fully or at all, and to hold back generally in their consideration of your questions. Such power is substantial. Its extent indicates how dependent you are on the respondents' willingness to be available and forthcoming.

You cannot dictate the particulars of your interviewer–interviewee relationship: if you will meet; where, when, and how often you will meet; what you will discuss, for how long and how often. However, for as long as the interview remains the means to ends you have fashioned and are pursuing, you will remain dominant—notwithstanding that you are submissive (as characterized above), dependent, and sit relatively quietly alongside a respondent whose flying words bring joy to both of you (to you for being able to hear the words and to the respondent for being able to say them).

Should you try to be less dominant? Young began to share her record of her interviews with Tardif in regular "have-I-got-you-straight?" sessions (Young and Tardif 1988). Such respondent involvement is most useful when all interviewing with a respondent is over and you ask him or her to review the transcripts and identify anything that should be changed or removed. Regular sharing of transcripts prior to the end is difficult because of the problem of transcript preparation. Depending on the respondent and the nature of the interview, regular sharing can also be risky because the respondent may develop second thoughts about being so frank or even about continuing the interviews.

As you reflect on the interview in the terms just presented, regard it as a curiously bilateral relationship. You choose your respondents, believing that they know something you need to know, and you choose the topic and direction of your discourse, but the respondents also have prerogatives. These prerogatives derive in the first place from the interviewees' control of the decision whether to cooperate, and in the second from their judgment that the research project merits their cooperation. (We assume that the respondents are not bound to remain in the interview relationship because of subordination to the researcher.) The relationship benefits the researcher most when respondents do most of the talking. In this respect, the researcher gives center stage over to the respondents, their questions being the pretexts for the lines they speak that become the "play's" script. The researcher assumes a role at the periphery, one that may expand and contract as the respondents and the interview situation require. We see no viable role for interviewers as cool, impassive, distant interrogators. We see them, rather, as multidimensional human beings, not so hellbent on data collection as to ignore the interview as an interaction between two human beings. Although friendship may eventuate from long-term interviewing, the interview typically is not an exchange between friends. Unlike in conversations, the interviewer means to keep attention, concern, and talk time shifted from self to others.

Nonreactive, Nondirective, and Therapeutic

An issue in interviewing is how much of your nonresearch self can be present without contaminating or distorting the interview. The issue is not whether you will in some way be different in the role of interviewer, but how you will be different—what tailoring of self, as we discussed earlier, you will manage as suitable for the demands and circumstances of the research act.

We assume that a distinction must be made: As researcher you apprehend what your respondents mean and feel, and you rightly communicate that to them. What you, as researcher, do not ordinarily communicate is that you also share (or do not share) these meanings and feelings. To do so would establish your meanings and feelings and enable your respondents to shape their comments in reaction to you. You want your respondents to be as awful, inconsistent, bigoted, antisocial, and nonconformist as they really are. If your respondents play good for your benefit, then you get play-good data for your efforts.

To be nonreactive is not to be zombielike, impassive, or neutral, which behaviors would indicate that you were unaware of the sentiments that your respondent expressed. From Carl Rogers' (1942) techniques for nondirective counseling, we have learned that interviewers can make comments which reveal that they have both heard and empathized with what their interviewees have said. Comments such as "that must've hurt," or "that must've made you feel good" (and their numerous variations) are nonformulaic combinations of the right thoughts to express.

The idea is to make clear that you did hear what your respondents said, and that you do grasp their feelings. Both are essential if you are to know how to proceed in your interview conduct. Being able to communicate, by verbal and nonverbal means, that you have heard and understood is not mere technique for the promotion of rapport and the facilitation of more respondent talk, though it will have that much-valued effect. It also demonstrates that the role of researcher as you fill it genuinely extends beyond the acquisition of data to a concern for the respondent's well-being.

Your need is to express this concern without saying, "I'm with you, on your side," and, of course, without saying, "I'm not with you." It is the clarification of where your side is, where your preferences, values, and antagonisms are, that will make you reactive. The danger of reactivity extends beyond its possible distortion of the respondents' comments to the more general hazard of being refused access to a whole set of potential interviewees who feel that you have taken sides. In research studies that involve sides, you must be able to learn about everyone's pains and pleasures without looking as if you have been recruited to anyone's cause. Some respondents may insist on knowing where you stand as a condition for continuing to talk with you. In such cases, it is best to say that you cannot disclose your position at this time and ask them please to understand.

All of the preceding discussion about the conduct of the interviewer done for the sake of promoting successful data acquisition has the concomitant effect of being therapeutic. The aforementioned way of listening, decentering, and celebrating what your respondents tell you is therapeutic. What specifically is therapeutic is the unburdening effect of the respondents' saying safely whatever they feel. This effect is enhanced by the Rogerian "*Mm hmm*," "How did you feel about that?" "Would you tell me more about that?" "That must have made you feel sad [happy, nervous, confident]." Much of what you do and say is feedback, which again has the effect of indicating to your respondent that you grasp what he or she is saying and feeling, as well as what you found informative (which is a crucial part of helping respondents play their unac-customed role of talker for research purposes).

We regard the therapeutic dimension of good interviewing as part of what you can return to your respondents. It will not be uncommon for you to receive words of gratitude from respondents who are pleased with the opportunity for the profound, prolonged expression of personal views that your multisession interviews afford. Knowing that it is a way of reciprocating, we suggest that you make the most of your interview's therapeutic aspect.

Patiently Probing

For qualitative inquiry, the interview is rightly conceived as an occasion for depth probes—for getting to the bottom of things. By so doing you do justice to the complexity of your topic. Qualitative researchers operate from the assump-tion that they cannot exhaust what there is to know about their topic. They may stop their investigation because they have run out of time, run out of wit for further productive exploration, or satisfied their particular research conceptual-ization. While the research remains in process, interviewing is a "what else" and "tell me more" endeavor. The next question on your interview schedule should get its turn only when you have stopped learning from the previous one and its spin-offs. This is where virtuous patience comes in.

You need to concentrate on being patient in order to give due, unrushed attention and deliberation to the responses you elicit from each question you ask. Rush and the world rushes with you: If you communicate your satisfaction with your respondents' short-shrift replies, then you teach them how little it takes to satisfy you. Say, "Tell me more," and your interviewees will learn to respond accordingly. You will find that the better you probe, the longer your interview time becomes. Short and few interview sessions are the mark of inexperienced, incompetent researchers (or interviews with unwilling, tight-lipped respondents). With experience and competence, the number of your sessions will increase (although this can also happen with forceful, garrulous respondents who turn your interview sessions into occasions devoted primarily to their personal needs to the neglect of your research needs).

Your probes are requests for more: more explanation, clarification, de-scription, and evaluation, depending on your assessment of what best follows what your respondent has said. Probes may take numerous forms; they range from silence, to sounds, to a single word, to complete sentences. Learn which forms work best for you. Silence is easy to use, if you can tolerate it. Too little silence, and you may fail to have made clear that you were inviting more respondent talk; too much silence, and you may make your respondent squirm. The magical right amount of silence indicates, "Go on. Take some more time to think about why children abuse their parents. I'm not in a hurry."

Silence literally leaves more time for thought. Its use saves you from the common practice of offering your respondents a multiple-choice menu from which to select an answer to your question. For example, you might ask, "How do teachers select their instructional materials when they have an ethnically diverse student group?" Then, it is best simply to pause in silence and await a reply rather than to jump in with "Do they just do what they would do if they were teaching in any school? Do they see what the library has for supplementary material? Or do they try to find a textbook that shows due respect for ethnic diversity?" Silence is better than a menu of choices, as is rephrasing the question if it elicits no answer, or saying, "We can come back to that later if nothing comes to mind."

Used judiciously (before the squirms set in), silence is a useful and easy probe—as is the bunched utterance, "*uh huh, uh huh*," sometimes combined with a nodding head. "Yes, yes" is a good alternative; variety is useful. Longer, more directive probes take various forms. A couple of examples of the many possibilities are, "I'm not sure I got that straight. Would you please run that by me again," and (accompanied by a summary of what you thought you heard), "Did I understand you correctly?" Both types invite a rethinking by the respondent, and with rethinking may come elaboration. The summary alternative can also be used to preface, "Is there anything more you'd like to add to this?" Probes also can be simple questions: "How did that happen?" "What made you feel that way?" And more complex conditional questions: "If you had allowed your child to stay longer at camp, would that have changed her abusive patterns when she came home?"

Clearly, it is not the form of your probe that is most critical. It is your intent to probe, supported by your patience to linger and inquire rather than get on with completing the interview. The more nervous you are, the less patient you will be to probe and the less you will find occasion to do so. Missed opportunities for probing, however, plague us all. We read our old interview transcripts and find many occasions to groan over opportunities foregone. We were too tired, we were satiated with ideas, or we just didn't grasp what was being said. Given the intent to probe, the requisite habit and skill will develop—although you will always probe less than you should (as you learn in the ex post facto replaying of your tape or reading of your transcript).

There are other good interviewer qualities, and we lump them together with little elaboration because we feel that their meaning and consequences are reasonably self-evident. Among them is the quality of being *nonthreatening*. Tardif comments on its corollary—the sense of safety she felt in talking to Young, a sense that Young could convey by being outside Tardif's personal and professional world:

> I found it easier to discuss my thoughts and feelings regarding some of my professional decisions with Beth [Young] than I did with many of my colleagues. There was a freedom of expression afforded me in these ses-

sions that was not present in my everyday contacts. Beth was not a threat to me in any professional sense—she did not have a stake in any of the issues that had been discussed. (Young and Tardif 1988, 8)

Young's advantages as an outsider are a large part of the case against doing research in your own workplace or with people with whom you already have a relationship.

Of course, you should never do anything to make your respondents look or feel ignorant. Equally obvious, you should be calm and reassuring. Your nervousness can exacerbate the respondent's own nervousness. You must always be attuned to the respondent's anxiety at the prospect of being interviewed. When you try to make interview arrangements, you will discover that respondents often try to excuse themselves on the grounds that they haven't had enough schooling or they don't know enough. Even otherwise sophisticated respondents will be diffident about their performance, saying, "I don't know if that is what you are looking for or not."

Respondents may perceive your questions as testing, in the way they thought of questions as students at school. You may inadvertently present your questions and respond to answers in tones that suggest you are testing. Accordingly, you need to reassure, not only when you present yourself at the outset of interview arrangements, but also in the course of the interviews when respondents understandably want to know if they are being helpful to you. You need to reassure that it is perfectly permissible to say, "I don't know," "I have no idea," or "I never even thought about that before." Respondents seldom have unfailing memories or are omniscient; they should know that, even so, you still appreciate them.

We close our list with the sensible good interviewer qualities of *warm and caring*. When you are warm and caring, you promote rapport, you make yourself appealing to talk to, and, not least, you communicate to your respondents, "I see you as a human being with interests, experience, and needs beyond those I tap for my own purposes." It should be more than just tolerable to be with you in your role as researcher. In an effective interview, both researcher and respondent feel good, rewarded, and satisfied by the process and the outcomes. The warm and caring researcher is on the way to achieving such effectiveness.

SOME TYPICAL PROBLEMS

Fortunately, it is only once that you can do something for the first time (or do we believe that because it is consoling?). Helen reflected in somber tones about the beginning of her interviews:

> Things don't always work the way you plan. It took me a month to get access. Then, when I got there, I learned the interview guides had not been passed out. I had asked the principal to identify teachers who knew a lot, and found he had simply told various people that they would meet with me. About a third of the way through the first interview, I realized that the pause button was still on on my tape recorder.

Everything that possibly can go wrong did not go wrong for Helen. None of her respondents, for example, had brought with them to the interview young children who could not sit quietly for an hour—so that the parent's attention was consistently drawn away from the interviewer's questions. Making the best of bad times may be all that you can manage as you try to salvage something from an interview, at least chalking it up as an occasion to get to know your respondent and promote rapport. Ideally, your respondent forgives your pause-button lapse, and sees the futility of being interviewed with a distracting child present, and comes alone to subsequent sessions. If it is a case of no child, no respondent, then your ingenuity is challenged to find ways to keep child happy (and quiet) and parent on track.

Remembering to check your tape recorder comes easier after your initiation. Beyond problems most commonly associated with the novice's early days are others that can occur to anyone at any time. For example, your respondents do not answer the question you ask. What is going on? The reason may simply be that the respondent has innocently (without a hidden agenda) taken a fancy to discussing something else. This innocent discussion may challenge your patience and your willingness to legitimate your respondent's interests that diverge from your research needs. If you can listen as gracefully to their off-target talk (in your terms) as you do to their on-target talk, then the time that you lose may be more than offset by the enhanced quality of your respondent's answers. Or it may simply be that your question was not clear or the respondent was too nervous to concentrate. You take all the blame for questions not correctly understood (even if you aren't culpable) and look for suitable other words in which to recast your question. If restating does not help, go on to other questions rather than risk the respondent developing feelings of inadequacy.

The reason for not answering a particular question, or for respondents turning the focus of talk to topics of their own, may be more complex. Jennifer had a respondent who brought the talk around to safety in the nursery school, when Jennifer had the virtues of outdoor play on her mind. In time, Jennifer realized that her respondent gave very little time in her program to outdoor play and was saving herself from embarrassment in an interview that was directed exclusively toward outdoor play. In still more time, Jennifer realized that she needed to preface her interviews with the clearest possible statement that her inquiry on outdoor play was free of advocacy, so that respondents could continue to feel good about themselves—whether they did or did not include outdoor play in their nursery school program.

Such prefacing is critical to effective interviewing, because respondents logically conclude that if you ask a lot about something, you must think it is important. This may be true. However, if you cannot disabuse your respondent of the conclusion that you are an advocate (of outdoor play), then you risk embarrassing respondents or compelling them to appear ''better'' than they are by telling you what they think you want to hear. Dissimulation aside, to the extent that you appear as an advocate, your respondents may become defensive. Try explaining to them that you believe there are both successful and unsuccessful teachers who emphasize outdoor play; that you are not in the business of making judgments about success; that you want only to understand the place of outdoor play, or lack of it, in their nursery school curriculum. If it is there, then why is it there? If it is not, then why not?

When respondents show a pattern of turning away from your questions, they may be saying obliquely what they won't say directly: ''I don't want to continue this interview.'' Other forms of resistance to being interviewed are missed appointments and monosyllabic replies. The resistance may be apparent or real. Apparent resistance may result from respondents being preoccupied with personal matters that preclude concentrating on your matters. If they want to talk about their personal problems, your listening may clear the deck for them to return to your questions. Cutting short your current session or postponing further sessions for a few weeks may suffice to return to normalcy. Do not prematurely conclude that respondent resistance is tantamount to their wish to terminate all further interviews. It may be that your questions are treading on matters too sensitive for them to discuss with you. We think it useful to be gently direct. If you observe resistance, then ask about it: ''It seems to me that you have not been comfortable. . . . Are there areas you would rather not talk about?'' You might even ask, ''Do you think we ought to stop the interviews?'' If you do not hear yes, then you can continue interviewing and judge the quality of what you are hearing. If it is poor, then shorten your list of questions and end the sessions as soon as you can manage to do so.

Far removed from the troublesome problem of resistance is the problem of the nonstop talker. Respondent fluency is wonderful if it is on your research topic, but if not, then you need to learn to curb what may be your respondent's innocent but unproductive behavior. Assume that the respondent does not mean to be disruptive, so that a sign from you will agreeably redirect him or her. Don't wait too long to seek this redirection. Making a wordless sound or a physical sign, such as a slightly upraised hand or forefinger, may stop the verbal torrent so you can get a word in edgewise. When your interviewee stops, your response must not draw attention to the nonstop talk. Instead, apologize for your interruption before picking up on something the respondent has said that you can probe. Or summarize what the respondent has said and then bridge to where next you wish to go. The idea is to avoid making an abrupt shift to a topic distant from where the respondent's talk had been.

At a more basic level, you might try informing the too-talkative respondent at the beginning of the next session that you might stop the talk from time to time, but only in the interest of getting things straight. You do not want to relinquish control of your interview to your respondent. But although some boldness may be necessary to keep in control, the way you react to any of your respondent's behavior should not undermine your rapport with that respondent or your access to others.

In interviews, as in ordinary conversations, people make contradictory statements. Although it may be entirely appropriate in conversations to point out the contradiction in the time-honored, confrontational, one-up,"got you" fashion, this has no place in interviewing. Consider the possibilities that contradictions connote: the evolution of the respondent's thinking about the topic; the respondent's confusion about the topic; the respondent's being comfortably of two minds about the topic. Is the topic generating the contradictions worthy of clarification? If so, then you need to probe further into the respondent's most recent statement, right then and there. In addition, you can raise the topic again at your next session, inviting more thought to it. If it is not too obvious, you can take the two contradictory statements and put them in the mouths of two hypothetical persons: "I've heard some people say. . . . I've heard other people say. . . . What is your thinking about these two positions?" When the respondent has replied, you can continue: "Is it possible that both are right?" Or, "Is there a third or even fourth position?" The point is, when you ask questions, especially about complex matters, you cannot reasonably expect complete, carefully considered responses to be ready at hand. You can easily get spontaneous, short answers, but is this what best serves your research purposes? If you allow respondents time to think, then you will get more trustworthy data.

Though not a problem in the same sense as those above, you may find it problematic to decide whether or not the interviews—a particular session or the entire series with one person—went well. In one sense, "going well" means getting answers that fit the questions you ask and that you can visualize as part of your forthcoming text; careful listening will indicate whether this criterion is met. In another, more serious sense, going well means getting trustworthy data. Trustworthiness, certainly a relative consideration, is likely to increase with time and the establishment of a trusting relationship with your respondent. Clearly, the more one deems a person trustworthy, the more he or she will speak fully and frankly to that person. What you learn, under the best of circumstances, may not be "true" when the reference is to external states (e.g., matters that were visible). Lapsed memory, disadvantageous angles of vision, poor concentration, strong commitments—all of these factors and more can delimit the trustworthiness of your respondent's reporting. What a respondent says may be reinforced or undermined by what you learn from other interviewees, as well as from other data sources such as documents and participant observation. Thus, judging how the interviews are going may be tentative at first—you feel good about the interview because the flow of talk was easy, smooth, uninhibited, and on target—and confirmed or denied later as you acquire data from other sources.

CONCLUDING CONSIDERATIONS AND SUMMARY

It is well to stay aware of what you have received from your respondents so that when your interview sessions are over you can conclude in sufficiently enthusiastic terms. The quality of your listening is surely one type of reciprocation that they will value. When you consider the time, effort, cooperation, and flying words that they give you, your level of appreciation is usefully enhanced so that you are able to communicate at the end the proper degree of gratitude. Leave time after your final interview for the expression of your gratitude and for other informal talk which demonstrates that you did not perceive the respondent only in terms of his or her data contribution. In fact, such informal time (with tape recorder unplugged) before, during, and after other interviews is of substantial value for communicating this perception and for promoting the quality of your research relationship. Think of small talk, off-target talk, and end-of-interview session talk not as a loss of time (though if overdone it could be that), but rather as a gain in the quality of subsequent responses from your interviewees, a gain that imaginably will extend to future interviewees. Do not be surprised if occasionally you learn more of value at these times than when you were plugged in. A combination of the tape recorder and the formality of the interview inhibits some persons who do not mind talking freely, but do so best under apparent noninterview conditions.

Your gratitude is the interviewees' deserved return for their investment in your research project; it is readily within your power to provide. Another type of return is not necessarily within your grasp, though it is not an uncommon by-product of the interview process. A Vincentian young man told Corrine in the course of an interview, "I tell you things I've never told myself." Given the amount of time qualitative researchers spend with their respondents, we must conclude that the research experience will often modify some aspects of the respondent's behavior. Questions raise consciousness, as in the example just cited. Respondents learn about themselves, you, research, and how to be a respondent.

Researchers get more than data from their interviews. They speak of the exhilaration of conducting interviews, and of the rewards of meeting new people and of coming to understand some they thought they might not want to meet. Andrea commented,

One of the most enjoyable surprises was finding common ground with those
respondents I was least inclined to interview. I would be struck, upon
leaving, at how pleasant a time we had together. . . . I wrote in my journal:
"Up close, these people don't seem so extreme to me as they appeared
before I met them."

The type of interviewing emphasized in this chapter is (1) structured—you
have specified questions you know you want to ask; (2) open—you are
prepared to follow unexpected leads that arise in the course of your interviewing; and (3) depth-probing—you pursue all points of interest with various
expressions that mean "tell me more" and "explain." The intent of such
interviewing is to capture the unseen that was, is, will be, or should be; how
respondents think or feel about something; and how they explain or account for
something. Such a broad-scale approach to understanding is drawn from the
assumption that qualitative research, notably nonreductionist, is directed to
understanding phenomena in their fullest possible complexity. The elaborated
responses you hear provide the affective and cognitive underpinnings of your
respondents' perceptions. With this picture you have obtained what is characteristic of qualitative inquiry: the native's point of view.

Interviewing is an occasion for close researcher–other interaction. Although the personal feelings of researchers of any paradigmatic loyalty can be
engaged from whatever distance they stand from their others, qualitative
research provides many opportunities to engage feelings because it is a
distance-reducing experience. The feelings in question are those that are
involved in the researchers' relationships with others—the matter of rapport—
and those that are involved in the researchers' reactions to what they are
learning in the world of their others—the matter of subjectivity (the issues in
Chapter 5).

The Personal Dimension: Rapport and Subjectivity

In qualitative inquiry, the nature of relationships depends on two factors: the quality of our interactions to support our research—or rapport—and the quality of our self-awareness to manage the impact of self on our research—or subjectivity.

RAPPORT[1]

The term *rapport* describes the character of effective field relationships. Just what that character is, however, is vague and sometimes confusing. This section does not delineate steps for achieving rapport; there is no such list, although we will talk generally about some apparent antecedents of rapport.[2] This section, rather, explicates some of the issues that complicate establishing and maintaining rapport. (For other references on rapport, see Gans 1982; Glesne 1989; and Gonzalez 1986.)

Definitions of Rapport

The dictionary defines rapport as the "relation characterized by harmony, conformity, accord, or affinity," and notes that it refers to the "confidence of a subject in the operator as in hypnotism, psychotherapy, or mental testing with willingness to cooperate" (*Webster's* 1986, 1882). Rapport is an attribute that is instrumental to a variety of professional relationships, from used-car salesperson to marriage counselor. Its function, however, varies with each relationship. For example, counselors establish rapport so that clients can feel sufficiently comfortable to disclose information; their intent is to attain ends shaped by the clients' needs, as they and the clients ascertain them.

Researchers, to the contrary, traditionally establish rapport to attain ends shaped primarily by their own needs. In qualitative research, rapport is a distance-reducing, anxiety-quieting, trust-building mechanism that primarily serves the interest of the researcher. Spradley gently acknowledges rapport's acquisitive function: "Rapport encourages informants to talk about their culture" (Spradley 1979, 78). Freilich is more pointed: "The researcher . . . 'engineers' people and situations to get the type of data required by the study" (Freilich 1977, 257). Rapport is a necessary but not sufficient condition for obtaining good data; researchers partake in the opportunities it enables by virtue of other skills.

Rapport is sometimes used interchangeably with *friendship* in the fieldwork literature. Although the line between the two is often hard to distinguish, they are not the same thing. A friend is "one that seeks the society or welfare of another whom he holds in affection, respect, or esteem or whose companionship and personality are pleasurable" (*Webster's* 1986, 911). Friendship means mutual liking and affection and implies a sense of intimacy and mutual bonding. We trust our friends; even more, we like them and will do things for them that we would not do for others. The concept *liking* also helps to differentiate rapport and friendship. A relationship characterized by rapport is marked by confidence and trust, but not necessarily by liking; friendship invariably is. "One can learn a great deal from people one dislikes or from people who dislike one" (Wax 1971, 373). You do not need to like or be liked by your others, although your work will be even more rewarding if mutual liking occurs. In research relationships, your ordinary need to be liked is overshadowed by the necessity of being accepted.

Control over the relationship also distinguishes the two concepts. Friends are (or should be) equal actors in establishing and maintaining their relationship. The rapport relationship is more asymmetrical, with control in the hands of the researcher. (We address rapport and friendship in more detail later in this chapter.)

Factors Bearing on Rapport

The literature and lore of fieldwork often portray consummate researchers as sensitive, shrewd, patient, nonjudgmental, friendly, and inoffensive. They have a sense of humor and a high tolerance for ambiguity; and they learn the other's language, wear appropriate dress, and maintain confidentiality. These factors affecting rapport are personal characteristics, which, to some degree, the researcher can manipulate.

You manage your appearance and behavior in rapport-building efforts in order to acquire continual access to information. Measor (1985) discussed the role of appearance and shared interests in her data collection in a British school. She found that how she looked mattered to both students and teachers, and that this in itself caused a problem because each group had a different notion of appropriateness. As a result, Measor sought a compromise that showed she was fashion conscious, but not too much so. About her overall presentation of self, Measor observed, "In a research relationship, one presents a particular front or a particular self. My own view is that it is important to come over as very sweet and trustworthy, but ultimately rather bland" (Measor 1985, 62).

In order to maintain access, you will continually need to act in culturally appropriate ways. This may mean "getting mad" or "causing a disturbance," as Pettigrew (1981) discovered while working among Sikhs in the Punjab. When someone made a derogatory remark, she could not ignore it with a tolerant, indifferent attitude. In keeping with cultural rules, she had to display her opposition in order to maintain respect and rapport. Conversely, when Pettigrew witnessed the blatant sexist treatment of women, she could not object, or she would not have been allowed to stay.

Your appearance, speech, and behavior must be acceptable to your research participants. This may be hard to manage at first because you are habituated to acting in certain ways that reflect your personal sense of propriety, dignity, and integrity—and to take offense when your strongly held values have been assailed. It is important to learn, however, that your strongly held values often are not appropriate guides for conducting your research. For example, teachers in the Christian day school we studied were actively involved in anti-ERA (Equal Rights Amendment) rallies. As researchers concerned with rapport, we not only had to keep our thoughts on this topic to ourselves, but we also were restricted from partaking in any pro-ERA rallies that might be televised throughout the state. We could not be seen endorsing what was antithetical to core fundamental Christian belief. Thus, rapport places limitations on the researcher's ordinary interactions and expressions.

Although the range of accommodations you make to be inoffensive in your research role do not ensure rapport, they do enhance the prospects of its establishment. You consciously monitor your behavior so that people who are unaccustomed to the presence of researchers in their lives will be at ease in your presence. Your challenge is to fit in.

Gender, age, and ethnicity—attributes over which the researcher has a lesser degree of control—can also make a difference in your access to data. For example, Banks, a black anthropologist, may have had an advantage in developing rapport among Malaysians who were resentful of the British (Lawless, Sutlive, and Zamora 1983). Your color is not amenable to manipulation, but you do have other attributes that are and which you can emphasize in the effort to overcome disadvantages that might result from gender, age, or ethnicity.

Perhaps to some extent it is possible even to control ascribed characteristics. By acting in ways that others do not expect women to act, Hunt (1984) modified the impact of gender in her study of city police. Appearing as if one is something that one is not can also extend some degree of control over ascribed and achieved attributes. For example, Thomas Robbins (Robbins, Anthony, and Curtis 1973) appeared to be a member of a proselytizing group known as "Jesus Freaks," even though he was not. The use of an as-if posture rests on the researcher's sense of what is feasible and ethical, not merely on the demands of rapport. Clearly, in research, as in other matters, what works is not necessarily good.

The ideal of rapport is developing sufficient trust for the conduct of a study. Sufficiency is largely contextual, depending on your goals; the personality, age, gender, and ethnicity of all participants; and the setting and time of the study (Glazer 1972; Gonzalez 1986; Spradley 1979). In the end, you will know when you have established rapport, because you will see it in the willingness of others to allow access to that part of their life of interest to you.

Developing and Maintaining Rapport

When asked, "How do you know when you have rapport," students replied:

> The way the interview goes shows rapport. When the interviewee keeps looking at her watch, you know you have not achieved good rapport.

> Rapport comes when the interviewee gets something out of the interview. One person told me, "No one has asked me this before." In good interview situations, people get to think about things that they have not put together before. They learn about themselves in the process. Another person told me, "I think I got more out of this than you did." You feel good then.

The first student describes how being attuned to the nonverbal language of your others can inform you about your research relationship, although people do check the time for reasons other than boredom. The second student introduces the concept of reciprocity into the relationship. Rapport is more easily achieved if both parties get something out of the interaction. Often your others will find being part of a study flattering; they will welcome the attention and enjoy the opportunity to reflect on matters of importance to them.

This willingness can be found where least expected. Andrea received a letter from one of her interviewees after their first meeting. The interviewee expressed sincere desire to get together again, sent information relevant to their discussion, apologized for being too enthusiastic, and complimented Andrea on the approach she was taking to investigating change in a small rural community. The interviewee was a developer with whom Andrea had postponed talking because she feared her ability to keep an open, interested, learner perspective. Ironically, she found herself fascinated both by what he had to say and by his clear, logical, sensitive way of expressing his point of view. Rapport, obviously, had been achieved.

Generally, people will talk more willingly about personal or sensitive issues once they know you. In most cases, this means being perceived as someone who is willing to invest the time truly to understand them. Sometimes it simply means giving the person time to learn that you are an all-right sort of person. Dick tells of doing an interview with a teacher aspiring to be a principal. Dick had a single, 1 1/2 hour interview scheduled and felt dismayed going into it. "These people," he said beforehand, "will never tell a stranger all this information." But the interviewee was someone who talked easily, and Dick responded appropriately with *"umms"* and *"uh huhs."* After forty-five minutes, during which Dick thought he was getting good information, the interviewee asked, "Now that I know you, can we go back to one of the earlier questions?" Dick was delighted that he had been able to develop rapport sufficient for the interviewee to reveal deeper layers of information comfortably. He also learned that many layers of data existed and that, even though his single-session interviews might give him enough data for his purposes, he was getting "thinner" data than he could through multiple interviews.

Although contact over a long period of time does not assure the development of rapport, time may prove to be a determining condition once you have attended to other matters. If you are around long enough, you can verify that the self you have been projecting is an enduring self: You have said that you will maintain anonymity of respondents and you *always* do, and you have said that you have not come to find fault and you *never* do. Time allows you to substantiate that you will keep the promises you made when you were negotiating access, and that you will remain the person you have been showing yourself to be.

Like access, rapport is something to be maintained. Maintaining rapport means conscious attunement to the emerging needs of a relationship. An interviewee may become suspicious, distrustful, and uneasy after several sessions of interviewing. Pick up on these reactions and find ways to be more reassuring and to build trust (this may mean revealing more of yourself or your research thoughts). Alternately, you may find that in the interest of good data collection, you have to withdraw from certain research relationships. Many fieldworkers advise awareness and avoidance of a society's "marginals"— frequently the very ones who, because of their fringe status, are most open to rapport and friendship with researchers. It does not reassure your research participants if you are identified with someone whom they see as undesirable. Thus, when you realize that a close association is detrimental to your research, you may have to renegotiate the relationship or withdraw to some degree.

Developing and maintaining rapport involves more than consideration of one individual at a time; it calls for awareness of social interactions among participants. Researchers enter into social systems in ways which demonstrate that participants are valued, that is, that the worth of their time and attention and association are appreciated. Thus, if researchers are not equitable in the time they allot to participants, then they may risk bruising feelings or eroding relationships.

You often need to remain above the politics of your site, but this does not free you from understanding the political landscape and its pitfalls and mines upon which you might tread. Maintaining access is associated with becoming informed about your setting's social and political structure so that you can shape your conduct with the sure-footedness that such knowledge affords. It is no small matter to be aware of the formal and informal loci of power, of the issues that irritate, and of the history that continues to shape current behavior. All of this is part of rapport—both developing it and keeping it—for it is the knowledge on which we fashion fitting behavior.

Safety Valves

Given the stress of fieldwork, maintaining rapport may require safety valves. Immersed in a life that is not your normal one, which, accordingly, abnormally constrains you, you periodically need to get away to be with others from your own subculture and talk to those who have similar beliefs and ideas. You may need to blow off steam or simply disappear for a few days so that you do not destroy the rapport that has been developed.

Fieldwork accounts do not always address this need, but field notes or journals do. Malinowski's (1967) diary while among the Trobriand Islanders is a well-known example. It became the place for him to vent his feelings and make statements that would not have endeared him to his host community. You won't earn a merit badge if you persist in unbroken duty to the obligations of your study. Immersion is valued, but it can be overdone. Sustaining the needed degree of rapport depends on your capacity to continue making careful, considered judgments. Taking breaks promotes your ability to keep a sharp edge to the multitude of daily decisions that you make. Gaining distance by whatever means—trips, reading, strongly worded personal journals—is advised.

Rapport and Friendship

When a distinction between rapport and friendship is made in qualitative literature, the overwhelming tendency is to warn against forming friendships because of the hazards of sample bias and loss of objectivity. These hazards are linked to overidentification, also called "over-rapport" and "going native" (Gold 1969; Miller 1952; Shaffir, Stebbins, and Turowitz 1980; Van Maanen 1983).

Friendship appears to bias data selection and to decrease objectivity in three main ways (Gans 1982; Hammersley and Atkinson 1983; Pelto and Pelto 1978; Zigarmi and Zigarmi 1978). In the first situation, data bias may result from a somewhat unconscious subjective selection process. Researchers are tempted to talk primarily with people they like or find politically sympathetic. If they follow such impulses, Gans suggests that "the pleasure of participant observation [would] increase significantly, but the sampling of people and situations . . . may become badly distorted" (Gans 1982, 52). Or it may be that researchers talk to a variety of people, but overidentify with one group. They then hear what this group has to tell them, but less fully what other groups tell them. Therefore, they may censor their own questioning process to avoid alienating those with whom they are overidentifying. They also may be tempted to give such friends confidential information that would help them.

In the second situation, researchers are consciously aware of their best data sources, but they are denied access to some of them because of their friendship with others. Pelto and Pelto warn that "every firm social relationship with a particular individual or group carries with it the possibility of closed doors and social rebuffs from competing segments of the community" (Pelto and Pelto 1978, 184). In the Caribbean, Corrine attempted to maintain access simultaneously to alienated young adults, to unalienated young adults, to government officials, and to estate owners. She found herself frequently explaining to those of the unalienated group her time with the more alienated. Achieving a politically neutral presence is, however, easier in some settings than in others.

In the third situation, research participants overidentify with the researchers. In doing so, they may begin to act in ways that they perceive the researchers want them to act or in ways that impress them. Van Maanen (1983) cites the example of police he studied who used overly aggressive patrol tactics in an effort to increase their worth in the eyes of the observer. Gold (1969) suggests that the informant who becomes too identified with the fieldworker may even become an observer much like the researcher. In sum, friendship can affect the behavior of researchers or their others, with potential detrimental consequences for complete data collection and analysis.

It appears, therefore, that you should establish rapport but avoid friendships in the research setting or, at least, as Zigarmi and Zigarmi (1978) suggest, with research participants. Most prescriptions are easier to say than to follow. Many researchers do form friendships during fieldwork, most frequently with those who play the special role of key informant (West 1980). In other cases, the nature of the research requires getting to know a small number of people well. Friendship often develops in the process. Hansen's work is illustrative:

> That I did not remain fully detached from the flow of Danish life might be
> seen as a failure in my role as objective analyst. Yet to understand the subtle

dynamics of Danish behavior *required* as detailed a knowledge of the individual Danes as I had the capacity to acquire. Access to this information was made possible by friendship, and once established that relationship imposed standards of behavior at least as compelling (to me) as the rules of my discipline. (Hansen, 1976, 131–132)

The work of Hansen and others challenges the positivist paradigm's deep concern for objectivity. Contemporary qualitative researchers most often perceive subjectivity as a persisting dimension of the entire research process; thus, they acknowledge the invariable presence of personal factors. The issue is not whether personal factors will be present, but when, which ones, and with what impact (discussed in the next section).

As a researcher, you need to examine the assumptions underlying your relationships with your others. If "objectivity" is important, then friendship is a problem. Friendship entangles in that it conveys the impression that one has chosen sides, taken a stand, decided on preferences. Each such impression risks shutting down data sources or biasing the data collection process. From another perspective, however, friendship may be a goal that rapport helps to achieve. Friendship may assist you and your others to achieve and act on new perspectives in a negotiated fashion.

As a researcher, you also need to recognize the role of power distribution in your interactions. In the traditional research mode, those who are studied grant the researcher access and may benefit from the research process and product in a number of ways. The researcher, however, retains control over the project's purpose, methods, analysis, and use.

Collaborative modes of research attempt to distribute power more equitably among the various aspects of the research process. The researcher assists and facilitates rather than develops and executes. Since intent presumably lies with the group as a whole, the researcher is thereby exonerated from feelings of exploitation, deception, or guilt. But just how are research agendas actually set? What happens to established friendships when the researcher goes home?

The contribution of rapport to all modes of qualitative research remains *essential*. It is not separate from other aspects of doing good research, but an integral part of collecting data. Research could not succeed without the trust that rapport engenders.

SUBJECTIVITY

Reading about subjectivity is like reading about other aspects of the research process: It may represent the beginning of understanding, a necessary condition on the way to making the researcher's biases explicit and to grasping the place of subjectivity in research. Although we cannot absolutely specify what the sufficient conditions are for this to occur, we believe that the conditions relate to a personal encounter with self in the course of research. Aware that there is something to seek, to uncover, and to understand about yourself, you are ready to be informed through the research experience.

The voice of subjectivity takes an I, the first-person singular, the attestation that a particular person was in a particular place for a particular purpose. Accordingly, we organize our discussion of subjectivity in the voice of an I. It is Alan's voice as he recounts his experience with subjectivity beginning in rural Mansfield, continuing in fundamentalist Christian Bethany, and ending, for the time being, in multiethnic Riverview. Research in each of these settings became an occasion for considering subjectivity in general, and Alan's own subjectivity in particular. From this point on, we shift our voice to Alan's.[3]

I began my encounter with subjectivity by accepting, as I often had heard and read, that although there is no value-free research, objectivity is the researcher's ideal, and subjectivity, the prototypical orphan in the cinders, is just something to live with, avoid, and never, never be caught consorting with. I understood subjectivity in the way we understand something we hear a lot about, but hopefully remain distant from—things such as hunger, drought, poverty, and other forms of devastation. I could shake my head appropriately, make the right sounds in the right place, to such important acknowledgments as this one by anthropologist Robert Redfield as he explains why his study of Tepotzlan differed so much from that of his colleague Oscar Lewis (1951):

> I think we must recognize that the personal interests and values of the investigator influence the content of the descriptions of the study. . . . The hidden question behind my book is, "What do these people enjoy?" The hidden question behind Dr. Lewis' book is, "What do these people suffer from?" (Redfield 1955, 136).

And this one by Jean Strouse, who wrote about Alice James, sister of William and Henry James. After she had visited Alice's grave, saddened to tears at Alice's neglect relative to that of her famous brothers, Strouse wrote: "In fact, all these emotional responses that you have as a biographer are important parts of the work" (Strouse 1988, 195).

Indeed, what questions drive your work, what emotions you feel as you contemplate the subject of your research, are clearly important matters. Questions and emotions are not obscure abstractions. Applying their point to the conduct of your own inquiry, however, may be another matter altogether. What follows is my personal experience of coming to grips with subjectivity.

From 1972 to 1974, I studied the relationship between school and community in the midwestern village of Mansfield, a place of considerable distance from my upbringing in Chicago and my life thereafter in university towns. The longer I lived in Mansfield, and the more young and old Mansfield residents I interviewed, the more I felt at home there and admired the way of life the residents had created. These sentiments were evident to me in the course of the study. By the time I completed the study, and the book based on it was published (Peshkin 1978), other sentiments also were evident.

I realized that not only did I like the community of Mansfield, but also that I liked places characterized by a sense of community, places such as my neighborhood in Chicago where I spent the first twenty years of my life, and places such as the small resort town in southern Michigan where I spent all of my adolescent summers. "Discovering" community in Mansfield was for me like going home again, Thomas Wolfe notwithstanding. Moreover, I also realized that Mansfield, a village of only 1,300 or so, was vulnerable, facing an uncertain future because of population loss and economic decline. In this context, Mansfield High School assumed significance as a major contributor to the well-being of its host community, a point I acknowledged in my book's subtitle: "Schooling and the Survival of Community."

Because I liked Mansfield, thought it a special place, I rooted for its perpetuation. I concluded that state legislators, usually given to favoring consolidation as the answer to small-school financial and academic woes, should be alert to what they may be destroying—community—when they assume the role of educational saviors and pass legislation that closes all schools below a specified student enrollment. Not so fast, I cautioned; legislator spare that school because there is more at stake than just the education of children. Schools in Mansfield, and also in larger places, have communal as well as educative functions.

Beyond these substantive awarenesses of self was a procedural one: I thoroughly enjoyed the entire experience of long-term fieldwork. One day in Mansfield, my host and octogenarian friend Charlie Glancy, a retired coal miner and farmer, asked me if I got paid for the work he saw me doing. He was incredulous that anyone could get paid for going to meetings, church, and basketball games, and for sitting in classrooms. I confess to being a little incredulous myself, as if one should not get paid for doing what one so thoroughly enjoys. The point is that I like fieldwork, it suits me, and I concluded that rather than pursuing research with questions in search of the "right" methods of data collection, I had a preferred method of data collection in search of the "right" question.

In short, what I learned about a sense of community in Mansfield, what I made of what I learned about (tread lightly with school policy that may sever the school–community linkage), and how I learned in the first place (long-term participation, observation, and interviewing)—all were rooted in those personal orientations that I call subjectivity. They operate sometimes dispositionally, sometimes deterministically; and sometimes consciously, sometimes unconsciously. They derive from my life history, my biography. They are a complex composite of my values, attitudes, beliefs, interests, and needs.

Given the potential for many stories that could be told about Mansfield and Mansfield High School, I chose to tell one that centered on community. This was a far from random choice. Although I do not believe there is a one-to-one relationship between one's biography and research focus, the roots of the latter are most likely to be found in the former. If I know you well, I can't predict what you will study and how, but I am able to understand why you have made the decisions you have made.

With this level of understanding of subjectivity in hand, I came to my next school-community study in the fundamentalist Christian setting of Bethany Baptist Church and Bethany Baptist Academy (BBA). In research terms, this setting provided entry to the world of true believers, a world that I had never known before. Never before had I felt so alien, so distant from where I lived, while being geographically so close to home. I was proselytized by persons who were certain I was condemned to eternity in hell unless I was born again by accepting Christ as my personal savior. I had to learn to perceive proselytizing as the act of persons who sincerely wished me well, rather than as an act that offended my integrity as a Jew. At BBA, I became singularly conscious of my identity as a Jew and the threats to Jews in general from groups that assumed they were armed with God's Truth.

When I began to write chapter one of the book based on the Christian school (Peshkin 1986), I knew that I was annoyed by my *personal* (as opposed to research) experience at BBA. I soon became sharply aware that my annoyance was pervasively present, that I was writing out of pique and vexation. Accordingly, I was not celebrating community at Bethany, and community prevailed there no less robustly than it had at Mansfield. Why not? I was more than annoyed in Bethany; my ox had been gored. The consequence was that the story I was feeling drawn to tell had its origins in my personal sense of threat. I was not at Bethany as a cool, dispassionate observer (are there any?); I was there as a Jew whose otherness was dramatized directly and indirectly during eighteen months of fieldwork.

Looking back at Mansfield, I realized that of the many stories that could be told about Mansfield and its high school, I told one that drew on my attachment to community. I was aware of the facts for two other stories, but I referred to them only in passing. One was about a small minority of Mansfield residents who lived beyond the village's warm embrace of community. The other was about the racism of Mansfield residents, which I euphemized as their "antiblack sentiment." I further realized that if I had the outlook of a critical theorist, or if I were an African-American researcher, I most likely would have told other, verifiable stories.

Then, looking back at BBA, I realized that if I were a born-again Christian or a Christian apostate, I would have been enabled, no less, to see stories other than the one that I was moved to tell: the one that saw schools such as BBA as extraordinary opportunities for Christians of a particular ideological commitment, at the same time that they exemplified and challenged the principle of pluralism that undergirded their very existence.

In short, the subjectivity that originally I had taken as an affliction, something to bear because it could not be foregone, could, to the contrary, be taken as "virtuous." My subjectivity is *the* basis for the story that I am able to tell. It is a strength on which I build. It makes me who I am as a person *and* as a researcher, equipping me with the perspectives and insights that shape all that I do as researcher, from the selection of topic clear through to the emphases I make in my writing. Seen as virtuous, subjectivity is something to capitalize on rather than to exorcise.

One's subjectivity, however, has the capacity not only to enable but also to disable. It is necessary, therefore, to try to see what you are not seeing, to detect what you are making less of than could be made, so that you can temper as necessary that which your subjectivity is pressing you to focus on. Moreover, subjectivity should not be confused with subjectivism, which exalts personal feeling as "the ultimate criterion of the good and the right" (*Webster's*, 1986, 2276). By means of my subjectivity, I construct a narrative, but it must be imaginable by others, and it must be verifiable by others. The worth of my narrative cannot rest on its goodness or rightness in some private sense. It cannot be illusion or fantasy that has no reality outside of my own mind.

Having stumbled on my subjectivity as I began to write my Christian study, I resolved to look for it breaking out—like the measles, one red eruption after another—at the inception of my return to fieldwork. My next study took me to Riverview, a town of about 40,000 that caught my attention by the ethnic stratification of its high school. I intended to follow the play of ethnicity in school and community in order to learn how ethnicity operated in the lives of the students and their parents. Given my resolve, I looked for my subjectivity. On finding its manifestation, I took note of the feeling and the circumstance.

The results of this search for subjectivity I incorporated into a set of six subjective "I's," named as follows:

1. **Ethnic-Maintenance I**—This is my Jewish self, the one that values and means to sustain my own ethnic identity. It emerged when I observed activities in school and community that contributed to ethnic maintenance. I felt good when I saw others doing what I valued.

2. **Community-Maintenance I**—This is the self I had learned about first in Mansfield. In Riverview many were third-generation residents of the town. Their affection ran deep; they engaged in formal and informal activities that contributed to perpetuating a sense of community. Of course, I approved of such activities in Riverview, as I had earlier in Mansfield.

3. **E-Pluribus-Unum I**—This is the self that emerged my first day at

Riverview High School and that stayed with me throughout my period of data collecting. It resulted from seeing the high school students doing what they called "mingling." Their physical appearances signaled ethnic diversity, but it seemed that students, characterized by whatever expression of diversity, were together. Most particularly, color did not predictably separate students in this school, whose population was approximately 33 percent African-American, 33 percent white, 22 percent Hispanic, and 12 percent Filipino. The mingling cheered me; my subjectivity had been elicited.

4. **Justice-Seeking I**—This is a defensive self, the product of my identification with the well-being of Riverview's school and community. Once evident, it appeared repeatedly as I heard the stories of Riverview citizens being stigmatized by their wealthier neighbors whose children vied with Riverview's in football and basketball, and whose towns contained the malls where Riverview residents shopped. It seemed that no one was too young to escape the insults of outsiders directed against Riverview's poorer, nonwhite population. The sentiment aroused by this element of subjectivity was of the "my people" wronged, so "let's set the record straight" type.

5. **Pedagogical-Meliorist I**—This, too, is a defensive self. It is directed toward students, generally minorities, whom I observed getting nowhere in their classrooms. They were being taught by teachers who had not learned enough, often did not care enough, to make a difference in their students' lives. Class time for both students and teachers was an occasion for little more than marking time until the bell released both from their meaningless engagement. This circumstance, regrettably common, disturbed me more than I had ever been disturbed by the ineffective teachers I had observed at other schools. The difference at Riverview High School was that the students in such classes were usually minorities, those who came to school with two strikes against them. I found myself doing what I never before had done as I sat in the back of classrooms: hatching schemes that would alter the classrooms I was watching, schemes that were calculated to reorient instruction and make a difference in the lives of the students.

6. **Nonresearch-Human I**—This refers to the self who does not get left behind when the research self is at work. Its presence relates to the warm reception that Riverview residents extended to my wife and me as sojourners in their town. Feeling well received, I felt well disposed toward Riverview. This particular aspect of subjectivity is inclined to moderate otherwise sharp judgments. Its distance-reducing impact creates feelings of involvement and concern that develop a stake in the people and place under study.

These six subjective I's are points on a map of myself. They do not create a complete map because the experience of Riverview's school and community did not evoke all of my subjectivity. It is well, then, to speak of "situational subjectivity," of the personal aspects that arise for a particular person at a particular time and place. Some of these I's surely will appear again in other studies; just as surely, new I's will appear in other studies. I left Riverview with a record of my subjectivity. I was aware in the course of data collection, and thereby alerted as I proceeded to analyze and write up my data, of what within me was operative to shape, skew, distort, construe, and misconstrue what I was making of what I saw. My hope was to tame my subjectivity, to know it well, to get it in shape, so that I could use it in its virtuous capacity, while minimizing its negative potential. Undoubtedly, the book developed from my Riverview experience (Peshkin 1991) reflects my subjective I's.

We have no doubt that monitoring your subjectivity is a productive undertaking. Although it is not possible to be complete in this mapping of self, you can learn enough that is consequential about the selves generated in a particular research situation to be able to make use of this knowledge and to be responsible in reporting those selves to the readers of your work. How you pursue your own subjectivity matters less than that you pursue it; the means can be as idiosyncratic as the special, personal twist that all researchers give to the standard methods that they adopt to conduct their research. Reading, reflecting, and talking about subjectivity are valuable, but they are no substitute for monitoring it in the process of research.

RAPPORT AND SUBJECTIVITY

There is a connection between rapport and subjectivity: Your capacity and limitations for establishing rapport are affected positively and negatively by your subjectivity. Liking or not liking a person (or a place or event) presses you toward or away from that person, with the predictable consequence that you distort by under- or over-sampling. Being aware that you are so inclined suggests the need for moderation. Being aware that you are so disinclined suggests that you have an obstacle to overcome if you are successfully to pursue contact with people not to your taste; your others need not be to your taste. As observed earlier, friendship is not an essential condition for conducting research; being accepted and trusted is. Also essential is consciousness of your own subjectivity so that you can disabuse yourself of the fiction that, as the disembodied passive voice conveys, watching, listening, and reading are going on without a known human agent. Invariably, a sentient being does the watching, listening, and doing. We think it makes a difference who. The goal is to get as fully as possible in touch with the embodied self who performs the acts of research.

NOTES

1. This section on rapport draws on "Rapport and friendship in ethnographic research" by Corrine Glesne, from *The International Journal of Qualitative Studies in Education*, 1989, vol. 2, no. 1, pages 45–54, published by Taylor & Francis Group.
2. There are writers who presume to have nailed down the techniques for achieving rapport. From within the self-help literature, see Brooks 1989.
3. The section that follows is drawn from Peshkin 1982b, 1988a, 1988c. See also Barone 1990b; Couch 1987; Eisner 1990; Krieger 1985; LeCompte 1987; Riley, 1974.

CHAPTER 6

But Is It Ethical?
Learning to Do Right

As a group of students entered their second semester together in a qualitative research methods class, they reflected on the role that trial and error had played in their best-learned lessons. Ernie wondered, "Can we even consider the possibility of learning research ethics through trial and error?" With increased awareness of ethical issues, they deliberated over perceived ethical dilemmas and wondered about the unintended consequences of their work.

This group of students realized that ethical considerations should accompany plans, thoughts, and discussions about each aspect of qualitative research. Ethics is not something that you can forget once you satisfy the demands of human subjects review boards and other gatekeepers of research conduct. Nor is it "merely a matter of isolated choices in crucial situations" (Cassell and Jacobs, 1987, 1). Rather, ethical considerations are inseparable from your everyday interactions with your others and with your data.

Of course, ethical decisions are not peculiar to qualitative inquiry. Guidelines for ethical conduct grew out of medical and other types of intrusive research. The interactive nature of qualitative research, however, raises ethical questions that nonqualitative researchers ask less frequently. Lincoln points out that different philosophical systems give rise to different ethical concerns. The emphasis on separation between researcher and researched in logical positivism "prescribes a set of attitudes toward research subjects which fosters believing—on both sides—that researcher knows best" (Lincoln 1990, 290). According to Lincoln, both professional codes and federal law "assume the posture that researchers are in the best position to determine, within certain guidelines, what constitutes ethicality in social science research" (Lincoln 1990, 290). In contrast, interpretive approaches perceive reality as socially constructed and the researcher interacts with participants in order to understand their social constructions. This orientation "thrusts upon the respondent two new roles: that of agency, self-determination, and participation in the analysis and reconstruction of the social world; and that of collaborator in both the processes and products of inquiries" (Lincoln 1990, 290). This approach transforms the "researched from 'object needing protection' to 'person empowered to determine the direction and focus of participation'" (Lincoln 1990, 290). Lincoln speaks of the ideal here; many qualitative researchers do not work collaboratively with their respondents. Nonetheless, as qualitative researchers develop and maintain fieldwork relationships, they must continually ask what it means to be ethical within their research role.

This chapter focuses on ethical issues that arise out of the researcher–other relationship. It does not discuss ethical issues common to all types of research, such as falsifying results or publishing without crediting co-researchers. As in previous chapters, we find it difficult to give unequivocal advice on "right" or "wrong" ways to behave. Rather, the issues we raise here are meant to alert you to areas that need consideration and forethought, so that you can possibly avoid learning ethical lessons through trial and error.

ETHICAL CODES

Various professional groups have created codes of ethics. Cassell and Jacobs observe, "A code is concerned with aspirations as well as avoidances, it represents our desire and attempt to respect the rights of others, fulfill obligations, avoid harm and augment benefits to those we interact with" (Cassell and Jacobs 1987, 2). In general, research codes of ethics address individual rights to dignity, privacy, and confidentiality, and avoidance of harm (Punch 1986).

Nazi concentration camps and the atomic bomb served to undermine the image of science as value-free and automatically contributing to human welfare (Diener and Crandall 1978). Our image of science keeps changing. In light of today's codes of ethics, a number of studies from the 1950s and 1960s are questionable. Generally, subjects were drawn from low-power groups; in some cases, they gave information only to have the findings used against their own interests by people in positions of power (Punch 1986). Ethical codes help to mitigate this occurrence. Nonetheless, some researchers object to ethical codes because they can also protect the powerful. For example, Wilkins (1979, 109) notes that prisoners' rights are rarely a matter of concern for authorities until someone wants to do research in prisons. In effect, authorities can protect themselves under the guise of protecting subjects. Institutions that require explicit consent often have elaborate screening devices to deflect research on sensitive issues. Galliher asks, "Is not the failure of sociology to uncover corrupt, illegitimate covert practices of government or industry because of the supposed prohibitions of professional ethics tantamount to supporting such practices?'' (Galliher 1982, 160).

The ethical principles adopted by the Council of the American Anthropological Association address issues that potentially face qualitative researchers. The following portion is representative of their statement:

> In research, anthropologists' paramount responsibility is to those they study. When there is a conflict of interest, these individuals must come first. Anthropologists must do everything in their power to protect the physical, social, and psychological welfare and to honor the dignity and privacy of those studied.
>
> **a.** Where research involves the acquisition of material and information transferred on the assumption of trust between persons, it is axiomatic that the rights, interests, and sensitivities of those studied must be safeguarded.
> **b.** The aims of the investigation should be communicated as well as possible to the informant.
> **c.** Informants have a right to remain anonymous. This right should be respected both where it has been promised explicitly and where no clear understanding to the contrary has been reached. . . .
> **d.** There should be no exploitation of individual informants for personal gain. Fair return should be given them for all services.
> **e.** There is an obligation to reflect on the foreseeable repercussions of research and publication on the general population being studied.[1]

The Council of the American Anthropology Association's ethical statements include directives on the researcher's responsibilities to the public, the discipline, students, sponsors, one's own government, and the host governments. Many of the principles are general and open to interpretation; nonetheless, they provide a framework for reflection on fieldwork, sensitizing you to areas that require thoughtful decisions.

INFORMED CONSENT

Although informed consent neither precludes the abuse of research findings nor creates a symmetrical relationship between researcher and researched, it can contribute to the empowering of the researched. The appropriateness of informed consent, particularly written consent forms, however, is a much-debated issue that accompanies discussions of codes of ethics by qualitative inquirers. Through informed consent, potential study participants are made aware (1) that participation is voluntary, (2) of any aspects of the research that might affect their well-being, and (3) that they may freely choose to stop participation at any point in the study (Diener and Crandall 1978). Originally developed for biomedical research, informed consent is now applicable when participants may be exposed to physical or emotional risk. Sometimes the requirement of written consent is readily accepted, as in the case of studying young children by means of interviews. If it were required for all research projects, however, then much of the work of the qualitative researcher would be curtailed. Written consent would eliminate all unobtrusive field observations and informal conversations. The very record left by consent papers could put some individuals' safety at risk if they discuss sensitive topics (e.g., crime, sexual behavior, drug use).

Margaret Mead stated that, in contrast to research in the positivist vein, "anthropological research does not have subjects. We work with informants in an atmosphere of mutual respect" (in Diener and Crandall 1978, 52). Field relationships continually undergo informal renegotiation as respect, interest, and acceptance grow or wane for both researcher and other. As the relationship develops, the researcher may be invited to participate in ways he or she hoped but could not have sought access to in the beginning (from secret ceremonies to executive golfing rounds). When research becomes collaborative, cooperation, active assistance, and collegiality may exceed the demands of informed consent (Diener and Crandall 1978; Wax 1982). This sense of cooperation and partnership may be more relevant to the ethical assessment of qualitative fieldwork than whether or not informed consent forms were signed.

RESEARCHER ROLES AND ETHICAL DILEMMAS

In the beginning stages of research projects, novices tend to see their research role as one of data gathering. As they become more involved in fieldwork, they find themselves functioning in a variety of roles depending on research problems and procedures, their own characteristics, and the personal attributes of their others. Some of the roles may worry the researcher, while other roles may be attractive but perplexing in relationship to their data gathering goal. This section addresses several roles that qualitative researchers easily assume: exploiter, intervener/reformer, advocate, and friend. Different ethical dilemmas accompany each role.

Exploiter

Questions of exploitation, or "using" your others, tend to arise as you become immersed in research and begin to rejoice in the richness of what you are learning. You are thankful, but instead of simply appreciating the gift, you may feel guilty for how much you are receiving and how little you are giving in return. Take this concern seriously. Do researchers, as welcomed but uninvited outsiders, enter a new community, mine words and behaviors, and then withdraw to process those words into a product that serves themselves and, perhaps, their professional colleagues? Research participants usually remain anonymous. In contrast, researchers may get status, prestige, and royalties from publications (Plummer 1983). Researchers sometimes justify their actions with trickle-down promises such as "Through getting the word out to other professionals [special educators, educational administrators, teachers], we will be able to help other people like you."

Exploitation involves questions of power. If you are not engaged in collaborative research projects, then how do you decide if you are "using" your others? Mitzi began to interview homeless mothers about the schooling of their children. She agonized over questions of power and exploitation:

> What am I giving back to these homeless mothers that I interview? It seems so unfair that this middle-class privileged person is "using" this needy population. . . . Can someone in a shelter tell me they don't have time? Privilege allows my response [of no time] to others to be OK. For them, that response would be suspect. Am I "raping" the social issue of the moment?

Dick, in his study of first-year principals, felt he "used" his relationships, his contacts, and his friends all over the state to get data.

Although you may applaud Mitzi and Dick for their heartfelt sentiments, do not simply accept their harsh interpretation of their own behavior. Take Mitzi's case. Her homeless mothers may be counted among our nation's most unfortunate people. Mitzi's research will not bring them the security and support of a home, a job, and proper schooling for their children. But did Mitzi make such promises? To do so would be unethical. Did she treat the mothers with respect and dignity? This is ethical. Did she listen carefully, taking pains to understand what she was hearing? This is ethical. Did she intend to incorporate what she learned into her own professional conduct? This is ethical. Did she drop her topic once her dissertation was complete, never writing or talking about it again? This may be unethical.

If the standard of ethicality is solving the problems of the people from whom we collect data, and solving them right away, then much research is doomed never to begin. Were Mitzi to use the results of her research exclusively for her own good, she could be accused of being an exploiter, in the strict sense of the term. That Mitzi receives more good from her research— degree, job, status, income, attention—is not inevitable, but often it is unavoidable. When Mitzi's concern fastens exclusively on her personal gain, she is being unethical. When she writes honestly and cogently about the homeless mothers and the schooling of their children, sharing the knowledge that she gains, she is being ethical.

Perhaps Mitzi should have conceived of a collaborative study with the mothers. That she did not do so, that she created and maintained a power imbalance, does not condemn her as unethical.

Intervener/Reformer

Unlike the exploiter role, which researchers wander into but want to avoid, the intervener or reformer role is one that researchers may consciously decide to assume. As a result of conducting research, researchers may attempt to right what they judge to be wrong, to change what they condemn as unjust. Through observations at a zoo, Nancy grew increasingly concerned over what she considered to be inhumane treatment of certain animals and agonized over what to do with her information.

In the process of doing research, researchers often acquire information that is potentially dangerous to some people. Don was interested in the history of an educational research organization. As he interviewed, he lamented, "I'm hearing stuff that I neither need nor wish to know about attitudes and relationships." The process was complicated for Don because he was investigating an organization in which he himself was involved.

As Corrine interviewed young farmers about their practices, she learned about the illegal cultivation and marketing of marijuana. And as Alan interviewed students about life in school, he became privy to information such as the following:

> You know about the corner store, right? No? Gosh. They sell alcohol to anyone. Anyone. My friend and I went there to buy some chips, and the guy who was standing behind the counter said, "You guys drink? I'll sell you some wine coolers. I won't tell your parents. Don't worry about it. Want some wine coolers?"

When your others trust you, you will invariably receive the privilege and burden of learning things that are problematic at best and dangerous at worst.

Your ethical dilemma concerns what to do with dangerous knowledge. To what extent should you continue to protect the confidentiality of research participants? If you learn about illegal behavior, should you expose it? If the researchers in the above examples were to inform authorities of their knowledge, they would jeopardize not only their continued research in those sites, but also possible subsequent projects. None of them discussed their knowledge with other research participants, nor personally intervened. If what you learn relates to the point of your study, you must explore ways to communicate the dangerous knowledge so that you fully maintain the anonymity of your sources. Such advice is consistent with other researchers who suggest that continual protection of confidentiality is the best policy (Ball 1985).

The question remains, however, of how "wrong" a situation must be before you should intervene on the basis of your unexpectedly acquired knowledge. If, for example, as a researcher you become aware of an ongoing episode of child abuse, do you react differently than if your work puts you in contact with students being offered alcohol at the corner store? Could not the latter also be construed as a case of child abuse? How do you decide where the lines are between a felt moral obligation to intervene and an obligation to continue as the data collecting researcher?

We have no definitive answers to the above questions and again defer to judgments made on a mix of contextual elements and personal compulsions. We have learned, however, that some preventative measures will help avoid such dilemmas. Laurie, a nurse, conducted research in a hospital setting. She worried about what she should do if she observed malpractice while in her research role. Finally, she discussed her worries with her cohorts in a qualitative research methods class. By taking the worry seriously and putting it through a variety of configurations, the class urged Laurie to meet with her gatekeepers and with the nursing staff that she was observing and interviewing to get their advice on how she should proceed if she observed malpractice. In the earlier example, Nancy also appealed to colleagues after witnessing behavior at the zoo that she considered "wrong." After much debate, the group agreed that she should continue collecting data and become an animal advocate after she published the data.

Developing some sort of support group to discuss worries and dilemmas is a valuable part of the research process. Some researchers build a panel of experts into their research design. A student's dissertation committee can serve this function, but expert panels and dissertation committees do not necessarily know how to deal with ethical questions that arise in the qualitative research world. Ideally, the researcher has a support group made up of others who, although perhaps involved in substantively different topics, are all struggling with similar methodological questions.

Advocate

Advocates are like interveners in that they decide to take a position on some issue that they become aware of through their research. Unlike interveners or reformers who try to change something within the research site, the advocate champions a cause. As Lynne interviewed university custodians, she was tempted to become an advocate:

> I keep asking myself to what extent the research should improve the situation for custodians. This is magnified somewhat by my feeling that I have been a participant in the process, raising issues with custodians that many by now have come to terms with or raising expectations that some good will result. Even though my research was for the purpose of under-

standing and not "fixing," how can one come so close to what is judged to
be a very bad situation and walk away? I keep asking myself, "Do I owe
them solutions or at least some relief?" My answer is always "no," but
then I keep asking myself the same question, probably because I just don't
like my answer.

Lynne's research heightened her concern for the well-being of the custodians
she studied, and the "take the data and run" approach left her uncomfortable.
Qualitative researchers find that advocacy can take a variety of forms—
presentations and publications among the most readily available. Lynne needs
to decide whether such formats will serve her concern, or if there are others
within her competency that would be acceptable to the custodians.

Finch (1984) experienced a dilemma over publishing data she collected
through her study of play groups. She found that child-care standards differed
in working- and middle-class women.

> This evidence, I feared, could be used to reinforce the view that working-
> class women are inadequate and incompetent childrearers. Again, I felt that
> I was not willing to heap further insults upon women whose circumstances
> were far less privileged than my own, and indeed for a while, I felt quite
> unable to write *anything* about this aspect of the playground study. (Finch,
> 1984, 84)

Finch resolved her dilemma by distinguishing between the structural position
in which the women were placed and their own experience with that position.
This enabled Finch to "see that evidence of women successfully accommodat-
ing to various structural features of their lives in no way alters the essentially
exploitative character of the structures in which they are located" (Finch 1984,
84). Thus, she described the child-care practices of the working-class women
in a way that would support them in an unfair and unequal society. Finch did
not alter her data; she did not explain away the differences she uncovered. Her
ethical sensitivity led her to contextualize her findings, so that the behavior of
the two groups of women was framed within the differential realities of their
lives. This is not the politician's cynical "damage control," but the academic's
commitment to effective interpretation.

Friend

Researchers often have friendly relations with their others; in some cases, the
relationship is one of friendship. Whether friendship or friendliness is the case,
ethical dilemmas can result. You may gain access to intimate information
given to you in the context of friendship rather than in your researcher role.
Should you use such data? Both Hansen's (1976) exploration of Danish life and
Daniels' (1967) investigation within a military setting relied on personal

friendships as channels for information. Hansen expressed discomfort with her role as researcher and her role as friend: "The confidential information I received was given to me in my role as friend. Yet, I was also an anthropologist and everything I heard or observed was potentially relevant to my understanding of the dynamics of Danish interaction" (Hansen 1976, 127). Hansen refers to a particular confidential story told to her by one woman:

> Later that day I would record this conversation, alone, without her knowledge, in my role as anthropologist. In my role as investigator the conversation became "data." Would she have spoken so frankly about this and other more intimate subjects had she understood that I listened in *both* roles, not only as friend? (Hansen 1976, 129)

As she continued to gather data, Hansen grew concerned over how she would protect the anonymity of her interviewees and struggled with thoughts on whether public description of behaviors violates an individual's right to privacy. She and Daniels both experienced ethical dilemmas over publishing findings that would possibly discomfort their friends, if not betray their friendship relationships. In light of research data and publications, their friendships appeared utilitarian, a characterization that may be problematic for perpetuating friendship.

Both Hansen and Daniels need to ask, as do we all in similar circumstances, if their narrative truly has to include all that their friends tell them. Will the narrative hold up if the troublesome bits are excluded? Can these troublesome bits be presented in less troublesome ways? In the end, should we all not let our friends be judges, by submitting to them what we have written and taking our lead from their decision?

THE RESEARCHER–OTHER RELATIONSHIP

No matter how qualitative researchers view their roles, they develop relationships with their others. The relationships, however, are generally asymmetrical, with power disproportionately on the side of the researcher. Consequently, researchers must consciously consider and protect the rights of participants to privacy. They must reflect on and mitigate deceptive aspects of research and consider issues of reciprocity.

The Right to Privacy

In discussions of the rights of research participants, privacy is generally the foremost concern. Participants have a right to expect that when they give you permission to observe and interview, you will protect their confidences and preserve their anonymity. Respect confidentiality by not discussing with anyone the specifics of what you see and hear. When a principal asks what you are learning from the teachers, for example, you might respond with something like the following:

> I am really enjoying talking with your teachers. They seem to take both their jobs and my research seriously and are therefore helping me tremendously. It's too early yet to know what I can make of all the information I'm receiving, but a couple of themes have been emerging and I'd like the opportunity to discuss them with you. Do you have the time?

Such a response leads away from particular individuals and toward the discussion of general concepts, which respects the principal's interest in your findings without violating any of your commitments to teachers. Such discussions must balance your unqualified obligation to the teachers with your appreciation of the principal's natural interest in your findings. It also makes use of an opportunity for participant feedback or a "member check" (Lincoln and Guba 1985) on the researcher's analytic categories.

Researchers sometimes argue over whether unobtrusive methods, even in public places, invade rights of privacy. This discussion usually includes debates on the use of covert observation (to be discussed in more detail in the next section, "Deception"). One position is that covert observation in public places is permissible because people ordinarily watch and are watched by others in public places. Accordingly, social scientists should be able to do so as well. A counter point is that when such observations are systematic, recorded, and analyzed, they no longer are ordinary and thereby violate rights of privacy.

Similar arguments develop around less discussed means of unobtrusive data collection. Diener and Crandall (1978) describe a study in which researchers used both surveys and the contents of garbage bags to discover what people bought, discarded, and wasted in different sectors of Tucson, Arizona. The findings concluded that poor people waste less food than higher-income people, and that there is a marked discrepancy between self-reports on alcohol consumption and evidence from bottles and cans in the garbage. Although garbage content was not linked to particular households, the examined bags often included envelopes with names on them. Do such studies violate privacy rights?

The issue of privacy arises again during the writing phase of the qualitative inquiry process. To protect their anonymity, researchers use fictitious names and sometimes change descriptive characteristics such as sex and age. Fictitious names, however, do not necessarily protect participants, as demonstrated by two frequently cited cases: West's (1945) *Plainville U.S.A.* and Vidich and Bensman's (1968) *Small Town in Mass Society*. Despite made-up names, the towns were easily identified by descriptions of their characteristics and locations, and people in the towns easily recognized themselves in the descriptions of individuals. In both cases, the research participants were upset by the portrayals of the town and their inhabitants.

Critics (see Johnson 1982, 76) point out that West, for example, focused on the negative, that he looked with an urban perspective, and that he used offensive and judgmental words such as "hillbilly" or "people who lived like animals." Plummer states that although "confidentiality may appear to be a prerequisite of life history research; it frequently becomes an impossibility" (Plummer 1983, 142). He cites several examples: fifty years after the original study, Shaw's (1930) Jack Roller was located for reinterview, and after a month of detective work, a reporter tracked down Oscar Lewis' (1979) *Children of Sanchez*. For confidentiality, Plummer observes, "Sometimes the researcher must partially deceive his readership" (Plummer 1983, 144). These studies and others raise a number of ethical questions about the publication of data: What obligations does the researcher have to research participants when publishing findings? If the researcher's analysis is different from that of participants, should one, both, or neither be published? Even if respondents tend to agree that some aspect of their community is unflattering, should the researcher make this information public?

Despite justified worry about protecting anonymity, researchers may also have to deal with declined anonymity. Jacobs (1987) tells of an anthropologist who wrote about a community in Melanesia; she disguised villagers and their location through use of pseudonyms. Three years later, she returned to the field to distribute copies of her manuscript to those who had been most helpful and to ask permission to conduct further study. People liked the book and felt the accounts were correct, but told her that she had the name of the village wrong and the names of the individuals wrong. She was told to be more accurate in the next book. The author was faced with an ethical dilemma: Should she follow the wishes of the villagers or the conventions and cautions of ethical codes? When her second book was completed, she sent a copy to the village and asked for comments as well as whether they still wanted actual names used. When she did not get a direct reply to her question, she used the same pseudonyms in her second monograph.

Jacobs (1987) tells of another case of anonymity declined, this time within the United States. An applied medical anthropologist worked for three years in an urban African-American community. Before she published her articles, she asked community members to read, comment on, and criticize them. They complimented her on her accuracy, but they questioned her use of pseudonyms for the town, the health center, and the individuals who "struggle to improve the healthcare for our people" (in Jacobs, 1987, 26). The anthropologist explained the reasons for privacy conventions and how disclosing names could result in possible harm. In the end, she omitted the actual name of the center and its location, but she acknowledged the names of staff members in footnotes. This decision was made collaboratively.

Deception

Chris was interested in researching the gay community on a university campus. He attended a meeting of the Gay/Lesbian Alliance as a participant observer, jotting notes unobtrusively. Because the meetings were open to the public, he originally saw no reason to proclaim his role as researcher. As that first meeting continued, however, he struggled with feelings of deception and guilt. Finally, he quit taking notes and decided to meet with the organization's officers and obtain their permission to attend meetings in the role of researcher.

Conventionally, we regard deception as wrong. Nonetheless, its role in research is debated time and time again. Deception easily enters various aspects of research, and it can take the form of either deliberate commission or omission. For example, in covert studies, participants never know that they are being researched. Some researchers misrepresent their identity and pretend to be someone they are not; others present themselves as researchers, but misrepresent or do not fully explain what it is that they are researching. This latter practice is called omission or "shallow cover" (Fine 1980). The decision to deceive generally rests on a concern to ensure the most natural behavior among research participants.

Punch (1986, 39) raises two questions concerning the role of deception in research: (1) Are there areas in which some measure of deception is justified in gaining data? (2) Are devious means legitimate in institutions that deserve exposure? These questions summarize the ongoing debate over the use of deliberate deception in research.

Covert research gets its strongest support from those who advocate research of the powerful. As in investigative journalism, access to the workings of some groups or institutions with power would be impossible without deception. Van den Berge says of his research in South Africa, "From the outset, I decided that I should have no scruples in deceiving the government" (in Punch 1986, 39). If you, like Van den Berge, view an institution as "essentially dishonorable, morally outrageous and destructive," do you ignore it and study something more publicly acceptable in order to avoid being deceptive? Jack Douglas, a strong supporter of the utilitarian or "ends justify the means" approach, states,

> The social researcher is . . . entitled and indeed compelled to adopt covert methods. Social actors employ lies, fraud, deceit, deception and blackmail in dealings with each other. Therefore the social scientist is justified in using them where necessary in order to achieve the higher objective of scientific truth. (in Punch 1986, 39)

From the utilitarian perspective, deception in research may be justified by benefits to the larger society. Ethical decisions are made on the basis that moral action is that which results in the greatest good for the greatest number. Critics of this position argue that although costs and benefits may be estimated, both are impossible to predict and measure. Furthermore, they argue, who is to set the standards that determine when something is for the greater good of society? The decision maker in most studies is the researcher, who is never an objective participant, no matter what he or she claims.

Currently, the utilitarian position that one does what is necessary for the greater good is overshadowed by the deontological ethical stance, which posits that moral conduct can be judged independently of its consequences. The deontological framework holds up some standard, such as justice or respect or honesty, by which to evaluate actions. This position changes the nature of the researcher–other relationship and makes it unethical for researchers to misrepresent their identity to gain entry into settings otherwise denied to them, to misrepresent deliberately the purpose of their research, or to leave research participants feeling cheated. Bulmer (1982), for example, argues that covert research is not ethically justified, practically necessary, or in the best interest of social scientists. He views the rights of subjects as overriding the rights of science, thereby limiting areas of research that can be pursued. Bulmer suggests that the need for covert methods is exaggerated and that open entry may more often be negotiated than is commonly supposed (Bulmer 1982, 250). (See Flinders [forthcoming] for an in-depth examination of qualitative inquiry from the perspective of four ethical frameworks: utilitarian, deontological, relational, and ecological.)

Even when you are as honest and open as possible about the nature of your research, you will continue to develop ethical questions concerning your fieldwork. Many of the questions will be context-bound, arising out of specific instances in each study. For example, informed consent regulations indicate that you should disclose to potential participants all information necessary for them to make intelligent decisions about participation. Yet doing so is difficult in qualitative research because often you are not fully aware of what you are looking for, among whom, or with what possible risks. "The researcher is in a perplexing situation," states Erickson. "He or she needs to have done an ethnography of the setting in order to anticipate the range of risks and other burdens that will be involved for those studied" (Erickson 1986, 141). Although the partial nature of your knowledge does not obviate the propriety of informed consent, it does make implementing it problematic.

Certain ethical standards could encourage researchers to eliminate whole sections of their findings because publishing them could harm the individuals or groups they studied. Is this, too, a form of misrepresentation? Colvard (1967) suggests that reporting statuses and pseudonyms instead of actual names, paraphrasing quotations rather than presenting them verbatim, and withholding information obtained in more personal than official roles neither protects privacy adequately nor preserves knowledge adequately. We see

Colvard's observations as cautionary: We must always be aware of ways in which our work may be deceptive.

Reciprocity

In quantitative research, reciprocity is frequently assumed to be a matter of monetarily rewarding research subjects for their time. Although participants in qualitative research sometimes receive remuneration, the issue of reciprocity becomes more difficult because of the time involved and the nature of the relationships developed between researchers and their others. The degree of indebtedness varies considerably from study to study and from participant to participant, depending on the topic and the amount and type of time researchers spend with their others.

Glazer defines reciprocity as "the exchange of favors and commitments, the building of a sense of mutual identification and feeling of community" (Glazer 1982, 50). As research participants willingly open up their lives to researchers—giving time, sharing intimate stories, and frequently including them in both public and private events and activities—researchers become ambivalent, alternately overjoyed with the data they are gathering, and worried by their perceived inability to reciprocate adequately. As Corrine wrote up her Caribbean work, she reflected:

> Cultural thieving is what ethnographers do if their written product is limited in its benefits to the gatherer and, perhaps, his or her community. Also known as "data exportation" or "academic imperialism" [Hamnett and Porter 1983, p. 65], the process is reminiscent of past archaeologists carrying stone, pottery, and golden artifacts away from "exotic" places of origin to the archaeologists' homeland for analysis and display. What is owed to the people observed is the question. Are the terms of trade more than glass beads? (Glesne 1985, 55–56)

Researchers do not want to view people as means to ends of their choosing. Nonetheless, in noncollaborative qualitative work, they invariably cultivate relationships in order to gather data to meet their own ends. In the process, researchers reciprocate in a variety of ways, but whether what they give equals what they receive is difficult, if not impossible, to determine.

Equivalency may be the wrong standard to use in judging the adequacy of your reciprocity. What can you do for teachers who let you spend hours at the back of their classroom, or for students who come to your interview sessions week after week? Literally, their time is invaluable to you. Is there anything within your means to deliver that your others would perceive as invaluable to them? Probably not. They do not have a relationship with you that puts you in a position to have something that, typically, is of such consequence to them. What you do have that they value is the means to be grateful, by acknowledging how important their time, cooperation, and words are; by expressing your dependence on what they have to offer; and by elaborating your pleasure with their company. When you keep duty teachers company, assist participants in weeding their gardens, or speak to the local Rotary Club, you demonstrate that you have not cast yourself as an aloof outsider. By the quality of your listening, you provide context for the personal exploration of your interviewees. These are some of the critical commodities with which you, as a researcher, can deal in your exchanges with your research others. What else is within your capacity to deliver is, as always, a matter of circumstances. We believe in the need to be fully mindful of this miscellaneous category of commodities.

The interviewing process particularly provides an occasion for reciprocity. By listening to participants carefully and seriously, you give them a sense of importance and specialness. By providing them the opportunity to reflect on and voice answers to your questions, you assist them to understand some aspect of themselves better. If your questions identify issues of importance to interviewees, then the interviewees will invariably both enjoy and find useful their roles as information providers. One of the women that Alan interviewed in his ethnicity study told him, "You know I hadn't thought about high school in a long time. I can think about it this afternoon as an experience, but I also see how it lays the foundation for where I am today." In another example, Alan interviewed an administrator. They began at 4:00 P.M., and allowed forty-five minutes because the administrator had a board meeting that night. The three-quarters of an hour extended to an hour; and despite Alan saying, "Ok, let's stop here and I'll see you next week to continue," the administrator continued with another story. As Alan confirmed the same place, same time meeting for the next Tuesday, the administrator said, "How about starting earlier? How's 3:00?" Good listening with its attendant reinforcement, catharsis, and self-enlightenment are the major returns researchers can readily give to interviewees.

Although researchers do not wittingly assume the role of therapist, they nonetheless fashion an interview process that can be strikingly therapeutic. Obligations accompany the therapeutic nature of the interview. Self-reflections can produce pain where least expected, and interviewers may suddenly find themselves face to face with a crying interviewee. Tears do not necessarily mean that you have asked a bad or good question, but they do obligate you to deal sensitively and constructively with the unresolved feelings, without taking on the role of analyst. If appropriate, you might suggest people, organizations, or resources that may be of help. Follow up through letters or conversations to assist such interviewees in feeling comfortable with their degree of personal disclosure. When Dick interviewed first-year principals, one began to cry as he expressed his stress and frustration with the job. When Eileen interviewed nonwhite students about their experiences on a predominantly white campus, a young man began to cry as he talked about leaving his home community. At first, both Dick and Eileen were stunned, but then they empathically told of similar life experiences. Finally, they suggested people and organizations that might assist the interviewees.

The closer the relationship between researcher and research participants, the more special obligations and expectations emerge. For example, Cassell (1987) tells of an anthropologist who, during her initial fieldwork and successive summers, was accepted as granddaughter of an elderly southwestern Native American couple. Their children and spouses treated her as a sister. One summer, when the anthropologist returned to the reservation, she learned that her "grandfather" showed signs of senility, was drinking heavily, and was hallucinating. His children and their spouses left soon after her arrival, saying that they had cared for him all year and that it was now her turn. Although his care took full time and her work did not get done, the anthropologist felt she had no choice but to honor her "occasional kin" status. She also felt, however, even more a part of the family and free to bring with her an emotionally and educationally difficult nephew the next summer. Her "kin" helped tremendously in dealing with him. In another example, biographer Rosengarten (1985) wrote about his work with Ned Cobb and the form of his reciprocity: "There was one special reason why Ned Cobb's family agreed to busy itself with me, apart from the feelings between us. My work with Ned revived his will to live" (p. 113).

Interviews and other means of data collection can contribute to raised expectations in less intimate relationships as well. When researchers spend days and months asking people about their problems and aspirations, they elicit voices of dissatisfaction and of dreams. In the process, they may encourage people to expect that someone will work to alleviate their plight. If, as a researcher, you plan only to publish your findings, then you must find a way to make that clear to your others throughout the data gathering process. Through written reports, however, qualitative researchers frequently convey reciprocity by their tales of injustice, struggle, and pain. Reciprocity may also include making explicit arrangements to share royalties from publications.

NO EASY SOLUTIONS

By their nature, ethical dilemmas defy easy solutions. Researchers continue to debate whether or not some people or areas should be researched. They question whether or not fieldwork is inevitably deceitful. They argue over the role of conscious deception in fieldwork. They raise ethical questions over the issue of power relationships, particularly with poor and "deviant" groups. And they question whether codes and regulations can successfully shape research ethics.

Plummer (1983) identifies two positions in relation to ethics: the ethical absolutist and the situational relativist. The absolutist relies heavily on professional codes of ethics and seeks to establish firm principles to guide all social science research. The relativist believes that solutions to ethical dilemmas can not be prescribed by absolute guidelines but have to be "produced creatively in the concrete situation at hand" (Plummer 1983, 141). Pointing out weaknesses in both positions, Plummer suggests a combination: broad ethical guidelines with room for personal ethical choice by the researcher. We concur. Ethical codes certainly guide research behavior, but the degree to which research is or is not ethical depends on the researcher's continual communication and interaction with research participants. Researchers alone must not be the arbiters of this critical research issue. (For further discussion about ethics in qualitative research, see Burgess 1984; Ellen 1984; Eisner and Peshkin 1990; Guba 1990; Punch 1986; Rynkiewich and Spradley 1976; Whyte 1984.)

NOTES

1. From *Professional Ethics: Statements and Procedures of the American Anthropological Association*, Statements on Ethics, June 1983, November 1986 by the American Anthropological Association.

CHAPTER 7

Finding Your Story: Data Analysis

Work days of fairly long hours on the notes finally have come. These days are tedious and also something else when I come across a good bit from an interview. These days, I'm coding interviews with older folks who are inclined to feel tender toward their ethnic identity. Reading the notes recalls the day I sat in their living room or kitchen. Even when I'm feeling specially cheered by something I'm simultaneously thinking—now what to do with it and its numerous brothers and sisters sitting with the same code heading in a separate pile marked Black, Hisp, Fil, or Ital. I probably felt this way at the same point in earlier studies, but I don't remember. Is this the wise fellow tucked away in each of us that is selective about what it allows us to remember, knowing that to remember all is to possibly preclude ever getting into such a quandary again? I frequently remind myself that if I'm patient, inspiration will finally come with a plan to settle all the unsettled matters. I remind myself, but I can't always believe what I'm saying. (Peshkin, Letter, 13 January 1988)

Data analysis involves organizing what you have seen, heard, and read so that you can make sense of what you have learned. Working with the data, you create explanations, pose hypotheses, develop theories, and link your story to other stories. To do so, you must categorize, synthesize, search for patterns, and interpret the data you have collected. (See Bogdan 1972; Denzin 1989; Dobbert 1982; Erickson 1986; Fetterman 1989; Lincoln and Guba 1985; Miles and Huberman 1984; Strauss 1987; Tesch 1990.)

EARLY DATA ANALYSIS

Data analysis done simultaneously with data collection enables you to focus and shape the study as it proceeds. Consistently reflect on your data, work to organize them, and try to discover what they have to tell you. Writing memos to yourself, developing analytic files, applying rudimentary coding schemes, and writing monthly reports will help you to learn from and manage the information you are receiving.

Memo Writing

By writing memos (see Glaser and Strauss 1967) to yourself or keeping a reflective field log, you develop your thoughts; by getting your thoughts down as they occur, no matter how preliminary or in what form, you begin the analysis process. Memo writing also frees your mind for new thoughts and perspectives. "When I think of something," says Jackie, "I put it on a card. I might forget about the thought, but I won't lose it. It's there later on to help me think." Even as you become intimately familiar with your data, you can never be sure of what they will tell you until analysis and writing are complete. As you work with data, you must remain open to new perspectives, new thoughts. Gordon states,

> I have found that my analysis goes on even if I am not actually working with the data. Insights and new ways to look at the data arise while I am at work at other things. Probably the most productive places for these insights is on the long drive to class and during long, boring meetings when my mind is not actively engaged.

It is particularly important to capture these analytic thoughts when they occur. Keeping a battery-operated tape recorder in the car can help, as can jotting down your thoughts wherever you happen to be, day or night. The comments and thoughts recorded as field log entries or as memos are links across your data that find their way into analytic files.

Analytic Files

Analytic files (see Lofland 1971) build as you collect data. You may begin with files organized by generic categories such as interview questions, people, and places. These files provide a way to keep track of useful information and thoughts. As your data and experience grow, you will create relevant specific files on the social processes under investigation, as well as on several other categories such as subjectivity, titles, thoughts for introductory and concluding chapters, and quotations from the literature.

Each of these specific files serves a distinct purpose. The subjectivity file, for example, helps you to monitor, control, and use your subjectivity (see Chapter 5). Given the bearing of your subjectivity on the way you perceive your data, you cannot meaningfully separate the two (although you can forget their relationship). But by keeping track of your subjectivity, you will become attuned to the outlook that shapes your data analysis.

The title file contains your efforts to capture what your narrative may be about (see Peshkin 1985). Although your research project has a stated central focus (per your research proposal), you do not really know what particular story, of the several possibilities, you will tell. Conjuring up titles as the data are being collected is a way of trying out different emphases, all of which are candidates for ultimately giving form to your data. The titles become a way of getting your mind clear about what you are doing, in an overall sense, although the immediate application may be to concentrate your data collecting as you pursue the implications of a particular focus. In short, your search for a title is an act of interpretation. Titles capture what you see as germane to your study; but as your awareness of the promise of your study changes, so do your titles.

Files related to introductions and conclusions direct you to two obvious aspects of every study—its beginning and its ending. Regardless of the particular name that you give to your introductory and concluding chapters, you frame your study in the former—providing necessary context, background, and conceptualization. You effect closure in the concluding chapter by summarizing, at the very least, and by explicating the meaning that you draw from your data as befits the point of your study. It is never too early to reflect on the beginning and ending of your work, much as the formal preparation of these chapters may seem a distant dream when you are caught up in collecting data. Ideally, the existence of these files alerts you to what you might otherwise miss in the course of your study; they stimulate you to notions that, like your titles, are candidates for inclusion in your forthcoming text. Until the writing actually is done, however, you will not know which will be the surviving notions.

The quotation file contains quotations from your reading that appear useful for one of the several roles that the relevant literature can play. Eventually, they will be sorted out among chapters, some as epigraphs: quotations placed at the heads of chapters because they provide the reader with a useful key to what the chapter contains. Other quotations will be the authoritative sprinklings that your elders provide as you find your way through the novel terrain of your own data. By resourceful use of quotations, you acknowledge that the world has not been born anew on your terrain. The quotation file, like other files, is meant to be a reminder that reading should always inspire the question: What, if anything, do these words say about my study?

Analytic files help you to store and organize your own thoughts and those of others. Data analysis is the process of organizing and storing data in light of your increasingly sophisticated judgments, that is, of the meaning-finding interpretations that you are learning to make about the shape of your study. Understanding that you are in a learning mode is most important; it tells you that you need not be all at once as accomplished as eventually you need to be to meet the challenges of data analysis. It reminds you that by each effort of data analysis, you enhance your capacity to further analyze.

Rudimentary Coding Schemes

In sorting your data into analytic files, you are developing a rudimentary coding scheme. As the process of naming and locating your data bits proceeds, your categories divide and subdivide. Learn to be content, however, with your early, simple coding schemes, knowing that with use they will become appropriately complex. In the early days of data collection, coding can help you to develop a more specific focus or more relevant questions. For example, Bob was looking at the role of a principal in a problem junior high. Although he kept a daily log of his activities, he often felt that he was "missing the forest for the trees." He was collecting a lot of data, but he kept wondering if they were adding up to anything. When he began to give code names to main points in his log, he became familiar with what he was finding and, accordingly, with what he was missing. Through this process, Bob narrowed and shaped a focus that was both definable and manageable.

Cindy provides another example. Interested in the role of school boards in small, rural communities, she began by observing meetings of one rural school board and interviewing its members. After fifteen hours of data collection, she reread and began to code all of the data she had gathered. In the process, she reconceptualized her problem statement:

> My initial problem statement was so broad it was difficult to work with. The process of coding and organizing my codes has helped to determine an approach to solidify a new problem statement that will lead me in a focused exploration of two major areas of school board control—financial and quality education.

Unlike a squirrel hoarding acorns for the winter, you should not keep collecting data for devouring later. Rather, examine your data periodically to insure that your acorns represent the variety or varieties desired, and that they are meaty nuggets, worthy of your effort.

Establishing the boundaries for your research may be continuously difficult. Social interaction does not occur in neat, isolated units. Gordon reflected on his work:

> I have felt right along that it is questionable whether I am really in control of this research. As I immerse myself in the analysis of my data, I begin to be sure that I am not. I constantly find myself heading off in new directions and it is an act of will to stick to my original (but revised) problem statement.

In order to complete any project, you must establish boundaries, but these boundary decisions are also an interpretive judgment based on your awareness of your data and their possibilities. Posting your problem statement or most recent working title above your work space may help to remind you about the task ahead. Cindy used a computer banner program to print out her working title, which she taped to the wall over her desk. The banner guided her work whenever she lifted her head to ponder and reflect.

Monthly Reports

Throughout the data collection process, writing monthly field reports for yourself, for committee members, or for the funding agency is a way to examine systematically where you are and where you should consider going. Headings such as activities, problems, analytic thoughts, and plans help to review your work succinctly and realistically plan it. In reflecting on both the research process and the data collected, you develop new questions, new hunches, and, sometimes, new ways of approaching the research. The reports also provide a way to communicate research progress to interested others, keeping them informed of the whats and hows and giving them a chance for input along the way.

Maintaining Some Semblance of Control

By the end of data collection, expect to be overwhelmed with the sheer volume—notebooks, note cards, computer files, manila files, and documents—that has accumulated. You truly have acquired ''fat data''; their sheer bulk is intimidating. Invariably, you will collect more data than you need. The physical presence of so much data can lead you to procrastinate, rather than to face the seemingly endless task of analysis.

It may help to think of the amount of film that goes into a good half-hour documentary. Similar to documentary film making, the methods of qualitative data collecting naturally lend themselves to excess. You collect more than you can use because you cannot define your study so precisely as to pursue a trim, narrowly defined line of inquiry. The open nature of qualitative inquiry means that you acquire even more data than you originally envisioned. You are left with the large task of selecting and sorting—a partly mechanical but mostly interpretative undertaking, because every time you decide to omit a data bit as unworthy or locate it somewhere you are making a judgment. Gordon reflects on his experience with sorting data:

> Sorting the data is actually less difficult than I feared, and it certainly is not worthy of the apprehension I suffered before getting started or the procrastination growing out of the apprehension which has left me behind schedule. Before I began, the job seemed immense and endless. Once started, I found that it is not really one large task but more a series of small, discrete tasks. These tasks seem to be equal parts drudgery and intuition.

Dealing with fat data requires methodical organization. Keeping up with data organization during the collection process makes the bulk less intimidating and easier to manage, as Gordon further observes:

> Transcribe notes onto the computer after each interview and observation. This admonition has been prompted by my discovery that a fairly substantial part of my data is not in readily usable form. I have had to go back after three months and type my notes because I find it hard to use data that I cannot read easily. Drudgery. . . .

Keeping up with the data involves writing memos to yourself, making analytic files, and developing preliminary coding schemes.

At some point, you stop collecting data, or at least stop focusing on data collection. Knowing when to end this phase is difficult. It may be that you have exhausted all sources on the topic—that there are no new situations to observe, no new people to interview, no new documents to read. Such situations are rare. Ideally, you should stop collecting data because you have reached theoretical saturation (Glaser and Strauss 1967). This means that successive examination of sources yields redundancy, and that the data you have seem complete and integrated.

Recognizing theoretical saturation can be tricky, however. It may be, for example, that you hear the same thing from all of your informants because your selection of interviewees is too limited or too small to get discrepant views. Often, data collection ends through less than ideal conditions—the money runs out or deadlines loom large. Try to make research plans that do not completely exhaust your money, time, or energy, so that you can obtain a sense of complete and integrated data.

Later Data Analysis: Entering the Code Mines

In the early days of data collection, stories abound. Struck by the stories, you tell them and repeat them. You may sometimes even allow them to assume an importance beyond their worth to the purposes of the project. Making sense of the stories as a whole comes harder. You do not have to stop telling stories, but in data analysis you must make connections among the stories: What is being illuminated? How do the stories connect? What themes and patterns give shape to your data? Coding helps you to answer these questions.

When most of the data are collected, the time has come to devote attention to analytic coding. Although you may have already developed a coding scheme of sorts, you must now focus on classifying and categorizing. We refer to this as "entering the code mines." The work is part tedium and part exhilaration as it renders form and possible meaning to the piles of words before you.

Alan's words, extracted from field reflections, portray the somewhat ambivalent psychological ambience that accompanies entering the code mines:

> I have returned to coding with a vengeance and feel that it is taking revenge for long-time neglect. The tedium sends one off in all directions, including the refrig, but I intermittently persist and despair, the relative parts of each changing throughout each day.

Coding is a progressive process of sorting and defining and defining and sorting those scraps of collected data (i.e., observation notes, interview transcripts, memos, documents, and notes from relevant literature) that are applicable to our research purpose. By putting like-minded pieces together into data clumps, we create an organizational framework. It is progressive in that we first develop, out of the data, major code clumps by which to sort the data. Then we code the contents of each major code clump, thereby breaking down the major code into numerous subcodes. Eventually, we can place the various data clumps in a meaningful sequence that contributes to the chapters or sections of our manuscript.

Consider the example of writing this book. Before we discussed writing it, each of us had been developing and collecting notes on qualitative inquiry. In the prospectus we prepared for the publisher, we described the probable chapters of the book. These chapters—conceivable as large, general, analytic files—became our major working codes as we continued to collect data and make notes of our thoughts. Most of the material fell easily under major codes such as observation, interviewing, or analysis, but some of it at first did not seem to fit well. We therefore added major codes such as dissertation advice and miscellaneous, trusting that as we worked with the data we would figure out how to integrate, incorporate, or eliminate the information filed under these headings. Then, we reread the data scraps located in each major clump in order to develop minor code words or subcodes. Table 7.1 presents examples of the subcodes generated by data we had filed under the major code data analysis.

Each data scrap received both a code name and number. For example, each data scrap under the major code of data analysis that was related to the subcode of coding was marked both "8.2" and "DA/COD." As we worked through each major clump of data, we relocated some data scraps under other major headings. When we began writing, we continued the coding process: we merged, more finely divided, or relocated subclumps. Neither the assignment of a code nor the code name itself was inviolable; rather, we renamed and reassigned data as we saw fit to help us organize and manage the data—and learn what story we and the data could tell. After all, except when we are working with a team of researchers (see Liggett, Glesne, Hasazi, Johnson, and Schattman 1991), both acts are personal inventions in the interest of facilitating our personal creation.

TABLE 7.1   Subcodes of the Major Code "Data Analysis"

8. Data Analysis (DA)	
1. TRU	trustworthiness
2. COD	coding
3. STO	finding one's story, conceptualization
4. GEN	generalizations as products of qualitative inquiry
5. OUT	anything related to possible outcomes
6. THE	theory
7. DIS	data display
8. PRO	continuous nature of analysis process
9. SUB	implications of subjectivity for DA
10. INTRO	introductory material
11. STR	strategy for conducting; different forms
12. COM	use of computer in data analysis

When working with data gathered through qualitative inquiry, each major code should identify a concept, a central idea, though not necessarily a chapter or section of the final product, as in the book example. There should be as many major codes as needed to subsume all of the data, appreciating that more may develop than will hold up as separate codes. The blending of codes occurs over and over as you reread and reinterpret.

To facilitate developing and working with a coding scheme, make a code book. Assign each major code its own number and page, as shown in Table 7.1. Below the major code, list the number assigned to the subcode, the subcode name, and an explanation of the subcode. Start the code book soon after beginning to collect data so that it will reflect the emerging, evolving structure of your manuscript. It is highly personal, meant to fit you; it need not be useful or clear to anyone else. Although there may be common features and a common intent to everyone's data analysis process, it remains, in the end, an idiosyncratic enterprise. The proof of your coding scheme is, literally, in the pudding of your manuscript.

Begin by reading through whatever data you have—your observation notes, log, transcripts, documents, and literature. Identify what appears to be important and give it a name (code). The length of the coded sections will vary from parts of sentences to several pages. Because coding is an evolving process, it is advisable in the early stages to use a pencil to mark both data scraps and the code book. Be overgenerous in judging what is important; you do not want to foreclose any opportunity to learn from the field by prematurely settling on what is or is not relevant to you. In marking sections and giving them a name, you make judgments about which items are related and therefore belong under the same major code. The same subcode (such as anxiety, or theory, or ethics in our codebook, for example) may appear under several major codes. This indication of themes that may run throughout the work alerts you to look for their presence or absence under other major headings.

When you have collected and coded all of your data scraps, keep your code book in front of you and proceed to the next phase of data analysis: arranging your major code clumps into a "logical" order by asking yourself which clumps, or parts of clumps, belong together in the final code arrangement for your manuscript. Through such analysis, you sort out what you have learned so that you can concentrate on writing up your data.

The following are reflections of Andrea and Jill, who, after ten to twenty hours of fieldwork, undertook the coding/analysis process for the first time. In their descriptive portrayals, you may see your own struggles, achievements, and realizations.

> *Andrea:*   Alan Peshkin calls the act of coding "being in the code mines." I approached my first attempt at coding with that vivid analogy in mind. Beginning the process was indeed like preparing to descend into a mine shaft. The thought of dropping into the dark, cold abyss of twelve interviews and countless reflections made me shrink from the task. Perhaps, in the lightless confusion of data, I would not be able to sort out any meaning to it all. Perhaps, after seven months of collection, I would find no gold nuggets of wisdom in the walls of my code mines. Perhaps, like the miner, I needed to better prepare myself for entering the bowels of my notebooks and field logs.
>
> Hence I consciously entered into a series of avoidance tactics that kept me in the light of day as yet another week flew by. I finished transcribing my last three tapes. I backed up my [computer] disk. I reorganized my files. I considered reflecting more on my previous reflections. I even flipped through my Word Perfect [software] manual, on the pretense that I might find an ingenious way to manage my codes, someday. I kept a fire going in the wood stove to ward off the cold I constantly felt in my bones.
>
> Finally, the day came. I could put it off no longer; indeed, I was dreadfully remiss in waiting so long. I approached my first-semester notebook of interviews with images of Tolkien's Bilbo Baggins approaching the cave of Gollum. I must retrieve the precious ring, or never return to class and Professor Gandolf Glesne. I laid open my first interview next to my new, brightly colored coding notebook.
>
> Anticipation far exceeds the event in the exploration of the unknown. Three pages of codes flowed from my pen from the first interview. They were familiar words, words repeated on paper, on tape, and in my mind throughout my whole study. Like the Hobbit with his ring on, I disappeared into my interviews for hours.
>
> After the initial showering of codes, each interview added fewer to my list. That was comforting. I had a sense that the list would be manageable. The second interview added only one page of new codes, the third a half page. After that, each interview produced one new code and usually elab-

oration or clarification on some previous codes. Before I was done, the maze of words began organizing themselves in my mind. I flipped to a clean page and began jotting down umbrella phrases to collect subcodes under.

I am no longer a Pennsylvania coal miner dreading my life's work. I am no longer the Hobbit with but one precious ring. Today I am Smog the dragon sitting upon a mountain of jewels, stolen from my interviews. They lay, however, disheveled beneath me and hard to account for. So today my task is to organize my treasures that I might know what I have before I go on. The task is a bit easier because I made some notes as I was coding. I began clumping my codes into broader categories. They fall into neat piles, with only a few exceptions. These I place temporarily until I can consult with my fellow researchers. So ends, for me, the dreaded imagery of life-threatening mind shafts. I have much real work ahead, but I have dealt with the anxiety of passing the test.

Jill: I have reshuffled and reshuffled the cards. I have marked and arranged the deck carefully, so that when I lay my hand on the table, I will have played a winner.

First create the codes, the markings for the deck. Then mark the cards. It seemed straightforward at the start. Code the interviews; make the cards; deal out the marked hands. Only the marks kept shifting, and cutting and pasting to create the deck was tedious, not mindlessly relaxing as hoped.

It was not an auspicious start! I wasn't having a good time. In fact, by the time I was finished I was sure I never wanted to see, or shuffle, or deal those cards again. And worse, Card King Peshkin had betrayed me. The glory of index cards indeed! Eight-and-one-half × 11 slices of paper simply do not fit neatly on 5 × 8 index cards. I descended into the bowels of the code mines, where nothin' comes easy and canaries die a long, slow death.

But, the King wasn't all wrong. Once the cards were ready for play, I began to understand his game: build the deck and cut the cards so you can shuffle and deal, shuffle and deal, and then shuffle and deal again. So forgiving! A game of solitaire with more than one right way, and more than one chance to lay out the hands. In fact, about halfway through the play, when I imagined all my cards laid out on the table, I knew that the house was about to win the game. So I shuffled the deck, and dealt them out again.

The game makes sense now. The dealer groups and regroups the cards into playable hands. Sometimes she shuffles and deals it all out again. By the time she's done, the cards are not so crisp to the touch, but they sure play smooth and easy.

The game of qualitative research has general guidelines, but house rules vary, casino to casino. Solitaire is a dealer's game, after all.

Current house rules at the novice's casino are as follows:

1. One notion to a card. Peeling quote slivers off the cards slows the play of the game.
2. No color coding the cards. The whiteout budget is insufficient.
3. No multiple copies of passages from interviews. One quote to a card,

one category to a quote. Forced choices speed the game, while the redeal option protects against premature folding.

4. No dealing hands to please subjective eyes. And one last rule that every good player should know:

5. "Know when to hold 'em, and know when to fold 'em."

This game calls for time and patience. For me, it is best played a few hands at a time, with time to ponder the cards in between. The trick, I think, will be not to let the deck get cold.

Jill refers to the problem of transferring 8-½ × 11 paper to 5 × 8 cards when using note cards for coding. It is a tedious matter, one that can be avoided by using computer programs to code and segregate data bits. Or the paper scraps can simply be cut and put into file folders. Cards are, however, easier to handle than slips of paper and not as apt to get lost or misplaced.

DATA DISPLAY

Miles and Huberman (1984) have created a comprehensive text on using data display in the analysis of qualitative work. They describe data display as "an organized assembly of information that permits conclusion drawing and action taking." Making an analogy to "you are what you eat," they claim that "you know what you display" (Miles and Huberman 1984, 21, 22). Matrices, graphs, flowcharts, and other sorts of visual representations assist in making meaning of data, as well as in exposing the gaps or the areas where more data are needed. Data display is, therefore, another ongoing feature of qualitative inquiry. It can be a part of developing the problem statement, data collection, analysis, and final presentation of the study.

As you begin to conceive your research by working out the problem statement and plans for data collection, data displays help you to identify the elements of your study. Expect the displays to change as you learn more. After data collection has begun, urge Miles and Huberman (1984), create diagrams that reflect some risk; that is, use one-directional arrows that indicate potential cause and effect. Doing so forces you to begin to theorize about the social phenomenon under study.

After becoming absorbed in using a computer graphics program to display her work, Andrea teased another student about her sixty-one pages of notes: "Want me to reduce it to one good graph?" Data display provides the skeleton of your work. Just as observing the Earth from a satellite allows you to see the overall pattern of geologic structures and human adaptations to these structures, data displays help you to see the overall patterns in your research without getting lost in the details.

When thinking about displaying your data, experiment with a variety of forms. Tables provide detail, but bar and line graphs often portray patterns more vividly. If comparing two or more groups over time, line graphs are particularly useful. Matrices that use symbols such as + and o rather than numbers also can aid in uncovering patterns. For example, if investigating perceived constraints to effective education in six rural schools, you might, after a round of interviews, develop a table similar to Table 7.2.

With the table before you, you would look for patterns and begin to form some hunches about what was going on, using your knowledge of each rural town and school. For example, you would notice that schools 2, 3, and 5 all perceive their tax base as a problem, but not their communication between school and community. Schools 1, 4, and 6 are just the opposite. Returning to your data, you would try to figure out possible explanations. Although the communities are similar in size, you would note that the communities which host schools 1, 4, and 6 have a sizable proportion of nonnatives who have moved to the area in recent years. The communities that host schools 2, 3, and 5 do not. You would then hypothesize that the newcomers are bringing more money into the towns and, along with it, strife in school governance decisions. In reflecting on possible reasons for the pattern of responses in the categories of access to information and access to experts, you would wonder whether distance from the state's largest city makes a difference. Developing a new matrix, you would then map your hunches as demonstrated in Table 7.3. Such matrices-forming work serves to suggest both new questions and people or sites for investigation, as well as to make sense of the data collected.

Borrowing from the natural sciences, cognitive anthropologists use taxonomies to assist in displaying social phenomena. In this approach, the researcher seeks to understand how others classify "cognitive domains" or salient aspects of the world. Structured interviews are used to elicit indigenous classificatory schemes. Each category is, in turn, probed for subcategories and sub-subcategories until the interviewee's categorization scheme is fully

TABLE 7.2   A Matrix Example of Constraints to Effective Education in Six Rural Schools

School	Tax Base	Communication with Community	State Policy	Access to Information	Access to Experts
1	o	+	+	o	o
2	+	o	+	+	+
3	+	o	+	o	o
4	o	+	+	+	+
5	+	o	+	+	+
6	o	+	+	+	+

Key: + = perceived as a constraint by school personnel
       o = not perceived as a constraint by school personnel

TABLE 7.3 A Matrix Example of Data Patterns and Researcher Hunches Regarding Constraints to Effective Education in Six Rural Schools

School	Tax Base	Communication with Community	Access to Information	Access to Experts
native/near city (3)	+	O	O	O
native/not near city (2, 5)	+	O	+	+
mixed/near city (1)	O	+	O	O
mixed/not near city (4, 6)	O	+	+	+

Key: + =   perceived as a constraint by school personnel
      O =   not perceived as a constraint by school personnel

mapped. For example, Janet Davis (1972) investigated eighth graders for categories of the cognitive domain she called "things kids do at school." Through interviewing, she found that major categories included picking on other kids, sitting in classes, being nice to teachers, and acting up. Davis went on to investigate subcategories, such as all the ways that kids are "nice to teachers." She then probed for sub-subcategories such as how a student becomes a teacher's pet. Table 7.4 is extracted from Davis's taxonomic chart of the domain of "things kids do at school" (Davis 1972, 115–116). Taxonomic charts help researchers to see what they know and don't know about a particular cognitive domain.

A student at the University of Vermont investigated the types of undergraduates enrolled there as defined and categorized by undergraduates. Although categories were not necessarily mutually exclusive, the interviewer

TABLE 7.4 Partial Taxonomy of the Domain "Things Kids Do at School"

Take tests	
Sit in classes	
Be nice to teachers:	Do what you're told
	Turn in assignments
	Talk nice, use good grammar
	Don't talk out of turn
	Don't smoke
	Don't talk during lectures
	Stay in places
	Try to become a pet (get in with teacher) ⸢ Do extra stuff / Volunteer / Sweep floor / Kiss their butts ⸤

found that, according to interviewees, there were preps, japs, punkers, out-of-staters, Vermonters, granolas, squids, nerds, smarts, intelligents, and jocks. Many of these categories had subcategories such as both normal and progressive granolas or positive and negative jocks. Such information lends itself to a taxonomic chart that can then be used as a type of guide for discussion of the cognitive domain. (See Spradley 1970; Spradley and Mann 1975; Spradley and McCurdy 1972.)

Mathematics also can be useful in determining patterns. Regarding the use of mathematics in anthropology, Agar comments:

> Anthropologists, more than other social scientists, have mathophobia. One of my favorite wisecracks is to define mathematical anthropology as what happens when anthropologists number their pages. . . . Most of the points I need to make are made with simple frequency distributions. If that is all you need, stop there. . . . If you choose not to use statistical procedures in your systematic testing, it should be because you know enough about them to know they are inappropriate, not because the very thought causes you to break out in a rash. (Agar 1980, 132)

Simple frequency counts can help to identify patterns. For example, imagine that you have been inquiring into the attitudes of young people toward agriculture in the rural Caribbean. Through interviews with eighty-five persons, including twenty-five employed in town, fifty working in agriculture, and ten living in rural areas but not working in agriculture, you receive mixed answers to the question "How do young people feel about working land?" Your first frequency distribution (represented by Table 7.5) suggests that young people are not very interested in doing agricultural work. Yet, by listening to and rereading the interviews, you form the hunch that the attitudes are linked to land tenure. You go back to your interviews and rework the frequency counts, taking into account the relationship of each interviewee to the land. This time your frequency distribution demonstrates a definite pattern in the relationship between attitudes toward doing agricultural work and land tenure (see Table 7.6). The numbers assist in shaping a more specific hypothesis about attitudes toward farming.

TABLE 7.5 Frequency Distribution of Perceived Attitudes toward Working the Land

	Positive Attitudes	Negative Attitudes
Town employees	4	21
Agricultural workers	21	29
Other rural people	0	10

TABLE 7.6 Frequency Distribution of Perceived Attitudes toward Working the Land by Dominant Land Tenure Situation of Interviewee

	Positive Attitudes	Negative Attitudes
No land worked	0	25
Agricultural laborer	0	13
Works family land	5	5
Shares crop/rent	2	17
Works land rent-free	10	0
Works own land	8	0

USING COMPUTERS
IN QUALITATIVE RESEARCH

We are only beginning to grasp the possibilities for computer use in qualitative research. Researchers primarily use the computer as a tool to facilitate what they have been doing manually. Some, however, are experimenting with the technology available to develop new approaches for managing and making meaning of data. This section presents an overview of the advantages and disadvantages of computer use in qualitative research, discusses in general terms the use of computers at various stages in the inquiry process, and introduces some of the microcomputer software that assists in handling qualitative data. (See also Becker 1984; Conrad and Reinharz 1984; Pfaffenberger 1988; Tesch 1990.)

Computers have revolutionized the handling and manipulation of quantitative data. Because qualitative researchers work with words and without discrete variables, they have found it more difficult to use the machines efficiently in applications other than word processing. As computers become more affordable, more transportable, and more usable through the development of software, more qualitative researchers are looking to computers to assist in the research process. As with most things, there are advantages and disadvantages in developing a partnership with the computer.

Advantages and Disadvantages

Computer users tend to praise the machine, saying that it helps them to save time and relieve the drudgery. No longer must one cut up field notes and glue them to cards. No longer must one spend hours manually sorting through the cards to clump and reclump as codes develop and change. Users also claim that computers force organization and planning and encourage systematic work. Thereby, issues are explored in greater depth and with more consistency (Becker 1984).

The process of using the computer documents, to an extent, the researcher's decisions and logic. The concreteness and specificity necessary for computer use require the researcher to be clear and explicit about analysis decisions, responding, in part, to urgings by Miles and Huberman (1984) and others that qualitative researchers delineate their analytic methods. Computer use can therefore help to demystify qualitative analysis and contribute to its accountability.

Nonetheless, because manual approaches are so time-consuming, some argue that researchers who do not use computers will carefully think through their analysis schemes, while computer users may allow their data analysis to be guided by computer programs rather than by thinking about the data. Computer users argue, however, that the laborious manual analyses might incline the researcher to continue with a poor coding scheme simply because of the investment already made.

Some people have expressed concern that confidentiality may be compromised by computer use, particularly if data are kept on a hard disk drive in an office. The same issue, however, exists if data are stored in boxes and filing cabinets. In either case, the researcher needs to take care in storing data and protecting the anonymity of participants, and the computer actually makes it easy to change real names to pseudonyms wherever they occur within a file.

Other people have suggested that computer use will contribute to the use of data out of context, because searching capabilities make sorting data by specific words so easy. This is not solely a computer problem, however. In addition, they warn of the potential to use the quantitative facilities of computers inappropriately because computers make it nearly effortless to count. For example, one could easily compare how many times a particular word appeared in the interviews of two separate groups. This might appear interesting, but it may not be particularly meaningful. Whether or not one uses a computer, data can be used appropriately or inappropriately. The responsibility lies with the researcher.

Without dispute, computers make the writing and rewriting process easier. They can also make even the most preliminary sketch of ideas look polished and organized. This is advantageous in that printed drafts invite reading and can be easily edited and changed. It can also be disadvantageous, if one is lulled by the look of completion and prematurely ceases working. Pfaffenberger (1988) suggests minimizing this temptation when printing drafts by using paper of lower quality or of a different color and using the plainest printing options, such as no right justification and dot matrix or a very plain typeface.

A very real disadvantage of the computer is that through technical problems or inadvertent mistakes on the part of the operator, data or work can be lost. Users must systematically save and back up their work both on disks and on paper and keep copies in different locations.

Computer Uses

Computers assist in keeping a record of fieldwork activities. Forms can be developed for reporting data collection dates, sites, times, and people interviewed or observed. In this way, an account is kept not only of progress in data collection, but also of gaps in data collection since one can easily see where and with whom time is spent.

Computers can be used systematically to record field notes, interview transcripts, and observation notes. Some researchers carry their laptop or notebook computers into the field and eliminate taking notes by hand. The process of transcribing interviews from tapes into the computer refamiliarizes researchers with the data, and enables them to record new questions, thoughts, and hunches in files labeled as such. Because the computer forces the organization of data, it provides occasion for constant reflection. The data stored in computer files are easy to access for preliminary analysis that can further guide data collection.

Performing the mundane tasks involved in data analysis is easier with data recorded on computer files than it is with data recorded through manual means. Computers assist in sorting, referencing, counting, coding, and displaying data. Various types of programs, including word processors, data base managers, graphics, spreadsheets, and qualitative software, can be used.

Finally, computers are useful for writing the final text. Excerpts from files in which data have been recorded or analyzed can be inserted into the report text without having to retype long sections. And, again, computers facilitate the editing process.

Computer Software

Qualitative researchers have appropriated existing computer programs, adapting them to their own purposes, and are increasingly developing new software programs to meet their needs. We begin with examples of adapting other programs.

1. *Word processing programs* can be used (although inefficiently) to code and sort data. After reading the text and developing a code book, you can systematically code the text files by inserting code words or numbers where appropriate. The code should be a unique string of characters that would not normally appear in the text. For example, "tea" would not be a good code choice for "teacher issues" because, through search commands, you would get every instance of the three characters *t, e, a* in the text, including words such as "instead" or "tease." A better choice would be something like "TCHISS." Using

search, block, and move commands, you could later sort your files according to your codes, making sure to identify source and data information for each datum as you do so.

2. *Data base managers* are programs in which data are entered according to a structured format. Although best at handling numeric data, most programs will also accept a minimal amount of text data.

The general idea behind data base managers is that you design a form which simulates an index card marked by key words. After entering data on the form, you can sort by words or numbers (e.g., date, age, sex). Programs vary by how many characters are allowed per form. Some allow only one page, others up to ten pages. Also, depending on the software, it may or may not be easy to alter the format for recording data.

Data base managers are particularly useful for keeping records of fieldwork. You can create a form to record the fieldwork activities deemed important. For example, to keep track of interview procedures, you could record the number of the interview session, the date, the name (or pseudonym) of the interviewee, the time the interview took, the role of the interviewee, the date of transcription, and other information (see Table 7.7). Such a format would help you to keep track of your research activities. With each interview, you would add a line. Depending on the program, you might even add columns as you discover helpful aspects to include.

3. *Spreadsheets* were initially developed for accounting tasks. Spreadsheet programs create tables in which you label each vertical column and each horizontal row, and fill in the resulting cells with data. These programs produce matrices, which can be useful in various stages of data collection and analysis. For example, in the planning stage of a study in group homes for adults with developmental disabilities, the rows of the matrix could be the three group homes you intend to visit. The columns could be characteristics of the group homes that are of interest to you, such as size, number of residents, use of recreational

TABLE 7.7 Example Form for Keeping Interview Records

Number	Date Interviewed	Interviewee	Date Transcribed	Time	Role	Subject	Note
18	4/8/91	C. Perez	4/10/91	1.5	teacher	math	—
19	4/9/91	D. Brown	4/10/91	.5	admin.	—	late; not completed
20	4/9/91	M. Levine	4/20/91	1.0	teacher	history	—

facilities, and involvement in meal preparation. As data are collected, you could add more columns of relevant characteristics. The matrix helps to summarize the data collected, showing similarities and differences among the cases and illuminating missing information.

4. *Graphics* packages assist you in creating charts, tables, graphs, and diagrams.
5. *Qualitative software* programs developed particularly for use with qualitative data include *The Ethnograph*, *QUALPRO*, and *Hyper-Qual*. Each is used for coding, searching, and sorting as a part of data analysis; each has different features. We will briefly describe working with *The Ethnograph*, but we urge you to consult Tesch (1990) for more information.

When ready to begin the coding process, the researcher transfers all field notes and data files from a word processing program to *The Ethnograph*. *The Ethnograph* numbers the lines in a file and formats the file with a large right margin. Reading and rereading the data, the researcher creates a code book and then, on a printed copy of the numbered file, begins to assign codes to chunks of text. Using *The Ethnograph's* coding capability, the researcher then enters line numbers and the assigned code words into the program. More than one code word can be entered for the same start line number, allowing more than one code word to be assigned to the same segment or to overlapping segments. With code words and line numbers entered, the researcher can sort data files by codes or combinations of codes. Although more powerful than indicated by this brief description, the program's main contribution is in the sorting of coded data.

In summary, the computer is a tool for executing the mechanical or clerical tasks of qualitative research. It can help to make the researcher's work less tedious, more accurate, faster, and more thorough. It does not, however, think for the researcher. The researcher decides what to enter into the computer, what to ask it to do, and how to use the results of the computer's mechanical manipulations. The products of computer-assisted analysis are only as good as the data, the thinking, and the level of care that went into them.

MAKING CONNECTIONS

Data analysis is of course an invariable aspect of all types of research, qualitative or otherwise. It is the effort of researchers to manage and make sense of their data, to transform it from its acquired form—at which point it is perhaps more accurately called "information"—into a form that communicates the promise of a study's findings. These findings include (but are far from exhausted by) theory, which researchers may develop, augment, or contradict. Researchers' outcomes range across the domains of description, interpretation, evaluation, and verification.

Examples abound of esteemed work conducted by scholars in the fields of education (Lightfoot 1983; Metz 1978; Schofield 1989; Wolcott 1973), anthropology (Dube 1967; Liebow 1967; Mead 1930), and sociology (Becker, Geer, Hughes, and Strauss 1961; Gans 1962; Mills 1951; Whyte [1943] 1981) that testify to the considerable breadth of outcomes from qualitative research studies. Data analysis, accordingly, is the prelude to sensitive, comprehensive outcomes that make connections, identify patterns, and contribute to greater understanding.

TRUSTWORTHINESS OF OUR INTERPRETATIONS

In his article on James Agee, author of *Let Us Now Praise Famous Men*, Hersey cites reviewers of Agee's book, concluding with a quotation from Mrs. Burroughs, a woman from one of the tenant farmer families portrayed in the book: "And I took it home and I read it plumb through. And when I read it plumb through I give it back to her and I said, Well everything in there's true. What they wrote in there was true" (in Hersey 1988, 74).

James Agee would have been pleased to learn that Mrs. Burroughs affirmed his interpretations of her life. You want your interpretations to be trustworthy, to be affirmed by the Mrs. Burroughses in your research lives and also by your colleagues. Mrs. Burroughs may just be pleased that Agee understood her life. When your colleagues also believe this, they use your work in the range of ways that trusted outcomes can be used—to confirm, expand, and inform their own work—and thereby contribute to the accumulative nature of your knowledge.

Time is a major factor in the acquisition of trustworthy data. Time at your research site, time spent interviewing, time to build sound relationships with respondents—all contribute to trustworthy data. When a large amount of time is spent with your others, they less readily feign behavior or feel the need to do so; moreover, they are more likely to be frank and comprehensive about what they tell you.

Triangulated findings also help. For example, as Alan conducted interviews in the multiethnic school, he began to feel quite confident that social relationships crosscut ethnicity, and that they did so regularly. It seemed to be both readily observed and commonly mentioned in interviews. When Alan saw the results of his questionnaire that asked students to list their three best friends and the three most influential people in their lives, his hunches were confirmed. The triangulation of observation, interview, and questionnaire data corroborated his point. Without such tactics, it is sometimes difficult to know how much of what researchers see is a product of their earnest but unconscious wish to see it so.

Continual alertness to your own biases, your own subjectivity, also assists in producing more trustworthy interpretations. Ask yourself a series of questions, such as: Whom do I not see? Whom have I seen less often? Where do I not go? Where have I gone less often? With whom do I have special relationships, and in what light would they interpret phenomena? What data collecting means have I not used that could provide additional insight? To improve trustworthiness, you can also consciously search for negative cases. In the example of social relationships crosscutting ethnicity, Alan might have instructed himself to find evidence that this was not so and reread his notes with that perspective in mind. "I didn't confirm all my own opinions, which was nice," said Andrea in the final report of her community study. "Maybe there is some validity to what I found."

As you are planning, collecting and analyzing data, and writing up your findings, do not forget the invaluable assistance of others. Ask friends and colleagues to work with portions of your data—developing codes, applying your codes, or interpreting field notes to check your perceptions. To promote trustworthiness, Lincoln and Guba (1985) suggest a procedure for enlisting an outsider to "audit" fieldwork notes and subsequent analysis and interpretations.

You can also share the interpretive process with research respondents. Researchers, as a matter of courtesy, often give respondents copies of interview transcripts for their approval. Obtaining the reactions of respondents to your working drafts is time-consuming, but respondents may (1) verify that you have reflected the insider's perspectives; (2) inform you of sections that, if published, could be problematic for either personal or political reasons; and (3) help you to develop new ideas and interpretations. By sharing working drafts, both researcher and researched may grow in their interpretations of the phenomena around them.

Part of demonstrating the trustworthiness of your data is to realize the limitations of your study. Your responsibility is to do the best that you can under certain circumstances. Detailing those circumstances helps readers to understand the nature of your data. You need to discuss what documents or people or places were unavailable to you. You need to discuss what is peculiar about your site or respondent selection that could show the phenomena of interest in some lights but not in others. Approach the description of your study's limitations as part of setting the context. Limitations are consistent with the always partial state of your knowing in social research, and elucidating them helps readers to know how they should read and interpret your work.

CONCLUSIONS

Qualitative researchers must decide what the payoff of their research can and will be. Depending on the existing state of knowledge about their topic, they may make a contribution that includes a full range, from the descriptive to the theoretical. In *Cross Creek*, Rawlings writes, "A man may learn a great deal of the general from studying the specific, whereas it is impossible to know the specific by studying the general" (Rawlings 1942, 359). Qualitative inquirers look to the specific, both to understand it in particular and to understand something of the world in general. From the positivist's point of view, the respondent pool in qualitative research is too limited for development of generalizations. The particular case that you study in qualitative research, however, is likely to contribute to an understanding of similar cases, such that going beyond the case in your ruminations will not be farfetched (See Wehlage 1981 for more on making generalizations in qualitative inquiry.)

In short, researchers conduct qualitative studies not merely for their own sake, but rather in the reasonable hope of bringing something grander than the case to the attention of others. Researchers hope for a description and analysis of its complexity that identify concepts not previously seen or fully appreciated.

We conclude this chapter with an excerpt from a paper written by Gordon. He had completed his course-based research project and was reflecting on the analysis process, of which writing—the next topic for discussion—was a part.

> The paper is written, the computer clicks softly to itself as it cools after its long ordeal, and my cards lie scattered over the floor and desk. The paper lies in my briefcase in its bright blue cover, ready to be read and reviewed. It is done! It is over! Now what?
>
> After filling every waking moment with analysis and writing, leisure causes a kind of withdrawal. What does one say to one's wife and family? What does one do with all that time? I feel compelled to turn on the computer, to fill the blank screen with words once more. My mind is locked into the analysis mode, examining menus, cereal boxes, and junk mail and placing them in precise matrices. I compulsively buy and hoard 5 × 8 cards and glue sticks. I need to break the cycle, to fight my way back to the normal life of the nonresearcher. What to do?
>
> What else can I do? I'll analyze the process.
>
> My first thoughts concern the holistic nature of the process. There really is no way to separate the parts of research from one another. Data gathering includes parts of analysis, analysis leads to more data, writing leads to a greater understanding of both analysis and data. The process is totally holistic, each piece absolutely necessary to the whole. I am reminded of this as I stoop to pick up my cards, the various coding categories scribbled off,

edges bent, and the writing illegible. How do you analyze information you can't read? One thing seems to be certain: Next time I begin the analysis as I do the data gathering. To separate the two processes by three months doesn't work. All the soft nuances are gone, the tones and the shades of meaning are missing.

Another interesting discovery is that the writing process actually is an important part of the analysis. A lot of my insights and much of the understanding I gained from my research data came through the writing process. For me, writing is the final organization of my thoughts. Next time I will begin writing sooner.

A final thought is that matrices really help. By organizing my data into matrices, I was able to see in two or three dimensions. I realized only at this point that my really profound data concerned peer pressure on children, not parental pressures. Next time I will use more matrices.

This is a small first step on my way back to reality. By this time next week, the hours of writing and preparation will only be a fond dream that fades ever into the dust of newer crises. And yet, if I could only rewrite page 7, I bet I could. . . .

CHAPTER 8

Writing Your Story: What Your Data Say

So, with Auden, one hopes that one's case will touch others. But how to connect? Not by calculation, I think, not by the assumption that in the pain of my toothache, or my father's, or Harry Crosby's, I have discovered a "universal condition of consciousness." One may merely know that no one is alone and hope that a singular story, as every true story is singular, will in the magic way of some things apply, connect, resonate, touch a major chord. (Pachter 1981, 72)

Writing gives form to the researcher's clumps of carefully categorized and organized data. It links together thoughts that have been developing throughout the research process. The act of writing also stimulates new thoughts, new connections. Writing is rewarding in that it creates the product, the housing for the meaning that you and others have made of your research adventure. Writing is about constructing a text. As a writer, you engage in a sustained act of construction, which includes selecting a particular "story" to tell from the data you have analyzed, and creating the literary form that you believe best conveys your story (Denny 1978). It perhaps matters to some—but needs no resolution—whether the researcher's construction is more like that of an architect, proceeding from a vision embodied in a plan, or like that of a painter, whose vision emerges over time from intuition, sense, and feeling. For many, constructing a text is quite possibly some combination of both plan and intuition.

This chapter touches on intuition, but it focuses on strategies for writing, questions of form and style, and responsibilities of the writer.

ROLES OF THE WRITER

> By the time we finish reading a good ethnography, adroit rationalization has
> made familiar what at first seemed strange, the other, and has estranged us
> from what we thought we knew, ourselves. (Shweder 1986, 38)

A woman once asked one of us to review and provide feedback on her
dissertation work, which she was completing at another university. She had
developed her interview questions (both closed and open-ended) and had
scheduled her interviews with a number of administrators throughout the
nation, but had not yet collected any data. Nonetheless, she had compiled a
document of nearly 200 pages, divided into five chapters: introduction to the
problem, review of literature, methods, findings, and summary with recommendations. She had completed the first three chapters and much of the last
two, leaving blank spaces for percentages and applicable phrases once the data
were available.

We do not know how many dissertations and research reports are written
this way; not many, we hope. Those that are cannot do justice to the data in that
they forfeit interpretation. They neither show respect for the time and input of
the respondents, nor call on the creative and artistic qualities of the writer. And
they do not succeed in making the strange familiar or in estranging us from
ourselves.

This section addresses three roles of the writer of qualitative inquiry:
artist, translator/interpreter, and transformer. Although writers do not always
play all three roles, they nonetheless should keep them in mind.

Artist

To make meaning of data, writers employ technical procedures that are to some
extent routine and mechanical, but writers of good qualitative studies also are
artists who create their written work. In his edited book *Extraordinary Lives,*
Zinsser states:

> [Research] is only research. After all the facts have been marshaled, all the
> documents studied, all the locales visited, all the survivors interviewed,
> what then? What do the facts add up to? What did the life mean? This was
> the central question for the six biographers, and to hear them wrestling with
> it was to begin to see where the craft crosses over into art. (Zinsser 1988a,
> 17–18)

Craft involves the strategies and procedures authors use to write their story.
The form and style of the written presentation require artistic sensibilities,
which seem to involve a mixture of discipline and creativity. As artists,
qualitative researchers move into the murky terrain where nonqualitative re-

searchers may regard them as journalists, fiction writers, or worse. As artists, they seek imaginative connections among events and people, imaginative renderings of these connections, and imaginative interpretations of what they have rendered. They do this not just in the worthy cause of making their work most accessible, but, in addition, to do fullest justice to what they have endeavored to understand.

Translator/Interpreter

A currently popular way to speak of the qualitative researcher is as a translator of culture. The researcher works to understand the others' world and then to translate the text of lived actions into a meaningful account. Although the translator metaphor suggests struggle with representing the nuances of meaning, it also implies that the researcher is an objective middleperson, rather than someone whose perspectives and personality affect the portrayed account. To the contrary, qualitative researchers are interpreters who draw on their own experiences, knowledge, theoretical dispositions, and collected data to present their understanding of the other's world. As interpreters, they think of themselves not as authority figures who get the "facts" on a topic, but as meaning-makers who make sense out of the interaction of their own lives with those of their others. "An ethnography," explains Shweder,

> begins with an ethnographic experience: with your eyes open you have to go somewhere. Yet a culture is never reducible to what meets the eye, and you can't get to ethnographic reality by just looking. A culture is like a black hole, those compacted stars whose intense gravitational forces don't let their own light particles escape. You can never know it's there by simply squinting your eyes and staring very hard at it. If it is real at all, you can know it only by inference and conjecture. (Shweder 1986, 38)

Inference and conjecture are mainstays of the interpretive process. Inferences are made about the relationship of one thing to another, on the basis of carefully collected, carefully analyzed, trustworthy data.

Interpretations and their portrayal are limited by a number of factors that are increasingly acknowledged by qualitative researchers, but are not necessarily peculiar to them. In *Tales of the Field*, Van Maanen (1988, 4–6) discusses several of these limitations in depth:

First, in what ways does the experiential nature of the researcher in the research process shape the final story? The setting and the experiences of the researcher with research participants form the basis for the interpretive account.

Second, how do political relationships shape the final interpretation? If the research is funded, what do sponsors want studied? What role does academic politics play? If the researcher has more power than the researched, then what impact might the power relationship have on the data collected?

Third, what is the theoretical position of the researcher? Researchers all have a theoretical stance, although often somewhat implicit, which forms a lens through which they view social phenomena. They are also shaped by their disciplines and by academic trends and traditions. Their interpretations of social interactions and the readers' interpretations of their texts are limited or bounded by extant "structures of meaning" (see Clifford 1986; Marris 1974). If, for example, you view educational systems as "meritocracies," then you will interpret your data differently than if you see them through the conflict theorist's hegemonic eyes, a structure of meaning that is fairly recent to educational perspectives.

Fourth, how do narrative and rhetorical conventions limit the portrayal of the researcher's interpretations? Narrative and rhetorical conventions tend to be somewhat governed by the researcher's academic discipline. Political relationships may also play a role. For example, many dissertation committees are reluctant to allow a doctoral student to experiment with writing the work in any but traditional forms.

Fifth, in what ways does the historical situating of observations and interviews contribute to the limitations of the researcher's work? Culture does not stand still; it changes over time. An interpretive portrayal is often only several snapshots of a place and time and its people. It can be, however, a powerful and useful portrayal that focuses on processes that transcend static, descriptive accounts.

Sixth, and finally, how does the projected audience shape both the form and the substance of the researcher's product? The researcher may use tables and charts with one audience, but not with another. Or the researcher may use a disciplined-based language if writing for colleagues, but not for a more general group of people. Researchers tell different things in different ways to different people.

By being aware of forces that help shape your interpretations and their depictions, you can challenge some while simply acknowledging others. The point is to be as conscious as possible of both your prospects and your limitations.

Transformer

It is to the role of transformer—in the sense not of reformer but rather of catalytic educator—that writers of qualitative research rightfully aspire. As others read your story, you want them to identify with the problems, worries, joys, and dreams that are the collective human lot. By reflecting on themselves and their families, friends, and associates, they acquire new insights and perspectives on some aspect of human interaction. Although not your primary purpose, this process of learning about self through understanding others is a gift of qualitative research done well. Shweder states it poetically:

> Good ethnography is an intellectual exorcism in which, forced to take the perspective of the other, we are wrenched out of our self. We transcend ourselves, and for a brief moment we wonder who we are, whether we are animals, barbarians or angels, whether all things are really the same under the sun, whether it would be better if the other were us, or better if we were the other. (Shweder 1986, 38)

Writing up your work so that it contributes to transformative experiences requires the application of disciplined procedures and artistic creativity to meaningful data. We now turn to the disciplined procedures of writing.

STRATEGIES FOR WRITING

Getting Started

Most of us can find numerous excuses to postpone writing. We have to read more, see more, and talk more; we must recode and reanalyze; and, inevitably, we feel compelled to mop the floor, make a phone call, do anything to avoid sitting down and writing. That those who spend much of their life writing also experience anxiety over getting started may be of some comfort. The following words are Alan's, written January 18, 1988, while in the beginning stages of writing his ethnicity study:

> The demons of escapism loom large, but I will not weaken, I say weakly. Also weekly. Also daily. Writing, it seems, is primarily a matter of dealing with demons. It is good to give the enemy a name so he can be dealt with, except if the demon is cleverly chameleonlike so that you never know what new form he will assume. Each day I come to this place where work and the demons abide. They always are together, like dust balls under beds. Each day I feel like I'm going off to war, though the previous day's battle does not necessarily prepare me for the next day's. Each new day brings a surprise: what form will the demon assume? Will he bring fatigue within twenty minutes of beginning; will he shunt my attention to a book only vaguely related to my work that I can't resist looking at; will he leave me staring at a particular note card, fixated for no obvious reason on a point that at any other moment would not claim ten second's notice? The demon is clever; outsmarting him demands energy that he leaves me short of by diverting my attention and effort to other matters. I backslide, lord of writing. I desert your hallowed ranks for lesser gods parading in irresistible forms. I yearn for faithfulness, while doubting my yearning. Perhaps tomorrow I will be a warrior of the pen—whoever heard of a warrior of the

word processor?—wielding a mighty sword that vanquishes demons. But I know that when my pen becomes sword, the demon becomes liquid and my sword creates no more than a splash. From swish to splash is no way to subdue demons. Only writing is exorcism.

So, while the novice procrastinates (and, in the process, prolongs the anxiety), those with more experience write. As the Portuguese proverb goes, "When there is no wind, row."

It helps to know that writing, like data analysis, is not a discrete step in the qualitative research process. Ideally, and not at all unrealistically, you should write throughout the time of data collection and analysis. Long before you begin a phase of work that you can call "write-up time," you should be writing. In fact, it is useful to be conscious at the outset of a research project that it will culminate in words, sentences, paragraphs, pages, and chapters. Distant though it may be, this culmination will arrive. Aware that it will, you should look and listen, analyze and interpret, and be attuned to the prospect that the results will be words to be read. Every effort to collect data and make something of them should be in the spirit of a quest for what will appear in your words.

If you follow this advice, then you will have stacks of field notes and research memos, many containing well-developed thoughts in usable paragraph form. A time will come, however, when more of your effort will be put into writing than anything else. This time is often preceded by feelings of intense anxiety manifested in a variety of ways and labeled "writer morassity" by a student research support group in Vermont for whom metaphors of bogs, swamps, and slow drownings recurred. Woods refers to the "pain threshold" of writing, asserting that researchers must be masochists who confront the pain barrier till it hurts as they rework ideas that seemed brilliant before exposed to paper. He likens the suffering that the writer feels to that of other artists, and urges them to view the anxiety as a rite of passage that "is as much a test of self as anything else" (Woods 1986, 171). The writer gearing up for writing is unsociable and ill-tempered while sorting and resorting data, trying to organize thoughts for writing. A prewriting gloom descends. "I guess it is functional," says Alan, "The feeling is familiar, unwanted, and apparently unavoidable. I become hypercritical, self-esteem plummets, and I become snappish."

Writing is a lonely process. While writing about people and social processes, you paradoxically remove yourself from the world of human beings. This estrangement is functional in two ways: First, you need to be by yourself because you need time to concentrate on writing. Woods observes that "research may benefit teaching, but the converse does not apply" (Woods 1985, 88) because assisting others distracts one from focusing on one's own work. Those who try to write dissertations or other research reports while "on the job'' are likely to agree. Most writers do best with daily periods of extended time set aside for writing.

Second, estrangement is also functional in that it separates you from the research site. The distancing helps you to approach writing from a perspective that is more global than situation-specific:

> If one does not distance oneself from them [research participants], then there is a danger of being unable to dismantle the data, select from them, and re-order the material. One is left in the position of someone who, when asked to comment on and criticize a film or novel, can do no more than rehearse the plot. The ethnographer who fails to achieve distance will easily fall into the trap of recounting ''what happened'' without imposing a coherent thematic or analytic framework. (Hammersly and Atkinson 1983, 212–213)

So writers withdraw, immersed in their data and thoughts about their others, intending to give form and meaning to that which they have observed and heard and read.

There are several strategies that can help you to deal with the anxiety and the alienation that accompany beginning to write (see also Becker 1986b; Murray 1986; Wolcott 1990; Woods 1985, 1986; Zinsser 1988b):

1. Develop a long-term schedule with realistic deadlines. Expect to spend as much time, if not more, in focused data analysis and writing as you spend in data collection. You need time to play with the data and your words, to share drafts with research participants and colleagues, and to rework drafts a number of times. You need time, as well, to do justice to the considerable investment you have made in planning your study and collecting your data.
2. Develop a short-term schedule. Figure out when you are most creative in your writing. If possible, make appointments with yourself to write for three to four hours, four to five days per week. Expand the hours when you can. Some authors, with more flexible schedules, set a number of pages to be written each day rather than an amount of time to work. Somewhere around five double-spaced typed pages a day is a reasonable amount, unless you have nothing else to do but write.
3. Set aside a place for writing where you will be as free as possible of interruptions and distractions. When you go there, do not make phone calls, or write letters, or read books. Write.
4. Be prepared to write at other times and places. Many of our days become fragmented, with numerous short periods of unproductive time. Keep a notebook (or note cards) with you and stay open to ideas concerning your project. Jot down your thoughts when they strike you,

whether in the midst of a boring meeting, or riding the bus home, or working on something else. Murray (1986) suggests using fragments of time to make lists, notes, and diagrams; collect quotes; sketch outlines; and draft titles and key paragraphs.

5. Begin by editing yesterday's writing. Writers tend to need a gearing-up period before getting started. They find that editing what they wrote the day before helps them get into the new day's work, keeps the flow consistent, and assists in producing a better draft. Beginning by editing yesterday's writing not only lets you know exactly where to start today, but also allows you to revise that which seemed perfectly clear as it was written but may appear obscure a very short time afterward.

6. When stuck, write. Write without concern for syntax, coherence, or logic. Write to work out ideas and thoughts; play with form and style later. It helps to acquire the right "first-draft mentality," that is, the state of mind in which you give yourself permission to write without concern for appearances. You write this way knowing that you will revise later and clarify what may be very messy indeed. You write this way appreciating that it is best to produce a draft of any quality rather than be held back by premature concerns for form and style. A great obstacle to writing is holding inappropriately high standards for the quality of your early drafts, particularly your first draft. A standard that is too high will put you on the road to the paralysis of writer's block. Better to settle for a draft of *any* quality, trusting to the promise of revision to produce order, style, and worthy words.

    Murray finds that taking the attitude of conversing with one's peers facilitates the flow of words:

    > No publication is the final theological word on a subject. Too many academics believe they have to write *the* article or book on their topic. That is impossible. Each publication is merely a contribution to a continuous professional conversation. I was paralyzed by the idea that I had to deliver the Truth—Moses like; I began to write when I realized all I had to do was speculate, question, argue, create a model, take a position, define a problem, make an observation, propose a solution, illuminate a possibility to participate in a written conversation with my peers. (Murray 1986, 147)

    The written-conversation idea is easily extended by choosing a person that you know—a friend, relative, or colleague—and writing with that person in mind.

7. Finally, immerse yourself in exemplary ethnographies and qualitative studies, as well as in novels, poetry, and great works of literature (during nonwriting hours). Your reading provides models and sources

of inspiration. "Read widely as well as deeply," advises Murray (1986, 149).

Once you have started writing, keep at it. The clumps of notes carefully organized and segregated by paper clips and rubber bands are the makings for the qualitative researcher's text. As your "to do" clumps shrink in number and your "done" box fills, you have evidence of progress.

Keeping at It: Writing Your Story

In Beryl Markham's conception of progress,

> A word grows to a thought—a thought to an idea—an idea to an act. The change is slow, and the Present is a sluggish traveler loafing in the path Tomorrow wants to take. (Markham [1942] 1983, 154)

You should not wait until you know exactly what the words, thoughts, ideas, and acts should be before beginning to write. Knowing exactly, and knowing clearly, are unreasonably high standards. Writing "helps people generate, develop, organize, modify, critique, and remember their ideas" (Fulwiler 1985, 23). British historian Sir Steven Runciman captures this point in his description of the role of writing in forming ideas: "When I'm writing, I'm dealing with something being revealed to me all the time. I get the insight when I'm actually having to try to put it into words" (in Plante 1986, 78). Writing helps to develop your thoughts and ideas and to discover what you know and how much more there is to know. Therefore, it is best to begin sooner rather than later.

Although you may begin writing with an overall organizational plan in the form of chapters, the act of writing is likely to reshape the plan, reorganize the pieces, subsume some sections, and add others. For example, the process of writing restructured Alan's outline for his ethnicity book:

> I am feeling very immersed, and thinking I see benefits of being immersed. I think being immersed in writing is like being immersed in anything—you are never far from the work, you have continuity, thoughts get thought that might not get thought at all or not until much later. The latest appearance of a gain—breakthrough would be too strong—was the relegation of what was to be an entire chapter, Chapter 5, to a *part* of a chapter, Chapter 1. A chapter on the "town today" struck me as more fitting for the introductory stuff I have put in Chapter 1.
>
> So thinking, when I want to arrange the clump of notes, I was thinking small—part of a chapter, rather than big—an entire chapter. So thinking, I easily discarded lots of data that I'd originally put in the "town today"

clump. Which is to say, I have a lot less to write and can look forward to soon getting on to real Chapter 5, which now looks to be "education today," having done "education history" in Chapter 4. What is becoming clear is that my chapter outline, made when I had finished all coding, holds up only until I prepare to write a new chapter. Then, in light of the previous chapters done, I know whether the new one will fit next as the chapter, fit elsewhere as a chapter, fit somewhere as a part of a chapter, or fit nowhere at all. (Peshkin, personal notes, 24 May 1988)

As Alan's reflections indicate, writing up data seems to be a continual process of organizing and reorganizing the data as you work through what they are telling you. Begin on a macro-level: after coding all of your data, work with the codes to make an overall outline. The outline organizes the data and assigns data clumps (the coded bits of paper, note cards, computer print-outs, and documents) to chapters or major sections. Somewhat like the Russian doll within a doll, your organizational steps should be repeated within each chapter and then within each chapter subsection.

Once your writing begins, the bits of paper within the carefully sorted clumps will look different. No longer homogeneous, they must be sorted into subclumps that make up each subsection of the text. For example, suppose you have a major code on "resolving conflict" for a study of first-year principals. Under "resolving conflict," you further categorize the data by techniques used, such as "holding meetings," "using humor," "turning the matter over to others," and "ignoring the situation." Now suppose that within the sub-clump "turning the matter over to others," you learn that first-year principals sometimes turn budget conflicts over to the school board, but personnel conflicts over to the superintendent. Your data scraps could be arranged accordingly. To write up your data, you must continuously, progressively code.

Another excerpt from Alan's reflections on writing reinforces this point:

What is consistent in all the writing I have done is that I have to do a final coding at the time I prepare to write a new chapter, notwithstanding that I have my already coded clumps in hand, with each piece in the clump duly coded and located in a subclump that made sense at one time. What remains to do before writing is to decide on the order in which the subclumps will appear, and the order in which the individual pieces within a subclump will appear. (Peshkin, personal notes, 24 May 1988)

All data scraps do not necessarily end up where originally filed. As you work with the data, you may move individual pieces to a place that makes more sense now that you are writing; or you may relegate them to a miscellaneous pile that you scan at the beginning and end of each chapter or major section to see if something fits. Or you may file them in a discard box, concluding that they really are tangential to your story. Through this progressive coding process, you increasingly impose order on your data. Yet, at the same time, the order is flexible; it continuously changes, shaped by the ideas that your writing generates.

Discussing the organizational procedures of your writing is relatively easier than discussing what makes it more than a descriptive report of what you did and what you found. Your writing must develop how you interpret what you found by carefully integrating themes that support a thesis and create or augment theoretical explanations. No mechanical procedure exists for doing so. Rather, you must be so immersed in your data that you are open to those flashes of insight that come when least expected. Such moments make connections and provide perspectives that allow the pieces to fall into place.

Drafts and Revisions

Expect your work to go through a number of drafts before it reflects the polish of a well-crafted manuscript. The first draft of your manuscript is like the sculptor's roughly hewn form emerging from a block of wood. To make the form a work of art, the sculptor carefully continues to shape the form, creating details, smoothing rough spots, and polishing the overall piece. Successive drafts do the same for the author's words. When your first draft is completed, read it for overall cohesion and then add, move, or eliminate sections as needed. In another reading, focus on the clarity of your theories and descriptions. With more readings, tighten, sharpen, and brighten (Trimble, in Jeske 1984) your work: Tighten by eliminating unnecessary words. Sharpen by reworking passive statements and employing precise and lively words. Brighten by simile and metaphor, by wit and lively description. Grammar, spelling, and punctuation should also get a turn.

Do not overlook the contribution of a reading that attends to subheadings. Subheadings benefit both author and reader. Scan your subheadings to check the order of the parts within each chapter. Try listing all of your subheads on a separate page, then reconsider their most effective, most logical order. In addition, name any previously unnamed sections; then reexamine the content and the order of paragraphs and pages within that section. Although unnamed sections may be easy for you to make order of—easy because the words are yours and you are familiar with them—that is not the case for the reader. Alan had this experience in preparing the final chapter of his book on ethnicity. He sent the entire manuscript off for review but felt uneasy about the concluding chapter. With only two subheadings to structure its thirty-eight typed pages, too much of the chapter was left unstructured. A reading of the chapter for the sole purpose of locating namable sections led to the addition of three more sections and their subheads. As a result, Alan saw how to reorganize the writing within the sections so that each section could become a congruent set.

Artisans sometimes have assistants who help in certain stages of crafting a work. Qualitative researchers have colleagues or peers and research participants who play invaluable roles in polishing the final product. Enlist them to respond to your interpretations, ideas, and forms of expression, and allow time for such input in the shaping of your manuscript.

THE TEXT: QUESTIONS OF FORM AND STYLE

Types of Tales

The written reports of qualitative research take a variety of forms. Van Maanen (1988) discusses various ethnographic conventions, in particular, realist, confessional, and impressionist tales. We heartily recommend his book *Tales of the Field* for a more complete understanding and appreciation of ethnographic writing.

In *realist tales,* authors take positions of authority. They are absent from much, if not all, of the text, and they present their tales with an air of what Van Maanen calls "interpretive omnipotence." They do so by minutely documenting the details of the lives of people studied, using closely edited quotations to portray the "native's" point of view. Rites, practices, and beliefs are central to the tales and presented in an authoritarian "this is the way to say it" fashion. In realist tales, authors look at fieldwork as an observational and descriptive act.

In *confessional tales,* on the other hand, authors view fieldwork as an interpretive act, and they are very much present in the text. The point of view is not that of the native, but that of the fieldworker as interpreter. Such authors portray themselves as human beings who make mistakes and blunders, but who eventually "learn the rules" and come to see things in a new way. Accompanying the confessional tale is the "simple assertion that even though there are flaws and problems in one's work, when all is said and done it still remains adequate" (Van Maanen 1988, 79). Clifford observes,

> The new tendency to name and quote informants more fully and to introduce personal elements into the text is altering enthography's discursive strategy and mode of authority. Much of our knowledge about other cultures must now be seen as contingent, the problematic outcome of intersubjective dialogue, translation, and projection. (Clifford 1986, 109)

A confessional section is now an expected part of ethnographic writing, most commonly located with the description of methods or as an appendix.

Impressionist tales, says Van Maanen, "are not about what usually happens but about what rarely happens. These are the tales that presumably mark and make memorable the fieldwork experience" (Van Maanen 1988, 102). Impressionist tales make use of dramatic recall, artistry, and literary standards. A degree of tension builds while cultural knowledge is presented in a fragmented way. Characters are developed with names, faces, motives, and voice. The audience experiences what the fieldworker saw, heard, and felt, and, like the fieldworker, is left to interpret the events along the way.

Van Maanen also discusses critical and formal tales. *Critical tales* either explicitly or implicitly draw on neo-Marxist perspectives and demonstrate concern for the oppressed in a capitalistic society. They are fashioned to illuminate the larger social, political, and economic issues of the society of which the ethnographic study is a part. Van Maanen finds "something of a crusading spirit behind many critical tales" (Van Maanen 1988, 129), although other forms of writing, not at all grounded in Marxism, also may possess a "crusading spirit."

The authors of *formal tales* intend to build, test, or exhibit theory in some way. They are often specialists who belong to a particular school of qualitative inquiry, such as ethnomethodology or sociolinguistics. For the formal tale writers, the field setting becomes something akin to a science lab. "The members of the studied culture so artfully portrayed in good formal tales appear as they do in good critical tales: as rather automated figures who are pushed and pulled according to whatever theoretical scheme animates the tale" (Van Maanen 1988, 131).

These several formats are derived from ethnographic writing, but you can apply them to qualitative writing in general. They inform your commitment to description, analysis, interpretation, evaluation, or prescription, as befits your writing in the realm of social research. Think of Van Maanen's formats as alternatives that you can combine to suit the particular purposes of your own research and writing.

Variety in Text Organization

To some extent, the type of tale determines the voice and style of writing. To a lesser extent, it shapes text organization. Hammersley and Atkinson (1983) identify several strategies that authors use to organize their presentation of qualitative research. These strategies are useful starting points for thinking about text organization; you may choose to use more than one of the strategies within the same text, or use other organizational techniques altogether.

In the *natural history* approach, the text re-creates the fieldwork process of exploration and discovery. Through this technique, the author can dramatically portray a sense of people and place and their interactions with the researcher (typical of impressionistic tales). The natural history approach is not useful, however, for description and analysis of research themes.

In the *chronology* technique, "the pattern follows some 'developmental cycle,' 'moral career,' or 'timetable' characteristic of the setting or actors under investigation" (Hammersley and Atkinson 1983, 217). If the passage of time is particularly critical to the study, then the chronology technique is appropriate. For example, Peshkin's (1982a) book *The Imperfect Union* chronicles the struggle between a village and a school board over the closing of the village's only remaining school.

Another technique involves narrowing and expanding the focus. The author moves from descriptive detail to theoretical abstraction or vice versa. Like a zoom lens, the text glides through various levels of generality. Spradley advocates this technique when he identifies six levels of statements that he believes should be a part of ethnographic writing. The levels range from universal statements about human beings and their cultural or environmental situation to incident-specific statements (Spradley 1979, 207–210). The writer, says Spradley, must move back and forth through the various levels. Accounts written only at the more general levels will be dry and dull with no examples to ground theoretical statements. In contrast, those written at the more specific levels may make for interesting reading, but fall short of analyzing the cultural significance of the data.

Yet another organizational technique is to separate narration and analysis, as in Willis' (1977) *Learning to Labor*. He first engages the reader with a narrative account of the research setting that is rich in dialogue, events, and interaction. Then the writing style changes dramatically as he develops his theories with detailed analysis of the data.

Probably the most frequently used technique is organization by themes or topics. By analyzing the data, the researcher generates a typology of concepts, gives them names or uses "native" labels, and then discusses them one by one, illustrating with descriptive detail.

Some writers have found that amalgamations are useful to present certain descriptive data. Researchers who have spent months "shadowing" a few people may amalgamate the observed activities into a "typical day" for each participant (see Flinders 1987; Peshkin 1972). Ashton and Webb (1986) analyze interview and observation data from a number of people, discover categories or types of respondents, and then develop descriptive portraits of each type through amalgamation.

Glaser (1978) emphasizes the need to focus on the concepts and processes relevant to the study. Places, people, and their interactions are constantly changing, but concepts and processes have duration and are the building blocks of developing theory. Related to Glaser's ideas is the question of how to handle case studies. Barbara, for example, prepared four case studies of persons who had chronic lung disease. Her research question related to compliance with prescribed medical regimens. Should she organize her data to devote a separate chapter to each case; should she identify major concepts and processes from each case and devote a separate chapter to each; or should she do both, to some extent? An answer, such as there may be to these questions, would consider what is gained and lost by each of these three approaches. On one hand, the cases kept intact might illuminate understandings and insights about the process of compliance that would be lost if they were sliced up into corroborating data for general points. On the other hand, the general points about compliance might be what represent the greatest potential contribution of the cases. Beyond the agreement that our research must make a contribution, neither Barbara nor the rest of us have the luxury of an agreement that specifies what that contribution must be and what organizational procedure for writing thereby follows.

Data display in tables, charts, or graphs can supplement text by introducing or summarizing categories discussed in detail in the text. Table 8.1, adapted from Glesne's (1985) work in the Caribbean, exemplifies one way of illustrating theme categories that grew out of interviewees discussing their occupational desires for their children. (See Miles and Huberman 1984 for numerous examples of the graphic displays.)

However the substantive sections of a work are organized, they conventionally include an introduction and an ending. The introduction usually states the purpose of the paper or book, presents the problem of inquiry, gives a general context to the problem, and foreshadows what is to come. Since many authors do not know with sufficient certainty what is to come until after they have written it, they often write the introduction last.

The ending, we believe, should be a conclusion, which is quite different from a summary. "A summary is redundant and an affront to those readers who have actually read the paper, and a cop out for those who have not read it, however useful to them" (Glaser 1978, 132). Summaries reiterate what has been said; conclusions deal with the "so whats." They stimulate thought and transcend the substantive content presented earlier. Glaser recommends using the conclusion as an opportunity to show the contribution of the work to formal

TABLE 8.1 Example of Theme Categories and Illustrative Responses

Occupational Desire Category and Illustrative Response	Number Who Agree
Something good (economically or in self-satisfaction) "Any kind of occupation that gives them satisfaction and joy."	10
It's up to them "I would not choose for my children."	10
Schooling first "Right now they must first further their education"	6
A life unlike mine "I want to bring him up so he doesn't have to hustle as I do, and let him have an open mind so he can learn easily without having to lie or fool anybody."	4

theory by "brief comparative analysis with data from experience, knowledge and the literature, and by raising the conceptual level" (Glaser 1978, 133).

We recommend devoting special attention to the concluding chapter. Often, it gets short shrift because the author is exhausted from all that precedes it and feels pressed for time. The writing well runs dry just when it should be at its fullest. When authors fail to deliver adequately on the promise of their data, they fail to do justice to their investment in their research project. The concluding chapter then becomes the weakest production rather than the jewel in the writing crown that it should be.

Begin by appreciating the significance of your concluding chapter. Take care to schedule time for its completion—more time, in fact, than you may want to believe is necessary. Review all preceding chapters as preparation for writing the conclusion. Review your research questions so that you are certain to address all of them, and take note of what emerged as consequential that was not anticipated by your questions. And, finally, worry yourself continually with the questions: Am I doing full justice to what I learned? Am I saying enough for readers to appreciate what I intend as *my* contribution to the matter under study?

When you have completed your concluding chapter, read it and your introductory chapter together. Have you done in the end what you announced in the beginning that you meant to do? Have you discussed all of the questions you raised? If not, why not? Your opening chapter presents readers with expectations that they anticipate will be met in the course of subsequent chapters, and that will culminate in the final chapter.

Specifics of Style

As with the overall form of your work, no absolutes govern the shaping of your style. The closest you can get is to apply what guides "good writing" in general to your writing of qualitative research.

The following five guidelines for good writing seem specifically applicable to qualitative researcher writing (for more complete discussion see Becker 1986b; Strunk and White 1979):

1. Make sentences active. Give passive statements an actor and avoid "it is" and "there are" constructions.
2. Make images concrete. Use descriptive words.
3. Avoid the jargon trap. "It is a way to strike a pose as a smart, well-versed, current member of a hot and influential in-group. But more than one hot and influential in-group within ethnographic circles has become over time a cold and impotent out-group" (Van Maanen 1988, 28).
4. Use enough words to make your point.

5. Avoid wordiness. For example, the sentence "There is some question as to whether he is the person who should be in charge of running the school owing to the fact that he rarely reads or utilizes educational research findings" is better written, "Because he rarely uses research findings, some people question his role as principal."

Try reading your draft with a mind set for "making sentences active" and edit appropriately. Then read it again, but this time concentrate on clarity and concreteness of images and examples. Then read (and edit) for jargon, trite metaphors, and wordiness. With each reading, you shape your work, eventually forming a product that is worthy of your and your reader's time.

Schooled to write reports in a passive and authoritative manner with little, if any, of the researcher showing, you may experience some confusion as you let go of old habits. Even when students in our courses find some joy in their writing, they are often inundated with questions that they have not had to ask before. Following are some of the commonly asked questions. In response, we offer thoughts toward answers. In practice, a number of factors may influence the answers, including the demands of funding agencies, the expectations of supervising committees, the author's theoretical disposition or research tradition, and the degree of risk that the researcher is willing to take with experimental forms of presentation.

1. *Question:* Is it ok to use "I"?

Answer: Writing in the first person singular fits the nature of qualitative inquiry. When reporting research methods, your "I" is particularly appropriate. The researcher conventionally becomes less visible, however, as he or she focuses on descriptive analysis of the data. The presence of your "I" in your text reflects your presence in your research setting. Your "I" says that yours is not a disembodied account that presumes to be objective by virtue of omitting clear reference to the human agent who lived through a particular research experience and lived with other people in the course of that experience. Avoid the obtrusive "I" that says, "Look at me," because, after all, the story you tell is not foremost about yourself. Use "I" in the sense of saying that you were present; it is well for both writer and reader to remember this fact. Moreover, it would be foolish for you to hide behind veils of awkward sentence construction, particularly when your ideal is graceful, clear, and cogent writing.

2. *Question:* When I am describing and analyzing what I saw and heard, do I also evaluate what I experienced?

Answer: In discussing her biographical work on Alice James, Strouse states, "Getting brave enough to venture my own views was really what writing the book was all about" (Strouse 1988, 190).

Scholarly work is interpretive; to pretend otherwise is to fool yourself but perhaps very few others. Nonetheless, the purpose of qualitative research in general is to increase understanding, not to pass judgment. There may be a fine line between finding fault and finding meaning. Taking heed of this line is worthwhile. Tell the story that the data tell; do not use data to tell the story that a priori you want told.

3. *Question:* Can I tell a "story" in a dissertation, or do I have to follow the conventional format of problem statement, literature review, research methods, findings, and conclusion?

   Answer: The qualitative researching student has an advisor and committee whose judgments may set the guidelines and orthodoxy for the student's writing. In general, however, qualitative research has no conventional organizational format; we trust that none will develop. But telling a story, or following any particular chapter arrangement, is likely to be a matter of negotiation with your overseers, a negotiation, we suggest, that should be undertaken early. We do not personally endorse the conventional dissertation format because it is not congruent with the openness of qualitative inquiry and the variable forms that may best suit the stories we choose to tell.

4. *Question:* Should I include a section titled "literature," or should I integrate the literature throughout the text?

   Answer: Depending on your study and audience, you may find both useful. It is accepted practice to integrate the work of others with your own. As Glaser (1978) stresses, however, novices tend to turn to the literature as the source of an idea or theory even when their thoughts developed out of fieldwork. The attitude toward existing literature, advises Glaser,

   should not be one of adumbration, volume or reverence. It should be one of carefully weaving . . . theory into its place in the literature. . . . It is amazing how many authors try to find their best ideas in previous work in order to legitimate using it, as borrowed or derived as if they could not be allowed to generate it on their own. The proper attitude is simply to accept having discovered ideas. (Glaser 1978, 137)

   Since your work may build on and extend the theories of others, you should make due reference to these other works; but do not allow them to overshadow your own thoughts and ideas.

5. *Question:* What use should I make of historical and current documents pertaining to sites other than the one I am investigating? For example, in a study of a one-room schoolhouse, Jody collected

numerous historical documents pertaining to both her site and similar sites, including diaries of one-room schoolmarms. Can she use the documents from the similar sites? If so, how?

Answer: We respond with a generality: Use whatever materials, however collected, that enhance your cause. The question is not where the material came from, but whether it will help.

6. *Question:* If I am focusing on one school in one community, how do I reference local documents if I have been using pseudonyms for the school and community?

Answer: Use the pseudonym consistently in all citations so that confidentiality is respected, but explain to your readers that you are altering the citation.

7. *Question:* When quoting informants in the text, should I reference my interview notes? If so, how?

Answer: We never do, but your faculty overseers may insist that you do. It seems meaningless to provide such references when no one but you has access to your notes.

8. *Question:* If in a quote the informant uses the name of a person or place, do I change the names to provide anonymity? If so, do I use brackets or some other means to demonstrate that the name has been changed?

Answer: If by naming the person or place you will breach your commitment to anonymity, then the answer is clear: use pseudonyms. A general footnote at the beginning of your work can clarify your intent to alter names and places as needed. Thereafter, we see no need to call attention to the changes you make in the interest of preserving anonymity.

9. *Question:* When quoting someone, should I leave in every "umm," "you know," and other unconscious patterns of speech?

Answer: Use your judgment. Leave in enough of such sounds and words to capture the person's speech, authentically but not so much as to impose on a reader's patience. Authenticity can be overdone; how many "you know's" and "umm's" should readers suffer?

10. *Question:* How do you assure confidentiality and anonymity to a person who plays a major role in a study and whose position is singular and central to the study (e.g., a school principal or superintendent)?

Answer: "When total confidentiality or anonymity cannot be guaranteed, the issue becomes, in part, one of ongoing communication and agreement . . . between the investigator and research participants" (Johnson 1982, 85). This is a sensitive matter. You may feel particularly constrained in what you say because you cannot safely disguise the person's identity. Our suggestion is to begin by saying all that you would like to say. Then reread what you have written as if you were that person. Finally, send a copy of your prose to that person and take your cue from his or her reaction.

11. *Question:* How do you describe and report unfavorable attitudes toward a person, program, or site when that person, program, or site is identifiable by research participants and by others in nearby areas?

Answer: Ask yourself if it is at all necessary to report anything negative about persons and places that are identifiable. A commitment to scholarship does not provide a license to injure those who allow you access to their words and deeds. If your research, however, has a clear evaluative component and that component is a negotiated aspect of your entry arrangements, then the matter of negative findings assumes another perspective.

12. *Question* Should I use precise counts, or imprecise terms such as "a few," "almost all," or "a majority"? For example, if I interviewed twenty persons, how much do I count when analyzing and reporting the data?

Answer: Although some reference to frequency may contribute to your presentation, keep in mind that numbers do not play the same role in qualitative research that they do in quantitative research. Qualitative research has the potential to make many useful contributions, but these do not include generalizations derived from sampling in the quantitative tradition. Qualitative researchers do, however, very much include generalizations of the type that qualitative inquiry can generate (e.g., the writing of Coles 1977; Dillon 1989; Heath 1983; Lightfoot 1983). When to count and in what ways to count are other judgments that you make. To rule out all counting is to shut down a possible way of presenting your data that is fully warranted by your intent. To count as a basic way of structuring your data is to insert the rationality of the quantitative paradigm where, ordinarily, it does not belong. Nonetheless, counting not only may be useful, it also may be necessary, as Erickson and Mohatt (1982) clearly demonstrate in their study of two classrooms of Native American students. Their study exemplifies several methodological techniques, including microethnography, use of numbers, and linguistic analysis.

13. *Question:* Should I end my written report with a list of recommendations? Education is an applied field of study; shouldn't I be prescriptive?

Answer: The need to be useful is both understandable and desirable. Useful outcomes, however, do not always take the form of prescriptions. You must ask yourself: Have I designed my study for the purpose of being prescriptive? If so, then prescribe. If not, then the prescriptions, although interesting, are bootlegged onto a study designed to do other things. Do what you set out to do, and do it as well as you can. Attend to the matter of prescriptions when it is clearly suitable to do so. To focus on them when they are not integral to your design is to take effort away from where you planned it to be.

This set of questions and answers covers many of the practical considerations that arise in bringing a research process to fruition. They are important but secondary considerations, preceded in priority by commitments: to collect the best data you can; to have something to say—a matter of analysis, imagination, and boldness; to be enthusiastic about your topic; to intend to write well; and, not least, to revise and revise and revise.

RESPONSIBILITIES OF THE WRITER

Writing is a political act: carefully think through both the intended and the unintended consequences of your words. Your first responsibility is to your research respondents, those persons whose cooperation is the basis of your research. Ask yourself whether your choice of words results in judgments rather than in descriptions of a place and its people. Note the difference between saying the "community is backward" and "10 percent of the adult population can neither read nor write" (Johnson 1982, 87). Nagel, a biographer, also gives good advice: "Writing about another person's life is an awesome task, so one must proceed with a gentleness born from knowing that the subject and the author share the frailties of human mortality" (Nagel 1988, 115). As a researcher, strive to understand the complexity of social phenomena. In doing so, you will most likely discover that research participants are as human as you are—neither saint nor sinner. Portray that humanness, neither disguising it with a hidden agenda of your own, nor overlaying it with emphases and highlights that gild—or wound, damage, and denigrate.

Central to the responsibility to research participants is the following question:

> Are we placing research participants and their site(s) at undue risk because of our interactions with them? We should imagine a scenario in which the location(s) and their participants are revealed and ask ourselves what the possible consequences of that discovery would be. (Johnson 1982, 87)

How could the information be used either positively or negatively? Would individuals be subjected to unwanted publicity? Would the disclosure of data about identifiable individuals or groups with little power be exploited by others who have power? Are there things that should be omitted?

Another consideration is your responsibility to the larger community of social scientists. Ask yourself whether your portrayal will preclude another study at the same site, by you or by someone else. Will participants be reluctant, if not adamantly negative, about allowing another researcher in? If so, what harm have you done to scientific opportunities and fellow researchers, in addition to research participants?

You must also be responsible to yourself. Your research discoveries can have political ramifications for your job and your interactions with "superiors," particularly if researching in your own backyard. Bonnie, for example, gave a copy of her final report to the nursing supervisor who was both the gatekeeper to her research participants and her "boss." The supervisor was unhappy with the report findings and told Bonnie that if she published them, she could not return to work in the hospital. You must consider the consequences of your words on yourself as well as on your others.

How do you avoid the research complications that may disrupt your own life as well as those of research participants? The surest way is to anticipate complications and to work them out along the way by collaborative arrangements with research supervisors and research participants. Anticipate to whom findings of any but the most obviously laudatory type could prove disagreeable and include those persons in the preparation of the "controversial" sections. That is, treat your findings as tentative; discuss them in very general terms, not as *the* results. Solicit reactions to your words from research supervisors and participants. In addition, look for colleagues who will read your manuscript for examples of judgment, criticism, and potential ethical and political problems. The idea is to avoid complications, rather than have to get out of them.

It may not seem appropriate to conclude a chapter devoted to writing on the topic of responsibility. In fact, we could well have begun this book by saying, in parallel with this section's opening sentence: Research is a political act, involving, as it most certainly does, power, resources, policy, ethics. We strongly endorse a larger view of our research, one that takes us beyond the understandable "What will it do for my credentials and career?" inquiry, to the necessary "What impact will it have on others?" question. But we do not think that being a responsible researcher should detract from the joy of being a participant in the pleasurable adventure of serious research.

CHAPTER **9**

The Continuing Odyssey

The Road goes ever on and on
Down from the door where it began.
Now far ahead the Road has gone,
And I must follow if I can.
Pursuing it with weary feet,
Until it joins some larger way,
Where many paths and errands meet.
And whither then? I cannot say.[1]

Qualitative research explores the poorly understood territories of human interaction. Like explorers who seek to identify and understand the biological and
geological processes that create the patterns of a physical landscape, qualitative
adventurers seek to describe and understand the processes that create the
patterns of the human terrain.

Exploring demands near total absorption. In speaking of being a naturalist, a student-in-training in Alaska said,

> Somehow you've got to put your heart and soul into it—not just for personal
> reasons, but to really understand what's going on. The more you allow
> yourself to fall in love with a place, the more you see the connections.
> (Wilson 1989, 17)

Similarly, qualitative researchers find their lives consumed by their work as
they seek understanding and connections. Personal commitment, trust, and

time are key to rich data and useful interpretations. Few anticipate the exacting demands on their mind, heart, and soul. For example, Toni set out in a pilot project to interview wives of medical interns about their sense of self. Six months later she exclaimed:

> This project has really become bigger than me! It is everywhere. We talked about it in our social psych brown bag as we discussed feminist methodology. It comes up for me in almost all of my readings—at a conference I attended, in conversations. . . . I have so much in my head and noted down somewhere that I have not had time to think about. . . . This project has consumed my life to the exclusion of almost all else.

Another student agrees: "I went to a conference the other day and kept taking notes for my work, and the conference was on a topic not even close to my project." Although most of us do not have lives that adapt easily to the demands of qualitative research on our attention, it is when we find our "problem" everywhere that we can be assured we are getting somewhere.

As with any kind of exploration of the unknown, adventuring into the qualitative can be lonely. Even though you may discuss your work with colleagues, friends, and research participants, you are alone—unless, of course, you are part of a team. You are alone with the ultimate responsibility of fitting the pieces together and finding meaning in the whole, alone in the role of researcher at your research site. Toni reflected on the loneliness of her work:

> Talk about isolation! I'm feeling it in many realms. One is working with the data, being overwhelmed by it all. I feel isolated at times when I talk about this [lives of spouses of medical interns] because people seem to get uneasy as though I am saying something I shouldn't about medicine. Additionally, I am wondering about how the women [interviewees] will react when they see it . . . and how I will react to how they react.

As Toni suggests, the journey into the unknown can also raise self-doubts. You worry that people won't want to talk with you or won't let you observe. You wonder if you are asking the right questions. You suddenly panic over whether your towering stack of notebooks, note cards, and computer disks really tell you anything and, even if they do, whether you are capable of putting the data bits together in a meaningful way. And you worry that perhaps you will not like what you bring to light.

That you do not know exactly what you search for contributes to periods of confusion and frustration. In the midst of analyzing data on a school in a rural transitional community, Carlton sighed, "I'm not sure if the data confuse me or if I confuse the data." Both surely occur in all good research projects. As surely, all good research projects require courage and integrity.

These discontinuities, the disturbing pieces that do not "fit," are actually what may give you clues to your more interesting discoveries. You will need to learn to live with confusion, if not welcome it into your life—to see it as a harbinger of new mysteries to unravel. Mary Catherine Bateson (1984) recognized this in the work of her parents, Margaret Mead and Gregory Bateson:

> Both Margaret and Gregory developed a style that involved collecting observational material in the expectation that, however rich and bewildering it might seem at first, they would arrive at points of recognition when things would "make sense" and fall into place. In the search for such moments of insight they would be dealing with points of congruence within the culture they were looking at and also points of personal response. (Bateson 1984, 163)

Understanding involves getting at the actors' perspectives, but it is more than that. It is reaching some collective understanding that includes self, the researcher, and those researched.

Although the journey is often exciting, even exhilarating, it can also be tiring. Exhaustion seems to hit hardest when one is trying to make sense of the data. After weary pursuit, Tina wrote,

> I felt extreme fatigue when the interviews were over. That fatigue made transcribing even more deadly. I remember many nights falling asleep for a few minutes at my computer during the transcribing process and thinking that I would never get to the last page. Somehow I did, however, but it was always a temptation to leave it until the next day.

APPLICATIONS OF QUALITATIVE RESEARCH: THE OUTCOMES OF YOUR ADVENTURES

When teachers conduct a study of new students' adaptation to middle school, when mothers map their families' past, or when students challenge the university food service, they all engage in research for a reason. The applications of research are as varied as the researchers and their sundry studies. When we talk about applying research, we generally refer to making use of the final report: the research product. The research *process,* however, also has its own applications.

Using the Research Manuscript

Research manuscripts or texts can take you places that you have not had opportunity to go, exposing you to other cultures and to unique aspects of your own culture. They also help you to adopt new perspectives, to see something from a different point of view, and to reexamine your own theoretical constructs.

Barone cautions against using the tool metaphor to view the use of qualitative research texts: "A text of qualitative inquiry is . . . better viewed as an occasion than as a tool. It is, more precisely, an occasion for the reader to engage in the activities of textual re-creation and dismantling" (Barone 1990a, 306). If you view the text as a tool, then you may too easily accept it as fact and ignore what went into the research process, including the values of the researcher and the problems in the research design.

Instead of responding to research findings as though they represent reality and truth, use the findings as an opportunity to think about the social world around you. Like the English teacher who said, "The beauty of a good story is its openness—the way you or I or anyone reading it can take it in, and use it for ourselves" (Coles 1989, 47), a good qualitative text invites you in. It encourages you to compare description and analysis in your own experiences, and to use it in a way that makes sense of your own particular situation.

Qualitative research texts also assist in academic pursuits (i.e., hypothesis generation and theory development) and in creating solutions to practical problems. Toni's work with wives of medical interns extends a theory that explains the development of self in relationship to others. Her descriptive stories may also serve as a mode of support and consciousness-raising for research participants and interns' wives. As with many research texts, Toni's work has both theoretical and practical applications.

Policymakers, evaluators, and practitioners such as teachers, school administrators, nurses, and physical therapists can all use qualitative research to help answer questions or to find possible solutions.

> People can and have been moved to take specific action, advocate change, and make consequential decisions inspired or influenced by reports of qualitative inquiry. Like art, literature, poetry and music, qualitative accounts of the drama of teaching and learning can have profound and unpredictable effects on human thought and action. (Clark 1990, 338)

Undoubtedly, countless reports find their way into the forgotten corner of office shelves rather than become the moving, transforming experience that Clark holds forth as a possibility. Yet, many research reports have changed lives. Willis' (1977) work in England drew attention to the role of resistance to the dominant ideology in shaping the lives of working-class "lads" both in and out of school. Humphreys' (1970) work contributed to a more tolerant portrayal of homosexuality in America. Gilligan's (1982) work with the moral development of women paved the way for exploring the sex bias that permeates theories of human development, which, for the most part, have been generated from male data. These studies are not without their problems, yet they and others have contributed to how we perceive and interact with the world.

Using the Research Process

Unlike the research text, which may be meaningful to people living thousands of miles away from the research site, the usefulness or application of the actual process of doing the research is more limited to those involved. This, however, does not detract from its significance and contributions to improving practice, evaluation, policy, and understanding.

Unless asked to participate in someone else's funded research project, you will generally find yourself researching something within your academic or applied discipline (e.g., special education, nursing, social work, physical therapy). As you conduct the research, you will invariably learn things that will improve your practice. Dorothy, with nearly twenty years of experience in clinical nursing, stated that she already knew "the value of a carefully placed 'go on,' a contemplative 'uh huh.' " Nonetheless, in her study of the process of committing a loved one to institutional care, she discovered that her interviewees "seem to yearn for a listening ear." Her open-ended, probing questions allowed the participants' stories to be told. "For some," she stated, "I have the sense I am the first health professional to listen." In her research role, Dorothy learned more about her clients than she had in her nursing role. Seeing that her clients appreciated an extended opportunity to discuss difficult issues, Dorothy plans to incorporate longer, more probing interviews into her practice. (Similarly, Aamodt [1989] discusses using qualitative interviewing techniques with children who have cancer in order to provide more personally meaningful care.)

Dorothy also reflected on how the process of participant observation in qualitative inquiry expanded her concept of the potential usefulness of observation in nursing:

> Documenting observations comes as naturally to a nurse as listening. Attention to subtle detail is essential to comprehensive patient assessments. In nursing, however, the areas for observation are clearly prescribed. I know that observing the rate and depth of respirations along with the color of fingernails and mucous membranes will allow me to reach conclusions about lung function. But what specific observations must I record to eventually understand family decision making? Would posture, level of enthusiasm, appearance of fatigue all be useful information? I now consider what I see in general. I describe the apparent uneasiness with which a son relates his inability to keep his dad out of the hospital. . . .

By conducting qualitative research, Dorothy learned both skills and knowledge applicable to her nursing practice. Similarly, practitioner-researchers in other disciplines learn skills and knowledge that assist them in carrying out their practice, conducting program evaluations, and shaping policy.

Using Qualitative Research to Learn about Yourself

"I reached the wall," Charlie said. "I could not write another piece about the classroom. We were both tired—I of being there, and she of having me there." Charlie was in the midst of research on an ungraded classroom. He had been observing the classroom; interviewing children, parents, and school personnel; and discussing his thoughts in intense meetings with the teacher. After a short break, he returned to the classroom and was welcomed by the teacher and students; in the meantime, he had learned something useful about the process of doing research. Charlie began to schedule different kinds of breaks— reflective breaks that allowed him to take stock of his work, and absolute breaks that gave him a complete rest from the researcher role and gave his others relief from the intrusion that a researcher, no matter how loved, represents.

The act of researching teaches you about yourself as a researcher. You can take pride in the way that you carefully listen and ask probing questions, but you may also realize that you are not as observant as you had hoped. You may need to develop better strategies to record and remember unspecified interactions. In addition to learning about yourself as a researcher, however, you may also learn more about yourself in general. Jill reflected, "By looking at what problems interest us and at what questions we ask, we may discover an avenue that leads us to a better understanding of what is important and of meaning to each one of us." Your research is autobiographical in that some aspect of yourself is mirrored in the work you choose to pursue. Figuring out why Corrine's interests lie with the rural poor and their socioeconomic-political opportunity and why Alan's relate to community, for example, leads us to a greater understanding of our core values and beliefs. Such understanding, in turn, can provide greater direction for future undertakings.

Over the course of writing this book, we have reflected on such auto-biographical issues and their significance for our evolving research perspectives. Alan's quest is to understand the relationship between communities and their schools and to bestow, through his books, a sense of how the host community shapes its schools and what, in turn, schools contribute to their communities. He is, therefore, interested in social science approaches that assist him in exploring this question. Corrine's core values include a commitment to social justice, belief in human potential, and concern for environmental preservation. Moved to act on these values, she is attracted to collaborative and participatory modes of research in an effort to effect social and environmental change. Consequently, as our understanding of ourselves and research methods have developed through writing this book, we would each now shape a somewhat different text than we have constructed here. In keeping with our mutual commitment to pluralism and diversity, however, we believe that there is a place for both the more traditional approaches of description and analysis and the more alternative approaches of collaborative and participatory inquiry. We also believe that they can contribute to and complement each other.

CONCLUDING WORDS

A naturalist said, "You can love a landscape for a lifetime, and it will still have secrets from you" (Wilson 1989, 18). Whether researching a Caribbean village, a Christian school, or the superintendency of a rural school district, you will never understand it all, but you will know where next to look, what new questions to ask, and what sense it might have for yourselves and others.

Qualitative inquiry is an odyssey into our discipline, our practice, and perhaps our souls. We cannot be sure of what we will find, but we invariably get caught up in the search. Andrea wrote,

> There is so much I want to know. I feel as though each interview is a rosebud handed to me. As I take them home and transcribe them, they begin to bloom, and each petal is a new idea or a deeper understanding. Here I stand with three beautiful flowers in one hand and my other hand out-stretched. Tomorrow another bud.

And tomorrow another adventure; the true ones do not end. Instead, they point the way for yet another search.

NOTES

1. From THE FELLOWSHIP OF THE RING by J.R.R. Tolkien. Copyright © 1965 by J.R.R. Tolkien. Reprinted by permission of Houghton Mifflin Company. All rights reserved.

References

Aamodt, A. 1989. "Ethnography and epistemology. Generating nursing knowledge."
In *Qualitative nursing research: A contemporary dialogue,* edited by J. Morse,
29–40. Rockville, MD: Aspen Publishers.

Agar, M. 1973. *Ripping and running: A formal ethnography of urban heroin addicts.*
San Diego: Academic Press.

———. 1980. *The professional stranger.* New York: Academic Press.

Ashton, P., and R. Webb. 1986. *Making a difference: Teacher's sense of efficacy and
student achievement.* New York: Longman.

Ball, S. 1985. "Participant observation with pupils." In *Strategies of educational
research: Qualitative methods,* edited by R. Burgess, 23–53. Philadelphia: Falmer
Press.

Barker, R., and H. Wright. 1951. *One boy's day: A specimen record of behavior.* New
York: Harper & Brothers.

Barone, T. 1990a. "Using the narrative text as an occasion for conspiracy." In
Qualitative inquiry in education: The continuing debate, edited by E. Eisner and A.
Peshkin, 305–326. New York: Teachers College Press.

———. 1990b. On the demise of subjectivity in educational inquiry. Paper presented
at the annual meeting of the American Educational Research Association, Boston.

Bateson, M. C. 1984. *With a daughter's eye.* New York: Morrow.

Becker, H. 1984. Field work with the computer: Criteria for assessing systems.
Qualitative Sociology 7(1–2):16–33.

———. 1986a. *Doing things together: Selected papers.* Evanston, IL: Northwestern
University Press.

———. 1986b. *Writing for social scientists.* Chicago: University of Chicago Press.

Becker, H. S., B. Geer, E. C. Hughes, and A. L. Strauss. 1961. *Boys in white:
Student culture in school.* Chicago: University of Chicago Press.

Belenky, M., L. Bond, and J. Weinstock. 1991. From silence to voice: Developing women's ways of knowing. Unpublished manuscript.

Berg, D., A. Gordon, and R. LeBailly. 1985. "Anxiety in research relationships." In *Exploring clinical methods for social research,* edited by D. N. Berg and K. K. Smith, 213–228. Beverly Hills, CA: Sage Publications.

Bernard, R. 1988. *Research methods in cultural anthropology.* Newbury Park, CA: Sage Publications.

Bissex, G. 1987. "Year-long, classroom-based studies." In *Seeing for ourselves: Case-study research by teachers of writing,* edited by G. Bissex and R. Bullock, 31–39. Portsmouth, NH: Heinemann.

Bissex, G., and R. Bullock, eds. 1987. *Seeing for ourselves: Case-study research by teachers of writing.* Portsmouth, NH: Heinemann.

Bogdan, R. 1972. *Participant observation in organizational settings.* Syracuse, NY: Syracuse University Press.

Bogdan, R., and S. Biklen. 1982. *Qualitative research in education.* Boston: Allyn & Bacon.

Brady, J. 1976. *The craft of interviewing.* Cincinnati: Writer's Digest.

Brooks, M. 1989. *Instant rapport.* New York: Warner Books.

Bruner, J. 1960. *The process of education.* Cambridge, MA: Harvard University Press.

Bulmer, M., ed. 1982. *Social research ethics: An examination of the merits of covert participation observation.* London: Macmillan.

Burgess, R. 1984. *In the field: An introduction to field research.* London: Unwin Hyman.

Caro, R. 1988. "Lyndon Johnson and the roots of power." In *Extraordinary lives: The art and craft of American biography,* edited by W. Zinsser, 199–231. Boston: Houghton Mifflin.

Casagrande, J. B., ed. 1960. *In the company of Man: Twenty portraits by anthropologists.* New York: Harper & Brothers.

Cassell, J. 1987. "Cases and comments." In *Handbook on ethical issues in anthropology,* edited by J. Cassell and S. E. Jacobs, 37–75. Washington, DC: American Anthropological Association.

Cassell, J., and S. E. Jacobs, eds. 1987. "Introduction." In *Handbook on ethical issues in anthropology,* 1–3. Washington, DC: American Anthropological Association.

Clark, C. 1990. "What you can learn from applesauce: A case of qualitative inquiry in use." In *Qualitative inquiry in education: The continuing debate,* edited by E. Eisner and A. Peshkin, 327–338. New York: Teachers College Press.

Clifford, J. 1986. "On ethnographic allegory." In *Writing culture: The poetics and politics of ethnography,* edited by J. Clifford and G. Marcus, 98–121. Berkeley: University of California Press.

Cobb, A., and J. Hagemaster. 1987. Ten criteria for evaluating qualitative research proposals. *Journal of Nursing Education* 26(4):138–143.

Coles, R. 1977. *Eskimos, Chicanos, Indians.* Boston: Little, Brown.

Coles, R. 1989. *The call of stories: Teaching and the moral imagination.* Boston: Houghton Mifflin.

Colvard, R. 1967. "Interaction and identification in reporting field research: A critical reconsideration of protective procedures." In *Ethics, politics and social research,* edited by G. Sjoberg, 319–358. Cambridge, MA: Schenkman.

Conrad, P., and S. Reinharz, eds. 1984. Computers and qualitative data: Editors' introductory essay. *Qualitative Sociology* 7(1–2):3–15.

Couch, J. 1987. Objectivity: A crutch and club for bureaucrats/A haven for lost souls. *Sociological Quarterly* 28:105–110.

Council of the American Anthropological Association. 1987. "Principles of professional responsibility" (adopted May 1971; revised 1986). In *Handbook on ethical issues in anthropology,* edited by J. Cassell and S. E. Jacobs, 96–103. Washington, DC: American Anthropological Association.

Crisler, L. 1958. *Arctic Wild.* New York: Harper & Brothers.

Dalton, M. 1959. *Men who manage.* New York: Wiley.

Daniels, A. K. 1967. "The low caste stranger." In *Ethics, politics and social research,* edited by G. Sjoberg, 267–296. Cambridge, MA: Schenkman.

Davis, J. 1972. "Teachers, kids, and conflict: Ethnography of a junior high school." In *The cultural experience: Ethnography in complex society,* edited by J. Spradley and D. McCurdy, 103–120. Chicago: Science Research.

Denny, T. 1978. Storytelling and educational understanding. Paper presented at the national meeting of the International Reading Association, Houston.

Denzin, N. 1988. *The research act,* rev. ed. New York: McGraw-Hill.

———. 1989. *Interpretive interactionism.* Newbury Park, CA: Sage Publications.

Didion, J. 1988. Interview on "Fresh Air" program, 19 Jan. 1988. National Public Radio.

Diener, E., and R. Crandall. 1978. *Ethics in social behavioral research.* Chicago: University of Chicago Press.

Dillon, D. R. 1989. Showing them that I want to learn and that I care about who they are: A microethnography of the social organization of a secondary low-track English-reading classroom. *American Educational Research Journal* 26:227–259.

Dobbert, M. L. 1982. *Ethnographic research: Theory and application for modern schools and societies.* New York: Praeger.

Douglas, J. 1976. *Investigative social research: Individual and team field research.* Beverly Hills, CA: Sage Publications.

———. 1985. *Creative interviewing.* Beverly Hills, CA: Sage Publications.

Dube, S. C. 1967. *Indian village.* New York: Harper & Row.

Dubell, F., T. Erasmie, and J. de Vries, eds. 1981. *Research for the people—Research by the people.* Linkoping, Sweden: Linkoping University and The Netherlands Study and Development Centre for Adult Education.

DuBois, B. 1983. "Passionate scholarship: Notes on values, knowing and method in feminist social science." In *Theories of women's studies,* edited by G. Bowles and R. Duelli Klein, 105–116. Boston: Routledge & Kegan Paul.

Ebbutt, D. 1985. "Educational action research: Some general concerns and specific quibbles." In *Issues in educational research: Qualitative methods,* edited by R. Burgess, 152–174. Philadelphia: Falmer Press.

Eisner, E. 1981. On the differences between scientific and artistic approaches to qualitative research. *Educational Researcher* 10(4):5–9.

Eisner, E. 1990. Objectivity in education research. Paper presented at the annual meeting of the American Educational Research Association, Boston.

Eisner, E., and A. Peshkin, eds. 1990. *Qualitative inquiry in education: The continuing debate.* New York: Teachers College Press.

Ellen, R. F. 1984. *Ethnographic research: A guide to general conduct.* New York: Academic Press.

Enright, S., and J. Tammivaara. 1984. Tell me more: The elicitation of interview data in a microethnographic study of multicultural classrooms. Paper presented at the annual meeting of the American Educational Research Association, New Orleans.

Erickson, F. 1973. What makes school ethnography "ethnographic"? *Council on Anthropology and Education Newsletter* 4(2):10–19.

———. 1986. "Qualitative methods in research on teaching." In *Handbook of research on teaching,* edited by M. C. Wittrock, 119–161. New York: Macmillan.

Erickson, F., and G. Mohatt. 1982. "Cultural organization of participant structures in two classrooms of Indian students." In *Doing the ethnography of schooling: Educational anthropology in action,* edited by G. Spindler, 132–174. New York: Holt, Rinehart and Winston.

Fetterman, D. 1989. *Ethnography: Step by step.* Newbury Park, CA: Sage Publications.

Finch, J. 1984. "It's great to have someone to talk to: The ethics and politics of interviewing women." In *Social researching: Politics, problems and practice,* edited by C. Bell and H. Roberts, 70–88. London: Routledge & Kegan Paul.

Fine, G. A. 1980. "Cracking diamonds: Observer role in Little League baseball settings and the acquisition of social competence." In *Fieldwork experiences: Qualitative approaches to social research,* edited by W. Shiffir, R. Stebbins, and A. Turowetz, 117–132. New York: St. Martin's Press.

Firestone, W. 1987. Meaning in method: The rhetoric of quantitative and qualitative research. *Educational Researcher* 16(7):16–21.

Flinders, D. 1987. What teachers learn from teaching: Educational criticisms of instructional adaptation. Unpublished doctoral dissertation, Stanford University, Stanford, CA.

———. In press. In search of ethical guidance: Constructing a basis for dialogue. *International Journal of Qualitative Studies in Education.*

Freilich, M. 1977. *Marginal natives: Anthropologists at work.* New York: Harper & Row.

Freire, P. [1970] 1988. *Pedagogy of the oppressed.* New York: Continuum.

Fulwiler, T. 1985. Writing is everybody's business. *National Forum: Phi Kappa Phi Journal* 65(4):21–24.

Galliher, J. F. 1982. "The protection of human subjects: A reexamination of the professional code of ethics." In *Social research ethics,* edited by M. Bulmer, 152–165. London: Macmillan.

Gans, H. 1962. *The urban villagers: Group and class in the life of Italian-Americans.* New York: Free Press.

———. 1982. "The participant-observer as a human being: Observations on the personal aspects of fieldwork." In *Field research: A sourcebook and field manual,* edited by R. Burgess, 53–61. London: George Allen & Unwin.

Geertz, C. 1973. *The interpretation of cultures.* New York: Basic Books.

———. 1979. "From the native's point of view: On the nature of anthropological understanding." In *Interpretive science: A reader,* edited by P. Rabinow and W. Sullivan, 225–242. Berkeley: University of California Press.

Gilligan, C. 1982. *In a different voice.* Cambridge, MA: Harvard University Press.

Gitlin, A., M. Siegel, and K. Boru. 1989. The politics of method: From leftist ethnography to educative research. *International Journal of Qualitative Studies in Education* 2(3):237–253.

Glaser, B. 1978. *Theoretical sensitivity.* Mill Valley, CA: Sociology Press.

Glaser, B., and A. Strauss. 1967. *The discovery of grounded theory: Strategies for qualitative research.* Chicago: Aldine.

Glazer, M. 1972. *The Research adventure: Promise and problems of fieldwork.* New York: Random House.

———. 1982. "The threat of the stranger: Vulnerability, reciprocity, and fieldwork." In *Ethics of social research: Fieldwork, regulation, and publication,* edited by J. Sieber, 49–70. New York: Springer-Verlag.

Glesne, C. 1985. Strugglin', but no slavin': Agriculture, education, and rural young Vincentians. Unpublished doctoral dissertation, University of Illinois, Urbana.

———. 1989. Rapport and friendship in ethnographic research. *International Journal of Qualitative Studies in Education* 2(1):45–54.

Glesne, C., L. Ayers, D. Kucij, L. Murray, E. Nalette, and J. Weinstock. 1989. Collaborative learning: Experiences of a qualitative research class. Burlington, VT: University of Vermont (ERIC document Reproduction Service no. ED 314 344).

Glesne, C., and A. Peshkin. Forthcoming. "The Christian day school. The Bible and the state." In *Private schools and public concerns,* edited by P. Bauch. Westport, CT: Greenwood Press.

Goetz, J., and M. LeCompte. 1984. *Ethnography and qualitative design in educational research.* New York: Academic Press.

Goffman, E. 1961. *Asylums: Essays on the social situation of mental patients and other inmates.* Garden City, NJ: Anchor Books.

Gold, R. 1969. "Roles in sociological field observations." In *Issues in participant observation: A text and reader,* edited by G. McCall and J. L. Simmons, 30–39. Menlo Park, CA: Addison-Wesley.

Gonzalez, N. 1986. "The anthropologist as female head of household." In *Self, sex, and gender in cross-cultural fieldwork,* edited by T. L. Whitehead and M. E. Conaway, 84–100. Urbana, IL: University of Illinois Press.

Gorden, R. [1969] 1975. *Interviewing: Strategy, technique, and tactics.* Homewood, IL: Dorsey Press.

Goswami, D., and P. Stillman, eds. 1987. *Reclaiming the classroom: Teacher research as an agency for change.* Upper Montclair, NJ: Boynton Cook.

Gould, S. 1990. *Wonderful life: The Burgess Shale.* New York: W. W. Norton.

Griffiths, G. 1985. "Doubts, dilemmas and diary-keeping: Some reflections on teacher-based research." In *Issues in educational research,* edited by R. Burgess, 197–215. Philadelphia: Falmer Press.

Guba, E. B., ed. 1990. *The paradigm dialog.* Newbury Park, CA: Sage Publications.

Hammersley, M., and P. Atkinson. 1983. *Ethnography: Principles in practice.* New York: Tavistock.

Hamnett, M., and D. Porter. 1983. "Problems and prospects in Western approaches to cross-national social science research.'' In *Handbook of intercultural training,* edited by D. Landis and R. Breslin, 61–81. New York: Pergamon Press.

Hansen, J. P. 1976. ''The anthropologist in the field: Scientist, friend, voyeur.'' In *Ethics and anthropology: Dilemmas in field work,* edited by M. A. Rynkiewich and J. P. Spradley, 123–134. New York: Wiley.

Heath, S. B. 1983. *Ways with words: Language, life, and work in communities and classrooms.* Cambridge: Cambridge University Press.

Heldke, L. 1988. Coresponsibility and the academy: An uneasy companionship. Paper presented at the University of Illinois, Urbana.

Hersey, J. 1988. Agee. *New Yorker,* 18 July, 72–82.

Homan, R., and M. Bulmer. 1982. ''On the merits of covert methods: A dialogue.'' In *Social research ethics,* edited by M. Bulmer, 105–124. London: Macmillan.

Homans, G. 1964. ''Contemporary theory in sociology.'' In *Handbook of modern sociology,* edited by R. E. L. Farris, 951–977. Chicago: Rand McNally.

Horowitz, R. 1986. Remaining an outsider: Membership as a threat to the research report. *Urban Life* 14:409–430.

Howe, K. 1988. Against the quantitative-qualitative incompatibility thesis, or dogmas die hard. *Educational Researcher* 17(8):10–16.

Humphreys, L. 1970. *Tearoom trade: Impersonal sex in public places.* Chicago: Aldine.

Hunt, J. 1984. The development of rapport through the negotiation of gender in field work among police. *Human Organization* 43:283–296.

Hustler, E., A. Cassidy, and E. C. Cuff, eds. 1986. *Action research in classrooms and schools.* Boston: Allen & Unwin.

Hyman, H. [1954] 1975. *Interviewing in social research.* Chicago: University of Chicago Press.

Hymes, D. H. 1982. ''What is ethnography?'' In *Children in and out of school,* edited by P. Gilmore and A. Glatthorn, 21–32. Washington, DC: Center for Applied Linguistics.

Jacob, E. 1988. Clarifying qualitative research. *Educational Researcher* 17(1):16–24.

Jacobs, S. E. 1987. ''Cases and solutions.'' In *Handbook on ethical issues in anthropology,* edited by J. Cassell and S. E. Jacobs, 20–36. Washington, DC: American Anthropological Association.

Jeske, J. 1984. Demystifying the dissertation. Los Angeles: University of California (ERIC document Reproduction Service no. ED 268 529; CS 209 648).

Johnson, C. 1982. ''Risks in the publication of fieldwork.'' In *Ethics of social research: Fieldwork, regulation, and publication,* edited by J. Sieber, 71–92. New York: Springer-Verlag.

Jorgensen, D. 1989. *Participant observation: A methodology for human studies.* Newbury Park, CA: Sage Publications.

Kelly, A. 1985. ''Action research: What is it and what can it do?'' In *Issues of educational research,* edited by R. Burgess, 129–151. Philadelphia: Falmer Press.

Krieger, S. 1985. Beyond ''subjectivity'': The use of the self in social science. *Qualitative Sociology* 8:309–324.

Lather, P. 1986. Research as praxis. *Harvard Educational Review* 56:257–277.

Lawless, R., V. Sutlive, and M. Zamora, eds. 1983. *Fieldwork: The human experience.* New York: Gordon & Breach Science Publications.

LeCompte, M. 1987. Bias in the biography: Bias and subjectivity in ethnographic research. *Anthropology and Education Quarterly* 18:43–52.

Lewis, O. 1951. *Life in a Mexican village: Tepoztlan restudied.* Urbana, IL: University of Illinois Press.

————. 1959. *Five families: Mexican case studies in the culture of poverty.* New York: Basic Books.

————. 1979. *Children of Sanchez.* New York: Random House.

Liebow, E. 1967. *Tally's corner.* Boston: Little, Brown.

Liggett, A., C. Glesne, S. Hasazi, A. P. Johnson, and R. Schattman. 1991. Qualitative teaming: Lessons learned. Paper presented at the annual meeting of the American Educational Research Association, Boston.

Lightfoot, S. L. 1983. *The good high school.* New York: Basic Books.

Lincoln, Y. S. 1990. "Toward a categorical imperative for qualitative research." In *Qualitative inquiry in education: The continuing debate,* edited by E. Eisner and A. Peshkin, 277–295. New York: Teachers College Press.

Lincoln, Y. S., and E. G. Guba. 1985. *Naturalistic inquiry.* Beverly Hills, CA: Sage Publications.

Lofland, J. 1971. *Analyzing social settings: A guide to qualitative observation and analysis.* Belmont, CA: Wadsworth.

Maguire, P. 1987. *Doing participatory research: A feminist approach.* Amherst, MA: The Center for International Education, University of Massachusetts.

Maher, F., and M. K. Tetreault. 1988. Breaking through illusion: The intersection of feminist pedagogy and feminist ethnography. Paper presented at the annual meeting of the American Educational Research Association, New Orleans.

Malcolm, J. 1987. Reflections. *New Yorker,* 20 April, 84–102.

Malinowski, B. 1967. *A diary in the strict sense of the term.* New York: Harcourt, Brace & World.

Markham, B. [1942] 1983. *West with the night.* San Francisco: North Point Press.

Marris, P. 1974. *Loss and change.* London: Routledge & Kegan Paul.

Marshall, C., and G. Rossman. 1989. *Designing qualitative research.* Newbury Park, CA: Sage Publications.

McCall, G., and J. L. Simmons, eds. 1969. *Issues in participant observation: A text and reader.* Reading, MA: Addison-Wesley.

McDermott, R. 1987. "Achieving school failure: An anthropological approach to illiteracy and social stratification." In *Education and cultural process,* 2d ed., edited by G. Spindler, 173–209. Prospect Heights, IL: Waveland Press.

McMillan, J. 1989. Focus group interviews: Implications for educational research. Paper presented at the annual meeting of the American Educational Research Association, San Francisco.

Mead, M. 1930. *Growing up in New Guinea.* New York: Morrow.

Measor, L. 1985. "Interviewing: A strategy in qualitative research." In *Strategies of educational research: Qualitative methods,* edited by R. Burgess, 55–77. Philadelphia: Falmer Press.

Metz, M. H. 1978. *Classrooms and corridors: The crisis of authority in desegregated secondary schools.* Berkeley: University of California Press.

Mies, M. 1983. "Towards a methodology for feminist research." In *Theories of women's studies,* edited by G. Bowles and R. Duelli Klein, 117–139. Boston: Routledge & Kegan Paul.

Miles, M., and M. Huberman. 1984. *Qualitative data analysis: A sourcebook of new methods.* Beverly Hills, CA: Sage Publications.

Miller, J. 1988. Points of dissonance of teacher/researchers: Opening into emancipatory ways of knowing. Paper presented at the annual meeting of the American Educational Research Association, New Orleans.

————. 1990. *Creating spaces and finding voices: Teachers collaborating for empowerment.* Albany, NY: State University of New York Press.

Miller, S. M. 1952. The participant observer and "overrapport." *American Sociological Review* 17:97–99.

Mills, C. W. 1951. *White collar.* New York: Oxford University Press.

Mohr, M., and M. Maclean. 1987. *Working together: A guide for teacher researchers.* Urbana, IL: National Center of Teachers of English.

Moorehead, A. 1959. *No room in the ark.* New York: Harper & Brothers.

Murray, D. 1986. One writer's secrets. *College Composition and Communication* 37:146–153.

Myrdal, J. 1965. *Report from a Chinese village.* New York: Pantheon Books.

Nagel, P. 1988. "The Adams women." In *Extraordinary lives: The art and craft of American Biography,* edited by W. Zinsser, 91–120. Boston: Houghton Mifflin.

Oakley, A. 1981. "Interviewing women: A contradiction in terms." In *Doing feminist research,* edited by H. Roberts, 30–61. Boston: Routledge & Kegan Paul.

Pachter, M., ed. 1981. *Telling lives: The biographer's art.* Philadelphia: University of Pennsylvania Press.

Patton, M. 1990. *Qualitative evaluation and research methods,* 2d ed. Newbury Park, CA: Sage Publications.

Pelto, P. J., and G. H. Pelto. 1978. *Anthropological research: The structure of inquiry,* 2d ed. Cambridge: Cambridge University Press.

Peshkin, A. 1972. *Kanuri schoolchildren: Education and social mobilization in Bornu.* New York: Holt, Rinehart & Winston.

————. 1978. *Growing up American: Schooling and the survival of community.* Chicago: University of Chicago Press.

————. 1982a. *The imperfect union: School consolidation and community conflict.* Chicago: University of Chicago Press.

————. 1982b. "The researcher and subjectivity: Reflections on ethnography of school and community." In *Doing the ethnography of schooling,* edited by G. Spindler, 20–47. New York: Holt, Rinehart & Winston.

————. 1984. Odd man out: The participant observer in an absolutist setting. *Sociology of Education* 57:254–264.

————. 1985. From title to title: The evolution of perspective in naturalistic inquiry. *Anthropology and Education Quarterly* 16:214–224.

————. 1986. *God's choice: The total world of a fundamentalist Christian school.* Chicago: University of Chicago Press.

————. 1988a. In search of subjectivity—one's own. *Educational Researcher* 17(7):17–22.

————. 1988b. Understanding complexity: A gift of qualitative inquiry. *Anthropology and Education Quarterly* 19:416–424.

———. 1988c. "Virtuous subjectivity: In the participant-observer's I's." In *The self in social inquiry,* edited by D. Berg and K. Smith, 267–282. Newbury Park, CA: Sage Publications.

———. 1991. *The color of strangers, the color of friends: The play of ethnicity in school and community.* Chicago: University of Chicago Press.

Pettigrew, J. 1981. "Reminiscences of fieldwork among the Sikhs." In *Doing feminist research,* edited by H. Roberts, 62–82. Boston: Routledge & Kegan Paul.

Pfaffenberger, B. 1988. *Microcomputer applications in qualitative research.* Newbury Park, CA: Sage Publications.

Plante, D. 1986. Profiles: Sir Steven Runciman. *New Yorker,* 3 Nov., 53–80.

Plummer, K. 1983. *Documents of life.* Boston: Allen & Unwin.

Popkewitz, T. 1984. *Paradigm and ideology in educational research: The social functions of the intellectual.* New York: Falmer Press.

Porter, R. 1984. The financial risk faced by college undergraduates. Unpublished dissertation, University of Illinois, Urbana-Champaign.

Pritchett, V. S. 1987. Books: One of nature's Balkans. *New Yorker,* 21 Dec., 132–154.

Punch, M. 1986. *The politics and ethics of fieldwork.* Beverly Hills, CA: Sage Publications.

Purvis, J. 1985. "Reflections upon doing historical documentary research from a feminist perspective." In *Strategies of educational research: Qualitative methods,* edited by R. Burgess, 179–205. Philadelphia: Falmer Press.

Rawlings, M. 1942. *Cross creek.* New York: Charles Scribner.

Reason, P., ed. 1988. *Human inquiry in action.* Beverly Hills, CA: Sage Publications.

Redfield, R. 1955. *The little community.* Chicago: University of Chicago Press.

Reichardt, C. S., and T. D. Cook, eds. 1979. "Beyond qualitative versus quantitative methods." In *Qualitative and quantitative methods in evaluation research,* 7–32. Beverly Hills, CA: Sage Publications.

Reinharz, S. 1983. "Experiential analysis: A contribution to feminist research." In *Theories of women's studies,* edited by G. Bowles and R. Duelli Klein, 162–191. Boston: Routledge & Kegan Paul.

Riley, G., ed. 1974. *Values, objectivity, and the social sciences.* Reading, MA: Addison-Wesley.

Rist, R. 1977. On the relations among educational research paradigms: From disdain to detente. *Anthropology and Education Quarterly* 8:42–49.

Robbins, T., D. Anthony, and T. Curtis. 1973. The limits of symbolic realism: Problems of empathic field observation in a sectarian context. *Journal for the Scientific Study of Religion* 12:259–271.

Rogers, C. 1942. The non-directive method as a technique for social research. *American Journal of Sociology* 50:279–283.

Roman, L., and M. Apple. 1990. "Is naturalism a move away from positivism? Materialist and feminist approaches to subjectivity in ethnographic research." In *Qualitative inquiry in education: The continuing debate,* edited by E. Eisner and A. Peshkin, 38–73. New York: Teachers College Press.

Rosengarten, T. 1985. "Stepping over cockleburs: Conversations with Ned Cobb." In *Telling lives: The biographer's art,* edited by M. Pachter, 105–131. Philadelphia: University of Pennsylvania Press.

Rynkiewich, M. A., and J. P. Spradley, eds. 1976. *Ethics and anthropology: Dilemmas in field work.* New York: Wiley.

Sanjek, R., ed. 1990. *Fieldnotes: The makings of anthropology.* Ithaca, NY: Cornell University Press.

Schofield, J. 1989. *Black and white in school: Trust, tension, or tolerance?* New York: Teachers College Press.

Schuman, H. 1970. "The random probe: A technique for evaluating the validity of closed questions." In *Stages of social research,* edited by D. P. Forcese and S. Rocher, 240–245. Englewood Cliffs, NJ: Prentice-Hall.

Schwandt, T. 1989. Solutions to the paradigm conflict: Coping with uncertainty. *Journal of Contemporary Ethnography* 17:379–407.

Seidel, J. V., and J. A. Clark. 1984. The ETHNOGRAPH: A computer program for the analysis of qualitative data. *Qualitative Sociology* 7(1–2):110–125.

Shaffir, W. G., R. A. Stebbins, and A. Turowetz. 1980. *Fieldwork experience.* New York: St. Martin's Press.

Shaw, C. 1930. *The jack roller.* Chicago: University of Chicago Press.

Shweder, R. 1986. Storytelling among the anthropologists. *New York Times Book Review,* 21 Sept., 1, 38.

Sieber, J., ed. 1982. *Ethics of social research: Fieldwork, regulation and publication.* New York: Springer-Verlag.

Sindell, P. 1987. "Some discontinuities in the enculturation of Mistassini Cree children." In *Education and cultural process,* 2d ed., edited by G. Spindler, 378–386. Prospect Heights, IL: Waveland Press.

Smith, M. 1954. *Baba of Karo.* London: Faber.

Spradley, J. 1970. *You owe yourself a drunk: An ethnography of urban nomads.* Boston: Little, Brown.

———. 1979. *The ethnographic interview.* New York: Holt, Rinehart & Winston.

Spradley, J., and B. Mann. 1975. *The cocktail waitress: Woman's work in a man's world.* New York: Wiley.

Spradley, J., and D. McCurdy. 1972. *The cultural experience: Ethnography in complex society.* Chicago: Science Research Associates.

Stake, R., and D. Trumbull. 1982. Naturalistic generalizations. *Review Journal of Philosophy and Social Science* 7:3–12.

Strauss, A. 1987. *Qualitative analysis for social scientists.* Cambridge: Cambridge University Press.

Strouse, J. 1988. "The real reasons." In *Extraordinary lives: The art and craft of American biography,* edited by W. Zinsser, 163–195. Boston: Houghton Mifflin.

Strunk, W., and E. B. White. 1979. *The elements of style,* 3d ed. New York: Macmillan.

Sullivan, M. A., S. A. Queen, and R. C. Patrick. Participant observation as employed in the study of a military training program. *American Sociological Review* 23:610–667.

Tesch, R. 1990. *Qualitative research: Analysis types and software tools.* New York: Falmer Press.

Tolkien, J. R. R. 1965. *The lord of the rings.* Boston: Houghton Mifflin.

Turner, J. 1985. In defense of positivism. *Sociological Theory* 3:24–31.

Van Galen, J., G. Noblit, and D. Hare. 1988–1989. The art and science of interviewing kids: The group interview in evaluation research. *National Forum of Applied Educational Research Journal* 1(2):74–81.

Van Maanen, J. 1983. "The moral fix: On the ethics of fieldwork." In *Contemporary field research*, edited by R. Emerson, 269–287. Boston: Little, Brown.

———. 1988. *Tales of the field: On writing ethnography.* Chicago: University of Chicago Press.

Vidich, A. J., and J. Bensman. 1968. *Small town in mass society,* rev. ed. Princeton, NJ: Princeton University Press.

Wax, M. 1982. "Research reciprocity rather than informed consent in fieldwork." In *Ethics of social research: Fieldwork, regulation, and publication,* edited by J. Sieber, 33–48. New York: Springer-Verlag.

Wax, R. 1971. *Doing fieldwork: Warnings and advice.* Chicago: University of Chicago Press.

Webster's Third International Dictionary. 1986. Springfield, MA: Meriam & Webster.

Wehlage, G. 1981. "The purpose of generalization in field-study research." In *The study of schooling,* edited by T. Popkewitz and R. Tabachnick, 211–226. Westport, CT: Greenwood Press.

West, J. 1945. *Plainville, U.S.A.* New York: Columbia University Press.

West, W. G. 1980. "Access to adolescent deviants and deviance." In *Fieldwork experience,* edited by W. B. Shaffir, R. A. Stebbins, and A. Turowetz, 31–44. New York: St. Martin's Press.

Whyte, W. [1943] 1981. *Streetcorner society.* Chicago: University of Chicago Press.

———. 1984. *Learning from the field: A guide from experience.* Beverly Hills, CA: Sage Publications.

———. ed. 1991. *Participatory action research.* Newbury Park, CA: Sage Publications.

Wildavsky, A. 1989. *Craftways: On the organization of scholarly work.* New Brunswick, NJ: Transaction.

Wilkins, L. T. 1979. "Human subjects—whose subject?" In *Deviance and decency,* edited by C. B. Klockars and F. W. O'Connor, 99–123. Beverly Hills, CA: Sage Publications.

Willis, P. 1977. *Learning to labor.* New York: Columbia University Press.

Wilson, S. May 1989. Alaskan journal. *Vermont Quarterly,* 13–18.

Wolcott, H. 1973. *The man in the principal's office: An ethnography.* New York: Holt, Rinehart & Winston.

———. 1975. Criteria for an ethnographic approach to research in schools. *Human Organization* 34:111–127.

———. 1990. *Writing up qualitative research.* Newbury Park, CA: Sage Publications.

Woods, P. 1985. "New songs played skillfully: Creativity and technique in writing up research." In *Issues in educational research,* edited by R. Burgess, 86–106. Philadelphia: Falmer Press.

———. 1986. *Inside schools: Ethnography in educational research.* New York: Routledge & Kegan Paul.

Woolfson, P. 1988. Non-verbal interaction of Anglo-Canadian, Jewish-Canadian, and French-Canadian physicians with their young, middle-aged, and elderly patients. *Visual Anthropology* 1:404–414.

Yoors, J. 1967. *The gypsies.* New York: Simon & Schuster.

Young, B., and C. Tardif. 1988. Interviewing: Two sides of the story. Paper presented at the annual meeting of the American Educational Research Association, New Orleans.

Zigarmi, D., and P. Zigarmi. 1978. The psychological stresses of ethnographic research. Paper presented at the annual meeting of the American Educational Research Association, Toronto.

Zinsser, W., ed. 1988a. *Extraordinary lives: The art and craft of American biography.* Boston: Houghton Mifflin.

———. 1988b. *Writing to learn: How to write and think clearly about any subject at all.* New York: Harper & Row.

Index

193